THE PRACTICE OF COLLECTIVE ESCAPE

Spaces and Practices of Justice series

Series editor: **Agatha Herman**, Cardiff University

The Spaces and Practices of Justice series focuses on the intersections between spaces and practices to provide innovative and important interventions on examples of real-world (in)justice. The series explores food justice, scholar-activism, social movements, gender, sexuality, race, childhood, labour, trade, domestic spaces, environmental relations and consumption to open out different approaches to questions of justice grounded within everyday experiences and spaces.

Forthcoming in the series:

Researching Justice: Engaging with Questions and Spaces of (In)Justice through Social Research
Agatha Herman and **Joshua Inwood**, April 2024

Find out more at
bristoluniversitypress.co.uk/spaces-and-practices-of-justice

THE PRACTICE OF COLLECTIVE ESCAPE

Politics, Justice and Community
in Urban Growing Projects

Helen Traill

First published in Great Britain in 2025 by

Bristol University Press
University of Bristol
1-9 Old Park Hill
Bristol
BS2 8BB
UK
t: +44 (0)117 374 6645
e: bup-info@bristol.ac.uk

Details of international sales and distribution partners are available at bristoluniversitypress.co.uk

© Bristol University Press 2025

British Library Cataloguing in Publication Data
A catalogue record for this book is available from the British Library

ISBN 978-1-5292-2068-1 hardcover
ISBN 978-1-5292-2069-8 paperback
ISBN 978-1-5292-2070-4 ePub
ISBN 978-1-5292-2071-1 ePdf

The right of Helen Traill to be identified as author of this work has been asserted by her in accordance with the Copyright, Designs and Patents Act 1988.

All rights reserved: no part of this publication may be reproduced, stored in a retrieval system, or transmitted in any form or by any means, electronic, mechanical, photocopying, recording, or otherwise without the prior permission of Bristol University Press.

Every reasonable effort has been made to obtain permission to reproduce copyrighted material. If, however, anyone knows of an oversight, please contact the publisher.

The statements and opinions contained within this publication are solely those of the author and not of the University of Bristol or Bristol University Press. The University of Bristol and Bristol University Press disclaim responsibility for any injury to persons or property resulting from any material published in this publication.

Bristol University Press works to counter discrimination on grounds of gender, race, disability, age and sexuality.

Cover design: blu inc
Front cover image: Stocksy/ Léa Jones

For Felix and Mabel, my garden babies

Contents

Series Preface		viii
Acknowledgements		ix
1	Introduction	1
2	Urban Growing in Glasgow	18
3	The Rhythms of Urban Escape	31
4	Who Gets to Escape?	49
5	Ownership, Autonomy and the Commons	73
6	Escape into Responsibility	93
7	Field Dynamics and Strategic Neutrality	110
8	The Political Imagination of Common Justice	125
9	Escape, Crisis and Social Change	139
10	Conclusion	150
Notes		159
References		161
Index		180

Series Preface

Agatha Herman

Justice refers to a broad concern with fairness, equity, equality and respect. Just from the daily news, it is readily apparent how questions of justice or, in fact, the more obvious experiences of *injustice* shape our everyday lives. From global trade to our own personal consumption; living or dying through war and peace; access to education; relations in the workplace or home; how we experience life through a spectrum of identities; or the more-than-human entanglements that contextualize our environments, we need to conceptualize and analyze the intersections between spaces and practices of justice in order to formulate innovative and grounded interventions.

The Spaces and Practices of Justice book series aims to do so through cutting across scales to explore power, relations and society from the local through to international levels, recognizing that space is fundamental to understanding how (in)justice is relationally produced in, and through, different temporal and geographical contexts. It is also always practised, and a conceptual focus on these 'doings and sayings' (Shove, 2014) brings a sense of the everydayness of (in)justice but also allows for analysis of the broader contexts, logics and structures within which such experiences and relations are embedded (Jaeger-Erben and Offenberger, 2014; Herman, 2018).

References

Herman, A. (2018) *Practising Empowerment in Post- Apartheid South Africa: Wine, Ethics and Development*, London: Routledge.

Jaeger-Erben, M. and Offenberger, U. (2014) 'A practice theory approach to sustainable consumption', *GAIA*, 23(S1): 166–74.

Shove, E. (2014) 'Putting practice into policy: reconfiguring questions of consumption and climate change', *Contemporary Social Science*, 9(4): 415–29.

Acknowledgements

Much like raising a child, it takes a village to write a book. All errors in what proceeds are rightfully mine, but I have accrued a village-worth of thank yous and unpayable debts in writing this book.

First, it wouldn't be a book without the great folk at Bristol University Press – thanks especially Anna Richardson, Freya Trand and Emily Watt, as well as their less visible colleagues who indexed, copy edited, designed, printed and otherwise made this book function. Thanks also to Agatha Herman, who saw the merit in the book and supported it and me through the process. Her initial support as series editor made it a serious endeavour rather than a pipedream.

This book grew out of my doctoral work at the London School of Economics and Political Science, so thanks to the many colleagues there who helped develop the work, my classmates and especially my examiners, Emma Jackson and Andrew Cumbers. Thanks to the NYLON writing group who were my lifeline back to the university when living in London was not an option.

In particular, I owe thanks especially to Don Slater – who first believed in the idea, and helped shape it – and to my primary supervisor, David Madden – who pushed me to define and refine, and whose thoughtfulness, support and precision helped hone sprawling ideas into arguments. I am grateful too to the Economic and Social Research Council as this work was supported by a full doctoral studentship (grant number 1510541).

My time at the University of Glasgow has greatly shaped the book. Thanks especially are due to Andrew Cumbers who has been a brilliant support, mentor and principal investigator, and who encouraged me to develop my own work alongside his grants. Thanks also to the community gardens folk in the Adam Smith Business School – Deirdre Shaw (another fabulous principal investigator), Bob McMaster and Stephanie Anderson – for encouragement, collegiality and willingness to meet outside; and the broader municipalizations group, who made the day-to-day much more fun. Thanks to Kirsteen Paton, whose enthusiasm was a real boost at a critical moment, and to the Food Geographies Writing Group, who read sections of this book and read *with* it – thanks for wading through the postdoctoral soup with me. To the many others who spoke with me, asked awkward questions, and showed even the mildest interest – thank you. Academia would be nothing without you all.

I owe a huge debt of thanks to the whole host of people who believed I could write a book, especially the extended clan of Traills and Seatons who we rely on a great deal. Thank you to my many sisters; the real ones, Susan and Anne, without whom I'd be much less strange; to Julia Brainin, who never doubted and always turned up; to Sarah Crook, for sharing the joys and the aches of academic-parenting; to Claire Norman, for the various medical advice and moral support, despite my insistence she's not a real doctor; to Sophie Wawro, who let me chew her ear off and sleep on her sofa too many times to count.

Thanks most of all to my little family: to Andrew, Felix and Mabel, who kept me sane, made me laugh, kept my ego in check, and brought me motivational posters. I can't say it has been easy to balance a young family, academic life and a pandemic; but I wouldn't change it for the world. They keep me grounded and challenged in equal measure, and I love them all very much.

The biggest thanks of course I owe to the many folks at Woodlands Community Garden, Woodlands Community Café, the North Kelvin Meadow and the Children's Wood. Without them there would be no research, and I can only hope to have done justice to the brilliant spaces you have built.

1

Introduction

A meadow in winter, a garden in spring

In the mornings, the North Kelvin Meadow is a calm place, periodically enlivened by dog walkers and people passing through as a shortcut to destinations both nearby and further afield in Glasgow. A mother and daughter pass through on the way to school, greeting the dogs. For them, passing through creates a break between the clamour to leave the house and the pressures of work and school. Others climb through the gaps in fences or walk between cheerfully painted bollards to sit among the trees reading a newspaper in a slither of sunlight coming through the branches of the birch trees. For some the meadow is a place to linger, to embrace the slowness of seasonality; or to speed up the boredom of having little to do. In the summer, the meadow's tree-lined edge blocks out the surrounding houses, lending the space a sense of disconnection from the rest of the city. In the middle of the meadow, it opens out: raised beds along one side and into the corner, open grass in the middle, worn through by use in places to its previous red, crumbling sports surface.[1]

In my early research encounters with the meadow in December 2014, it was brittle with frost, the ground hard and the days short. Walking through with a local campaigner and long-time resident, Alasdair, who insisted that we leave the warmth of his flat where we were talking to take in the meadow around the corner in the early dusk of mid-winter, we spontaneously met others who wanted to talk about old shell casings found on the meadow, the history of the space. Alasdair was enthusiastic, garrulous even, in spite of the freezing temperatures. I had initially reached out to him to discuss the meadow's fight against the sale of the land for development but Alasdair insisted that to understand the space and its value, I had to appreciate its rich, common ordinariness in person and immediately. As he put it, "It's communal, everyone's entitled to use it." In the meadow, the intertwined threads of mundane use and political campaigning against its development highlight critical tensions around who makes the city and how it might be remade and reimagined.

The meadow is embedded in the rhythms of everyday life for many local people; an everyday green space in the fabric of the city. It reconnects them with the pace of meadow growth and seasonal change and offers a sanctuary of sorts. The meadow is a cyclical place, each year turning through the seasons. It has a collective rhythm of daily routines made up of moments of coalescence and dispersal. Connecting with these rhythms contains the potential for an escape from tarmac and concrete, from the dismal indoors, the frenetic or glacial pace of everyday life. It offers a change in tempo within everyday life (Sharma, 2014).

A brisk 20 minutes' walk from the North Kelvin Meadow, towards the M8 motorway that runs through Glasgow's heart, sits the Woodlands Community Garden. I first encountered the garden in the rain in April as it emerged from overwintering. Early in the growing season, there were few people about and most of the raised beds were under seaweed, a carpet of leaves or green compost. As the days got warmer, more people emerged to engage in collective cultivation and the beds too began to come to life. As a raised bed grower, Cathy, put it on a rare sunny day in spring, "The sun is bringing everyone out, they're just sprouting!" This seasonality brings an annual pattern of decay and rebirth to the lives of communal growers, each spring marked by a reconnection to the garden and a recurrence of activity.

The Woodlands Community Garden site consists mostly of raised beds, landscaped up to street level from the foundations of the tenement that sat there until it burnt down in the 1970s. An individual or family owns each raised bed, and there are around 40 raised beds in total. It is an unstable number, as beds may be subdivided, rot and are reimagined, or are crafted from scratch by the team that work in the garden. Around them, the fruit trees and bushes are communally owned and tended in the space, along with communal beds and a tyre wall with herbs cascading down one side. The mulching compost bays slumber for months under pieces of donated carpet, warm and full of worms, until they are ready to be used; people drop off food waste and chop and turn younger compost. A shipping container filled with tools and useful paraphernalia sits towards the back of the site, close to the building known as the Hub. The aptly named Hub becomes a social centre twice a week during growing sessions, a space to share a conversation, a cup of tea and a biscuit. After the sessions end, the garden quietens down, with an occasional visitor perhaps popping by to read a book under the fruit trees. These rhythms of life in the growing project mark moments of escape. Done collectively, it is a communal escape and indeed an escape from individualized lives into communality itself. The vagaries of this collective escape are the focus of what follows in this book.

Communal growing projects

Communal growing projects are collective spaces of cultivation with varying levels of organization around them, often considered as community gardens or a form of urban agriculture. Pudup (2008) uses the idea of 'organised growing projects' to encapsulate a very similar activity, preferring to steer away from the vagueness of community gardening as a term. Such terminological evasions would not suit here, as they turn away from rather than engage communality as a critical, if complex, idea within the practice. Here, I attend to community as a key mechanism by which spaces such as the meadow and garden are built into this fabric of urban time and space as punctuation and respite. Communal growing projects are also often contested places; places with rich histories of ordinary people organizing for change. As such, community green spaces like urban meadows and community gardens are both political and prosaic, both spectacularly contested and considered principally as a backdrop against which everyday life plays out. This makes them provocative and kaleidoscopic research objects, and spaces where much broader social dynamics can be explored in microcosm (Barron, 2017; Douglas, 2018).

Communal growing projects are important points of intervention in the local landscape and can offer a reimagination of everyday urban life. They do so through practices of being communal and inclusive, and through challenging relations to urban land. In the contemporary climate of suspicion around immigration and difference in the UK, community has the potential to become a nostalgic throwback, but it also presents a horizon of renewal. The reinvigoration of a sense of collective interconnection prompted by the COVID-19 pandemic that began in 2020 presents an opportunity to re-centre interdependence, as people such as the Care Collective (2020) argue is necessary to reimagining our politics. Others, such as Gregory Claeys (2022), see sociability and interconnection as critical to imagining a sustainable future. This book, in its humble way, contributes to this conversation through foregrounding the mundane ways that politics, justice and community intertwine in everyday spaces of sociality in the city. An attention to practice is necessary to unfold processes of exclusion, community and urban land development, and I argue that everyday urban politics must always be considered in context, rather than seeing urban gardens as automatically exemplifying a distinctive politics or space of urban (in)justice.

Collective escape

Thinking with the idea of collective escape can help open up a series of important questions about how the city is lived. Collective escape centres the relationship between communal growing's urban intervention and its politics, providing insight into the way people within the urban community projects understand their action. Communal growing projects necessarily engage with urban struggles in the city, shifting the experience of social exclusion and reshaping local development and aesthetics. That this happens often outside of the language of politics raises questions about what shapes the emergence of politicized (or otherwise) understandings of growing. Escape is in this sense an ambivalent terrain, capturing how communal urban spaces create both inclusion and boundaries, and are troubled by attempting to balance autonomy against the depoliticizing influence of grant funding.

Through boundary work and narratives of inclusion, growing is a site for contesting social categories but also reproducing them. To unfold the intersection of these exclusions requires engagement with gender, race, class, employment and disability. I raise questions about the limits of inclusion as a practice of justice through following how inclusivity plays into larger questions of claiming a right to the city (Lefebvre, 1996). This has important implications for how we think about urban resistance in the everyday, particularly in relation to the capacity of communities to prefigure a systematic alternative to capitalist urbanity and rebuild cities for more sustainable futures. Given the systemic emissions from food production, distribution, consumption and waste, spaces in which to reimagine food futures are critical and timely, but there is a need to understand the limits and contradictions of such collective urban spaces.

The pressures of the global pandemic highlighted in the popular and academic imaginations how our lives are fundamentally interconnected (Oncini, 2021). The flourishing of collective support groups, mutual aid, neighbourly WhatsApp groups and spectacles of common cause such as the UK's weekly 'clap for carers' demonstrated how deeply social even socially distant lives are. But the COVID-19 pandemic, with its emphasis on closing borders and imported variants, also emphasizes how the local is always connected within and beyond imagined communities across scales (see Anderson, 2006). With the challenges of what has been called the 'post-COVID decade' emerging, the importance of understanding communality is acute, as it underpins the challenges facing society in rebuilding common life (British Academy, 2021).

Commentators concerned with justice have variously called for solutions such as Universal Basic Income (Standing, 2017) or the need for a 'promiscuous ethic of care' (Care Collective, 2020). In disparate ways, such solutions are often about making more time and space for, and truly valuing, the relational work that underpins reciprocity and social connection (Berlant, 2016). Relating to others requires time, space and effort, but enriches and indeed gives a foundation for social life and social meaning, as the pandemic increasingly made clear through its absence. As such, while this book draws the majority of its data from before the pandemic, in taking communality seriously as a practice and an idea, it opens up a way of thinking about collective life that is alive to the challenges and hopes inherent in being communal that is highly relevant as we face the enormity of building sustainable futures (Claeys, 2022).

Given the international conversation within community growing literatures, with much of it emerging from gardens in the US, speaking from Glasgow's growing spaces can add a specific viewpoint on communal growing, theorizing from the mundane opportunities of a post-industrial city where the land-use politics offer perhaps more space for reimagination away from hyper-commoditization. Nevertheless, Glasgow faces its own distinct challenges of inequality, unevenly distributed poverty and austerity, which has decimated the council's capacity to fulfil services. Further, the continuities around the neoliberalization of cities and similar patterns of class and ethnic exclusion mean that questions raised in Glasgow have resonance across the global north. That strong political tendencies and justice questions emerge from the diverse contexts of the community growing literature suggests the broad applicability of thinking about growing as a common, collective practice that intersects with urban regeneration, practices of care and micro-level actions towards connection and inclusion, although it always does so within a particular set of local relations.

Exploring escape is a way of looking to what can be learned in the mundane everyday lives of alternative spaces. Davina Cooper's (2013) writing on *Everyday Utopias* reminds the reader of the hopeful, utopian moments of alternative subcultural spaces, the futures that might be imagined from marginal practices. Communal growing offers such a space, with a distinct imaginary in the Glaswegian context of both communality and justice, the latter primarily viewed through the idea of 'inclusion' but also latent in the practices of reshaping the city towards care and the natural world. As Douglas (2018) argues, in-depth studies of niche cultural moments can speak far beyond their immediate contexts. The prism of escape offers a way of conceptualizing practices of communality that positions community not as a problematic object, but as an ongoing practice and a utopian horizon. Escaping into communality presents a paradoxical kind of freedom, but it also demonstrates the interplay between mundane social connection as a much-sought-after but also ever-present aspect of urban life (Studdert and Walkerdine, 2016b, 2016a; Blokland, 2017). The practices explored in this book are thus at once unusual in that they present a mode of living the city that is posited on creating a better, more connected kind of urban experience, and at the same time the most basic human kind of behaviour: the collaborative building of meaning in space, the collective endeavour.

Cultivating communal life

While the present cultural moment seems to confirm the importance of the communal, the term *community* bears a rather heavy moral and political weight. Since the 2000s, community has been evoked in a policy setting as a solution to a growing social disconnection, with community as an idea valorized and utilized to promote a variety of policy interventions. Within UK politics and across different governance levels, from the Conservative Party's 'Big Society' through to Scottish legislation that has centred community empowerment, such as the Community Empowerment Act (Scotland) 2015, community was a resurgent policy idea (Wallace, 2010; Lawson and Kearns, 2014). These different interventions are obviously not continuous with each other, but they do reflect a political focus on community as a solution, whether to social breakdown in the 'Big Society' or to concentrated land ownership and disempowerment in Scottish community empowerment narratives. The COVID-19 pandemic that began in 2020 took this further, with narratives around community groups responding to the needs of each other praised from many sides as people around the world wrestled with the socially disruptive nature of a global pandemic.

The positioning of 'community' as a salve for social ills has made the idea increasingly vacuous and plastic. It challenges any sense of a singular concept or definition yet requires attention for its role in everyday social life. Drawing on work that considers community as a practice, such as Talja Blokland's (2017), and work that situates community as a kind of 'micro-sociality' (Studdert, 2016; Studdert and Walkerdine, 2016a) can open up the everyday instances of communal life that exist within and against these politicized discourses. Seeing community as a practice, or perhaps more precisely attending to *communality*, helps to ground the analysis in social life and recognize its plasticity as lively – and as a *lived* ambiguity, not only a slippery political signifier. As Neo and Chua (2017) point out in relation to community gardening, growing and community provide two poles towards which people are more or less closely aligned. But they are also co-emergent: gardening provides a reason for people to gather, but gathering enriches the gardening, giving people interlocutors with whom to reflect on growing and the natural world, arguably bringing them closer together with both the human and non-human within the space of the garden.

As such, growing as a *collective* exercise necessarily intersects with murky questions of community and its various meanings. Community as an idea creates a conceptual tension within community gardening. It embodies an idealized notion of 'morally valued social relations' but also a sense of geography (Kurtz, 2001, p 661). This sense of geographical scale within the idea of community is reflected in its use descriptively, as a synonym for neighbourhood or place. This has resonance with the rich vein of community studies (Elias and Scotston, 1965; Bell and Newby, 1971), which also tended to take communities as geographically given, if socially constructed. Taxonomical distinctions can be drawn between gardens which are interest-based or place-based, as Firth et al (2011) do, as a way of discussing the variation in the make-up of communities that emerge around growing together. Yet even self-defining communities come in a wide range of forms, from online chat groups through village idylls to middle grounds that defy easy categorization (Calhoun, 1998; Brint, 2001). Taxonomy may capture distinctions between social groups that identify with the idea of community, but the idea itself becomes stretched in this usage.

Despite, or indeed because of its ubiquity, community is an imprecise concept – to the point where the myriad of activities under that banner can lead to a conclusion akin to the philosopher Jean-Luc Nancy's (1991), which is to say that community is 'inoperable' as a concept. Nevertheless, the power of the term and its ability to shape social life remains significant, and processes of being communal remain central in accounts of everyday life (Walkerdine and Studdert, 2012; Mulligan, 2015). Thus, community is a symbolically important frame for action, but an impossible object. Here, Goffman's (1975) notion of the frame becomes useful as a way to suggest that community is not just a social construct, but a socially constructed frame towards which communal action is oriented. In Goffman's (1975) terms, community is the answer to the question, 'what is going here?' Frames can encompass a myriad of definitions and how well a frame resonates is an empirical question that is critical here in capturing how community can take on a multitude of meanings in everyday life.

If 'community' and 'growing' offer different (and sometimes contradictory) frames within collective growing enterprises (Neo and Chua, 2017), this can produce tensions particularly around how and whether gardens become 'inclusive'. Neo and Chua's (2017) explanation of community as a process of responsibilization in Singaporean growing spaces offers a great deal in explaining that tension, and the different moments of contradiction regarding the prioritization of communal behaviour or success in growing. Yet seeing community as a process of governmentality, while helpful in understanding how communal behaviour is cultural and learnt, doesn't engage with the full range of what communality *is*. Community is also the idea that makes possible the collectivity of growing, and its ambiguity lends its own difficulties and possibilities (Traill, 2021). Thus, I contend that more attention is needed to community as an everyday enactment that is central to the practice of growing together.

Although the research was framed around two growing spaces that self-identify as communities, only one is a community garden in the strictest sense. The other is an urban meadow and wood, introduced in the opening vignette. Thus, the book revolves around the idea of 'communal growing projects' as a way of spanning the commonality of growing collectively, without requiring a strict adherence to a particularly form, whether micro-allotments or collaborative cultivation. Taking a comparative view of collective growing here allows an exploration of how the different structures of organization and activity can shape communal growing, and the similarities that emerge despite formal difference. Pudup (2008) suggests the idea of the 'organized growing project' to address the multiplicity of phenomenon she was discussing, out of a certain frustration with the idea of a community garden as too broad a concept to be functional. However, the idea of community is important in shaping what emerged, and so to obscure its centrality in the referent object seems to obscure part of the core focus here.

The projects with whom I worked proved particularly aware of the difficulty and fluidity of the community idea, creating a fertile ground to explore how it works as a concept, and how people relate their actions to community as an idealized notion. In what follows, then, community will be used as a category of practice (Brubaker, 2013). This reflects the lack of analytical usefulness of using community to conceptualize the practices of being communal. Yet that community as an idea retains emotive and political power is important; it shapes what emerges in significant ways. As the book will explore in later chapters, this has ramifications for the politics of growing and has serious implications for whether growing can be a practice of justice. Rather than discuss this as community building or creation, however, it makes analytic sense to explore these as ways of *being communal*, as negotiations and struggles within the urban environment. This shift is intended to conceptually address the issue of the continued emotional valence of community while remaining sceptical of the relevance of community as a definable or discoverable social form. The questions in this context then become: what does this communing do, and what does it change? One answer to these questions that I want to explore in what follows is that it changes how we might think of practices of escape as a *collective* phenomenon.

Politics and growing

Exploring escape in growing opens a path beyond the stalemate reached within the literature around the politics of communal growing. Urban growing has invited a range of political interpretations. In notions of 'radical gardening' (McKay, 2011) and 'digging ... [as] anarchy in action' (Hodgkinson, 2005, p 67), the radical intention within some forms of growing is positioned as a kind of direct action. Into this category falls growing that foregrounds land use, resistance to global food, acts of refusing capitalist food systems and seeing growing as a form of imagining other ways of doing things. This radical interpretation of growing is akin to 'guerrilla gardening' and its implications of subversive action and land reclamation (Adams and Hardman, 2014). As Certomà et al (2019, p 1) note, '[p]lanting tomatoes – under specific conditions and in specific contexts – has thus been broadly appreciated as a political gesture'.

The contextual point is of course crucial – plenty of growing projects have a far more implicit politics, or certainly less radical ones. Nettle (2014), in response to this, restricts her work on community gardening as direct action across Australia to those projects whose politics are overt and whose position is clear. Recognizing the limited impact of community gardening at even an urban scale, she situates growing as demonstrating an alternative way of living the city and relating to other urban dwellers, a politics of prefiguration and example. Yet in this a question arises about whether any kind of an alterity is posed in community gardening more broadly, and what role intentionality and taking an overt political position plays in how we assess the urban interventions of communal growing. It also raises the question of what precise contexts and conditions lead to the emergence of a political growing space. These are questions this book begins to offer an answer to.

Any consideration of the politics of growing also intersects with its relation to broader systemic shifts, particularly around welfare state retreat. As St Clair et al (2020) note, in increasing the competition between organizations for funding, the broader austerity context in Manchester, UK, makes it hard for organizations to collaborate on urban agriculture projects. Neoliberalization has often been used to reference the shifting complex of policy and economic decision-making reshaping contemporary cities. Described as a 'hegemonic project' by Stuart Hall (2011, p 728) and a 'new religion' by Peck and Tickell (2002, p 381), neoliberalism is the dominant driving discourse in this context promoting free market ideology, which David Harvey (2007) has explored as a class project. It is however disputed because of its shape-shifting nature, tied as it is to particular 'path-dependencies' that provoke specific urban manifestations that bear only family resemblance to each other (Peck et al, 2009). It is questioned as a result by radical geographers such as Gibson-Graham (2008) who see focusing on neoliberal processes as counterproductive because of the way it creates a false unity and can be disempowering. Equally, though from a different angle, Barnett (2010, p 269) has argued that critiques of neoliberalization have tended to 'reduce the social to a residual effect of more fundamental political-economic rationalities', thus questioning whether centring economic ideations is beneficial in the study of social processes. For communal growing, neoliberalism is an inescapable context in which growing emerges, yet it is not always central to the politics that emerge there.

A more subtle politics of growing is found among scholars who have questioned the role of community gardens under neoliberal conditions. It has been suggested that growing projects may be unwittingly (or unwillingly) supportive of neoliberalizing governance strategies, even while expressing a collectivity that runs contrary to its vaunted individualism (McClintock, 2014). Community garden activists and organizers often reproduce a narrative of growing as a (temporary) way to ameliorate urban vacancy, despite seeing community gardens as good in and of themselves (Drake and Lawson, 2014). It would be possible to read this as the internalization of a neoliberal discourse, but it seems more akin to Tonkiss' (2013) discussion of the anti-utopianism of temporary projects in the neoliberal city: a willingness to work between, rather than against, the dictates of contemporary capitalism. This suggests the need for a deeper consideration of the live politics of communal growing projects – not only as an analytical category but as a live phenomenon, often making concessions in the face of less-than-perfect conditions (see Ginn and Ascensão, 2018).

In working with escape, my contention echoes this moment of pragmatism, to deliberately turn away from orientations to political economic narratives to attend from the ground up to a more everyday politics. Similarly, Pudup (2008) questions the automatic resistance associated with community gardening, suggesting a more complex idea around the potential production of neoliberal subjectivities in gardening under certain conditions. These subjectivities vary, and need not be totally depoliticized, but depend on the context of their production. Within both Pudup's (2008) and Drake and Lawson's (2014) work, their slightly pessimistic analyses are still about a tension between tacit support of neoliberal policy and the radical intent of projects themselves. This core tension around whether or not growing can be situated as political is often addressed at an analytical level but is not directly explored as a lived phenomenon. In what follows, I want to stay with the everyday (de)politicizations of communal growing. Gibson-Graham (1996) suggest that the unity and power that scholars attribute to capitalism is often a result of that work, rather than a real coherence or unity in the hegemonic project. In sympathy with such an ethic, I want to stay with the ambiguities of political tensions as a lived phenomenon negotiated in the everyday life of communal growing projects.

Situating the culture of the field sites as escapist is a way of characterizing its politics as neither contesting nor complicit, but as deeply ambivalent to questions of politics and justice. While analytically there is a case for the radical potential of growing spaces, it remains a potential and as the case studies here suggest – particularly through the practical conditions affecting the emergence of these two projects – that potential is not always realized. Escape offers a way to characterize this ambivalence; a route into considering the limitations as well as the possibilities of the land politics of communal growing.

Common garden justice

Where there is a radical element to the projects, it centres on reimagining the spaces, and resituating a place for communality within the city (Cumbers et al, 2018). It is naturally not a universal prospect, located and reproducing distinctly narrow community practices around growing. Yet the work of community gardens can still be seen to be aiming at justice. As such, they constitute imperfect actualizations of justice in the city, emerging in situated and contingent ways. I am building here on a vein of community gardening literature that sees the spatial claims of growing and their interventions in the food system as claims on the grounds of justice (Barron, 2017).

The everyday practices of justice in growing are expressed in cultures of inclusion and exclusion, and often in the literature focused on spatial justice. Gardening projects are not always geared overtly towards overcoming exclusions, but the communal in community gardening can be helpful in improving social capital and bridging racial or class barriers (Glover, 2004; Cumbers et al, 2018). But community gardens have also been linked to rising local house prices (Voicu and Been, 2008) and argued to demonstrate gentrifying behaviours (Egerer and Fairbairn, 2018); leading to arguments around the need to be 'just green enough' to make aesthetic improvements without creating adverse gentrifying dynamics (Wolch et al, 2014). Given the increasingly accepted terrain of urban greening as a process replete with political tensions, this book responds to calls to consider the ways urban greening projects and interventions, of which community growing projects are but one type, are limited from becoming radical projects of justice (Anguelovski et al, 2020), while remaining critical terrain for the production of the sustainable city, embedded in the Glaswegian context in tree planting, growing and sustainable food strategies. Through considering inclusivity as the key terrain on which justice is imagined in the field, I explore the pathways taken by community projects towards imagining the just city.

Justice has been understood as consisting in multiple cross-cutting ways, and approaches such as those building on the work of Nancy Fraser (2008) delineate justice as 'multidimensional and intersectional, composed of socio-economic redistribution, cultural recognition and political representation' (Herman, 2021, p 428). Not only, Fraser argues, must we take account of how social goods are shared out, but justice scholarship must also take account of the distribution of equal respect and the ability of all to take part in political life. Fraser (2008) also suggested that the frames of justice are critical – thus it is not just what she calls the *what* of justice that is contested, but the *who* – which is to say, who is considered to be a valid claim-maker, and how the boundaries of claim-making are established, often in stabilized and implicit fashion. Rather than setting up a range of criteria to be met, I treat justice as an empirical topic, tracing the articulation of inclusivity as a way that justice is imagined and practised in the field.

Questions of distribution, recognition and membership in bounded, localized communal practices are highly pertinent. Yet following these concerns through a localized and situated phenomenon does require a certain degree of care, noting as Williams (2016) does the ways in which actually existing practices of justice are 'always becoming' (p 519). This reflects Fraser's (2008) notion that making claims and adjustments to the ways in which justice is framed is iterative:

> Granted, as I noted before, any frame will produce exclusions. But the question arises as to whether these exclusions are *unjust*, and if so, whether there is a way to remedy them. Granted, too, any remedy will produce its own exclusions, which may generate claims for further reframing, if the newer exclusions are seen as unjust. Thus, in the best-case scenarios, we should envision an ongoing process of critique, reframing, critique, reframing, and so on. (Fraser, 2008, pp 149–50)

Through tracing often-imperfect articulations of justice, it is possible to engage with the utopian element of communal growing, the reimagination of city and urban life, that is inherent to community growing as a practice and to recognize processes of critique and reframing on the ground. This is to stay with the attempts, however imperfectly, to envision a more communal urban life to include as many as possible, recognize difference and to represent heterogeneous neighbourhoods; rather than to critique communal growing for failing to reinvent the world without a hitch (Ginn and Ascensão, 2018).

In recognizing the many facets of justice theoretically, and calls to get beyond operationalizations of justice that focus on distribution, recognition and participation (Anguelovski et al, 2020), in what follows, I attend to the micro-processes of attempting to actualize just spaces in the city. In exploring such everyday justice, this book benefits from temporal distance from the initial research. A period of five years between the end of the initial fieldwork and another wave of interviews and visits allows for a reflection not only on the ways in which the ethnographic fieldwork offered a snapshot in time, but offers too a window onto the continued and iterative work of community growing organizations in reflecting on their practice and aiming to improve. Organizations are not static, and they do not remain as they were. They are inherently seasonal, and tend to evolve and mutate as the years pass and as events shift their meaning and purpose.

Tracing practices of justice within communal growing draws out the tensions and possibilities inherent within the projects; and highlights the interlinkages between the challenges of the localized scale and broader urban (in)justices. Concerns have emerged about what is asked of community gardens when they are held to seemingly impossible standards (Ginn and Ascensão, 2018). To get away from a critique from an unreasonable Archimedean point requires an excavation of the utopian moment within communal growing as a way of considering justice as a horizon and a live practice.

Time, place, practice

Contestation and challenge within communal urbanism emerge through the production of a specific escapist space and time. Critical questions arise about what relation this space and time has to the wider urban environment in which it is enmeshed. Is it supportive of dominant temporal narratives, or a source of real contestation? When space is appropriated, when it is enlivened, and lived, it is not always contrary – even if the use of that space is counter to its intended use. This is the point Alistair Jones (2013) is making when he talks about ludic space. Important here is not that contrary spaces, as in some extremely critical formulations, are actually part of the neoliberal urban production of space (Spinney, 2010). It is that some engagements with space are playful rather than subversive, avoiding rather than engaging with power structures. Jones quotes Thrift (1997a) who sums this up perfectly: 'Play eludes power, rather than confronts it' (Jones, 2013, p 1147). Using space is not itself enough: there is a need for a deliberate consciousness and practised subversion in order for a use of space to be deliberately resistant in this sense (cf perhaps the Situationist movement). In the context of crafting communality, this is about the intention as much as the action: community itself is hardly a radical term. As such, the question becomes not just what kind of alternative social practices are produced in the context of communal growing, but what relation they bear to the outside dynamics of the city and what intentions focus the projects.

The concept of rhythm is a useful tool in opening up the relation between internal dynamics and experiences of the broader city. A Lefebvrian notion of 'rhythmanalysis' provides a basis for this in the understanding that '[e]verywhere where there is interaction between a place, a time and an expenditure of energy, there is *rhythm*' (Lefebvre, 2004, p 25, emphasis in original). Relating in part to the therapeutic aspect of gardening, the spaces of the case studies arguably reflect a rhythmic break from the experience of the wider urban landscape. The emphasis on seasonality and slowness, certain experiences of being present with others, offer a different experience not only of space but also of time. In this respect, it could be seen to critique contemporary time-relations, a rejection of accelerated time, or time-space compression, of liquidity (Bauman, 2000) and of the disruptive effect of technologies and practices which disconnect from what Ellison (2013) called 'thick time'. Thick time refers to a specific kind of experience of temporality associated with clock time and fixed, continuous spatialities.

The relation communal growing has with time however is more complex than simply offering a bucolic respite from the experience of contemporary time-pressure, especially since this latter itself is problematic, with the acceleration of some depending on the temporal fixity and slowness of others (Southerton, 2009). The regulation of time and the rhythmicity of the field sites play an important part in the structure of their community practice, curtailing as well as creating opportunities for escape. Creating spaces of difference, of other ways of living, as I will explore in what follows, needs to be understood in its class context. Rhythm is not just a site for the production of alternatives but also a space for the production of exclusion (see Sharma, 2014). In this vein, the alterity of communal growing's urban intervention will be discussed here: as potential sites of exclusion, and as potentially problematic escapes for the White middle classes.

Researching community growing projects

The idea of escape as a way to characterize the practice of communal growing in Glasgow grew out of sustained engagement with two such sites over two years in 2015 and 2016; and regular visits to the sites since. Although the term ethnography has been increasingly questioned, the research here involved 'open-ended commitment, generous attentiveness, relational depth, and sensitivity to context' (Ingold, 2014, p 384), all of which are associated with ethnographic methods. During the research, I lived in the West End of Glasgow where the research was carried out. In this sense, I was enmeshed in the broader milieu of both sites. As Swann and Hughes (2016, p 686) note, quoting Elias, this brings 'problems of involvement and detachment'. I was for the most part a stranger to Glasgow initially, but research touched my life in ways that were daily, readily eroding its peculiarity. As Fraser (2013) found in his work on Glasgow gangs, I would regularly bump into people from the field in my daily life. Fraser notes that '[d]uring the fieldwork period, [he] could scarcely go out for a pint of milk without bumping into one or more of them' (Fraser, 2013, p 975). Participants were my neighbours; others' paths crossed mine seemingly randomly in the West End.

I carried out over 200 hours of participant observation and 36 interviews across the two projects, focused on how people used, thought of, felt, organized, worked, relaxed, cared, shared, and otherwise incorporated into their daily lives, the spaces and practices under consideration. Taking an ethnographic approach that combined interviews and observational methods allowed me to explore communality and community, without relying on what people say they do as a good indicator of their behaviour (Jerolmack and Khan, 2014), while giving space to their narrations and understandings.

An ethnographic approach offers a way to be sensitive to the local specificity of the projects (Byrne, 2005; Hall, 2013) in ways that resonate with the relationships gardens had with their neighbourhoods and broader contexts – including the relevance of Scottish politics, Glasgow City Council and the various struggles around neighbourhood distinctions. Utilizing multi-sited research allowed for comparison between similar phenomena, allowing for reflections on the particularities and continuities between the different locales (Carney, 2017). Comparing growing sites is common in community gardening research precisely for its value in teasing out the particular and the specific (Pudup, 2008; Ghose and Pettygrove, 2014; Crossan et al, 2016).

Two case studies were selected from a range of community gardens mapped by what was then known as the Glasgow Local Food Network (it has since become the Glasgow Community Food Network, with many of the same actors involved). Both case studies present established gardens on the edge of the middle-class West End, allowing for the exploration of the evolving dynamics in these edge neighbourhoods. I spent time throughout the active growing seasons of 2015 and 2016 (roughly March to September) volunteering, observing and attending community events, as well as interviewing key organizational figures at both sites. The data gathered differed across the sites. At Woodlands, I took part in regular volunteering at their gardening sessions, whereas at the meadow this tended to be irregular, project-focused volunteering such as shed painting. This inevitably led to a skew in the participant observation data towards Woodlands, and the resultant gap was filled through a focus on interviews with activists and users of the meadow. A slightly different approach across the sites was designed to capture better their distinct characters.

As Coffey writes, '[t]he image of the heroic ethnographer confronting an alien culture is now untenable, and fails to reflect much of what ethnographers do, if indeed it ever did reflect the lived reality of fieldwork' (Coffey, 1999, p 22). In engaging in this research, I was regularly positioned not just as researcher, but as a mother, and as a White, middle-class person. At any given moment, I was talking to those I was similar to, those I differed from, along many axes, and, for the sake of rapport, I often emphasized different personal narratives to reflect this – as Sultana (2007) has argued, difference is constructed in the research moment, and negotiated in the process. Seeing reflexivity as a critical and ongoing practice (Benson and O'Reilly, 2022) helps situate the research as a fluid set of encounters that shift over time.

Parenthood also lent me a personal prism through which to see motherhood particularly, and certain discomforts I felt in the field informed some of the analysis in those sections. I reflect on those moments in what follows, where it becomes relevant. However, as Matthew Desmond (2016) argues in a postscript to *Evicted*, there's a danger of ethnographic writing becoming about the researcher in first-person narratives. As far as possible, I focus on other people's stories, feelings and doings to illustrate the narrative. Nevertheless, there are notable ways in which I became to some extent part of the fabric of the garden and meadow: not least because as a White European with a child occasionally in tow, I blended in. I am sure I owe some of the material on parenting to this; yet what I hope to foreground in what follows is the many interweaving lives, ideas and concepts that might illuminate how we understand spaces of urban escape.

The original ethnographic fieldwork for this book finished in 2016, and although I have been writing about the work since then, I only returned to live in Glasgow again in 2019. Becoming a gardener again at the Woodlands Community Garden, and returning to the meadow, required developing a new relationship to the space – less focused on analysing and unfurling the relations of the space in situ, though still attending to shifts over time. This allowed me to appreciate the spaces in new ways, and in particular the peace of both places became hugely important to myself and my small family during the COVID-19 pandemic until we moved again in 2022. In returning to the material to form the book, my writing is now, as ever, positioned through and within this sensibility – not only as an academic but as a parent and Glasgow-resident. As Farhana Sultana (2007) reminds us, the intricacies of who we are in relation to the field are neither simple nor static.

Woven throughout the following chapters are the way that the concept of escape illuminates the practices of communal growing as an urban intervention that has a distinctive politics that is contradictory (McClintock, 2014; Ginn and Ascensão, 2018) – at once radical and not, liberating but connecting people in tighter webs of obligation, both inclusive and exclusive. In order to pursue this in the pages that follow, the book begins with an opening chapter that offers brief histories and sketches of the case studies and their constituencies, upon whose experience this book necessarily rests. It also introduces the broader context of Glasgow, its growing project networks and its present and recent historical forays into regeneration. Chapter 3 takes off from the idea of escape, offering an ethnographic exploration of the concept and its grounding in everyday experiences. Chapter 4 then asks the question of justice begged in much of this: who gets to escape? In doing so, it fleshes out the inclusionary discourses around both case studies and asks what can be learned from the boundedness of the projects. The next chapter then develops this picture, expanding on the concrete interventions communal growing makes in urban space in order to draw out the materiality and discourse of situating the case studies in order to understand escapism as a performance of a specific kind of urbanism. Chapter 6 looks at communal escape's paradox – the idea of escaping into care and responsibility to each other. This draws out contemporary community theory and notions of positive freedom to expand on this initially contradictory idea. Chapters 7 and 8 ask what politics might be situated within the practice of escape, the former engaging with strategic neutrality as a policy for negotiating the field of community gardening; while the latter explores the subjective political imaginations of the project. Both chapters thus deal with the political ambivalence of urban escapism between narratives of justice, imaginations of politics and practices of closure. Chapter 9 then takes a longer view on changes over time, arguing for a longer temporal view on communal growing as necessary for considering how community, politics and justice emerge.

The book concludes with considerations around how this contributes to our understanding of coming challenges around sustainable cities. Throughout, thinking with escape is a way to think with the ultimate ambivalence of growing as a practice, and this opens up to an array of similar community-oriented practices whose collective politics are inherently obscured.

2

Urban Growing in Glasgow

Dear green place

> Glasgow means green place,
> but it's kaleidoscopic, and I mean
> that with glossy, glassy, hallucination.
> Places that are nobody's property
> are everybody's property, up in the
> air. That's what's mesmeric. There are
> places in a place.
>
> Herd (2021, np)

Part of the escapist appeal of communal growing spaces such as community gardens and urban meadows lies in the sense of different ways of living the city. They offer what the poet Colin Herd, in a poem for a green space map from 2021, might call 'places in a place'. Urban growing spaces open up a reconnection with natural rhythms and a disconnection from putatively urban pressures of time and space. This is read within a narrative of Glasgow as the 'Dear Green Place', a naming which sits strangely against its industrial (and post-industrial) history and its colonial heritage as an important city in the British Empire.[1] Yet the number of parks, river fronts and increasingly long-term stalled spaces reclaimed by nature (like the Cuningar Loop in the East End, or the former Claypitts site in north Glasgow) reinstate a connection between a supposedly natural history and a human one. Glasgow's 425 hectares of derelict and vacant land in 2018, the largest urban concentration in Scotland, offers an interesting view onto this, often reclaimed first by buddleia and other invasive plants, and eventually, if left to it, renaturalized.

In Glasgow, proximity to wild places can be as simple as proximity to abandoned space, which is abundant, especially in poorer areas of the city. The future of such spaces seems to be mixed – with enthusiasm from the Scottish Government for turning such spaces to economic and housing uses balanced against recognition that some spaces are better suited (in the short to medium term) as green spaces and indeed wild spaces (Glasgow City Council, 2019). In the right conditions (environmental, cultural, economic and policy), a place of rubble can become an urban wilderness, with potential to address a range of social issues, not least a limited access for some to urban green space – which can be an acute issue especially in working-class areas of Glasgow. Such a wilderness is a construction, something Jorgensen (2011, p 2) notes when she says that wilderness 'can be seen as an idea, a way of thinking about urban space' that centres the agency of the natural world over the human. Indeed, the way that grass and buddleia grow from the cracks in crumbled industrial leftovers speaks to the way human architecture is temporary, always to be maintained against the incursion of plants and urban natures. The illicit uses of such spaces could also lay claim to a different kind of wildness, in the connotative sense of untamed behaviour, edgelands and derelict spaces where different value regimes may develop (Anderson et al, 2018). Yet the 'wildness' present in urban growing places is carefully cultivated, both in its human behaviours and its plant life, constrained and disciplined through community itself, as later chapters come to demonstrate.

Despite the perhaps unhelpful dichotomy of nature and urbanity (Angelo, 2021), the idea of nature and being able to be close to it, even attuned to its rhythms, is at the heart of what is often deeply valued by users of both case studies in this book. Yet contrary to this notion of natural agency, the spaces explored here are cultivated collectively to offer that proximity in a way that feels safe. Such safety is predicated on a boundary policing that says some bodies may remain there, but others cannot. As such, while they can offer a way to embrace the natural world within the city, as a contrast for some to the entrapment of the walls of inadequate housing and lonely lives, it remains one dominated by human actions both past and present.

Glasgow's history as a city of industry and the British Empire shaped the city in profound ways. Certainly the industrial legacy, the productivity from which fuelled the expansion of the Empire, has marked the city with contaminated land and a built heritage that often speaks to long-gone industries of ship building and manufacturing, and the legacies of historical inequalities that locate such industries away from centres of wealth. Glasgow is also home to entrenched structural problems, endemic poverty and health inequalities. Known as the 'sick man of Europe' (Whyte and Ajetunmobi, 2012), the city has high early mortality rates and large swathes of derelict and vacant land. At the height of the COVID-19 pandemic, Glasgow was the area of Scotland under restrictions for the longest, due to persistently high case rates. The outcome of this on health more broadly is yet to be known, but given the high mental health impacts of the pandemic and historic health inequalities that build on years of austerity that have been causally linked to decreasing life expectancy, the long-term impacts of the pandemic on the city may be severe (Whyte et al, 2021).

Derelict and vacant land and buildings in Glasgow persist, but they do so unevenly. In 2015, when the research began, Scottish national statistics suggested that 61.8 per cent of people in Glasgow lived within 500 metres of a derelict site. But taking proximity to dereliction at 1,000 metres, in 2013 it was claimed that almost everyone in the city lived close to a derelict site (Maantay, 2013). Given the small shift in the Glasgow dereliction rate indicated by a drop of 1.7 percentage points between 2016 to 2018, this seems likely to still hold. Dereliction is not evenly distributed, however – some neighbourhoods in the east and north of the city have much higher rates of dereliction. The Calton electoral ward in the east of the city had a level of 99.1 per cent living within 500 metres of a derelict site in 2018. Dereliction and poverty have been linked, although the exact causality of the link between poor health, poverty and derelict land is disputed (Crawford et al, 2007; Maantay, 2013; Walsh et al, 2016).

Given the structural inequalities that haunt Glasgow, focusing on two case study sites that sit, not in the working-class neighbourhoods of the city, but on the edges and interstitial spaces of the wealthy West End, may seem obtuse. Yet the aim of this research was to focus on disentangling the relationships that interventions in derelict space (communal gardens) have with wider urban social processes, particularly around communality, who gets to belong, reorienting urban development and social exclusion. The two case studies are to some extent iconic – offering insight into patterns of ownership, protest and their relation to communal growing. This centres the implications of claiming space and how such spaces exclude, including the subtle dynamics of community, care and justice that are tied up in everyday practices of cultivating a space of escape. Further, the privilege of the neighbourhoods studied here should not be overplayed, although they are not situated directly in areas of high urban deprivation. One of the crucial questions that emerged in both case studies was around diversity and belonging – around who comes to shape the city, and who does not; who comes to belong, and who does not. The interstitiality of the spaces allowed for attention to the daily negotiations in these edge spaces.

Nevertheless, derelict sites in the West End are less common than in other previously more industrial areas to the east or near the river. Vacant sites are however still high. Within walking distance of both field sites in this research, gap sites where tenements have come down stood filled with rubble, buddleia and wildflowers, and an old church demolished into crumbled stone sits beside a play park, which remains a pile of rubble even in 2022. The West End is an area of Glasgow with relatively high property prices, although this drops off fairly quickly around the boundaries. Under these conditions, vacancy becomes a possible opportunity for profit (Weber,

2002; Drake and Lawson, 2014), though it often faces local opposition against housing development. How strident the opposition is differs across disputes. One could point to the difference between the activism around the meadow's potential loss and the much smaller mobilization around the potential loss of high rises in adjacent Maryhill as a way of highlighting class disparities between mobilizations; but also issue disparities. As later chapters attest, the power of an urban green space symbolically is different, and much easier to make common, than a protest against the demolition of high-rise housing. The council claims a projected housing shortfall that must be met, which often overrules local opposition. Yet Glasgow's long-term large-scale vacancy problem has provoked not a rush to infill housing in the many hectares of derelict land, but a focus on temporary land uses, particularly within a series of focused council-run regeneration attempts called the Stalled Spaces programme.

This must be understood within a historical shift in regeneration attempts in Glasgow, moving from a more social focus (improving housing and amenities) to one driven by economic measures of city success, inviting foreign investment, iconic developments and celebrating globally visible urban spectacles with 'legacy' projects (Paddison, 2002; Mooney, 2004; Crawford et al, 2007; Paton et al, 2012, 2016), Particularly these efforts have been criticized for stigmatizing areas as beyond help, blaming 'problem people' (Paton et al, 2012), and also for a particularly thin notion of consultation, a veneer of participation, but with a real focus instead on economic goals and city marketing (Paddison, 2002; Mooney, 2004; Crawford et al, 2007; Macleod, 2012). These efforts have primarily focused on the East End (where the Commonwealth Games were hosted in 2014) and the centre of Glasgow, including the development of an area promoted as the International Financial Services District. The West End's relative affluence means that it has not been the focus of such large-scale regeneration attempts, although it retains a Glaswegian level of vacancy. If anything, the West End has begun to encroach down to Partick (documented in Paton's [2014] work on the gentrification of Partick and its effect on working-class residents) and northward into Maryhill, though it does so in incomplete and complicated ways. These broader dynamics are critical for understanding the field sites and their emergence. Both field sites sit on the edge of the West End, one to the north on that Maryhill border, and the other to the east in an interstitial area between the West End and the centre of town. Their interstitiality is notable in that it provides a space for potentially heightened dynamics of contestation, but it also opens up space to see how justice and the right to the city play out in spaces of relative affluence. Within the context of the valorization of Glasgow's West End, it also provides fertile ground for exploring who gets to determine Glasgow and whose voice matters in those conversations.

Within this, it is worth questioning the narrative of 'dereliction' that comes to define the spaces that are to be turned into high-rise offices or community orchards. Communal growing projects are most often engaged in revitalizing land that has lapsed into disrepair, leading Drake and Lawson (2014) to question their association with vacancy, and the potential complicity in regeneration this implies. Behind this criticism is a question: what does it mean to be derelict? A counter-reading of dereliction would parallel Weber's (2002) work on the purposive use of the term 'blight'. Writing about redevelopment in the United States, she highlights the use of the organic metaphor of blight to invite in creative destruction and redevelopment. Dereliction as a result of creative destruction, in the phraseology borrowed from Schumpeter, has been argued to be a normal part of capitalist development (Harvey, 2007; Németh and Langhorst, 2014). 'Derelict' does much the same work as 'blight' – it devalues current uses of the land (by plant life, illicit uses by the homeless, or dog walkers), and stigmatizes it as problematic, as empty. The Scottish Vacant and Derelict Land Register, and other official registries, do not take into consideration unofficial uses, usually illicit as they are. In this respect, is land ever truly disused or derelict, or simply outside of the circuits of capital and bureaucratic definition? It would seem spaces become illegible outwith these discursive boundaries (Scott, 1998). This is a critical background within which collective growing projects work to position themselves as legible within systems that do not recognize illicit use or marginalize unofficial local representation, and whose predominant measure of success is economic or quantitative.

Research on creative urbanism has drawn a link between dereliction and the possibilities of what Loukaitou-Sideris (1996) called the 'cracks in the city', although this language emphasizes marginality and miscreant behaviour. Yet the dividing line between creative appropriations of space being seen as alternative or progressive, and their role in gentrification and capitalist development is thin (Andres and Grésillon, 2013; Tonkiss, 2013; Spataro, 2015; Kamvasinou, 2017). 'Meanwhile uses' are riddled with ambiguity. In the context of community gardens, it has specific implications: community gardens often utilize spaces which might be deemed derelict, vacant or 'under utilised' in the terms of Stalled Spaces programme, the Scottish Government's funding stream for meanwhile use (Glasgow City Council, nd). Given the focus on temporary use in this form of interstitial urbanism, that Németh and Langhorst (2014, p 144) speak of as 'intentionally time limited' use contrary to the 'preferred permanent option', one can question their conclusion that this can be a boon for communities. They do note, however, that meanwhile uses may cause all sorts of pitfalls, from the tension-wrought process of negotiating the end of a tenancy, to the potential for groups involved in the project to return to marginalization, after a brief period of 'community empowerment'. This latter tendency is indicative of the short-term view and low value placed on communities, particularly in reference to their engagement with their lived environment, but also in terms of the shallowness of any attempts to 'empower' or 'cohere' a community.

Growing Glasgow

Glasgow city has around 60–70 community gardens that have emerged from rubble and formal vacancy.[2] They are interconnected through staff mobility, part-time contracts meaning staff sometimes work at more than one site, and informal and formal networks like the Glasgow Local Food Network, which later became the Glasgow Community Food Network. Gardens also often support each other's campaigns and gala days. Community gardens have tended to emerge in Glasgow through local groups organizing around empty spaces, although increasingly local housing associations show interest in creating them. A preponderance of community gardens in Glasgow must partly be apportioned to the scale of dereliction and available space, but also to a movement associated with environmental interest and community-level concern. Networks of activists work together, sharing funding advice and growing knowledge, as well as practically supporting each other through things like where to source half whisky barrels and soil for raised beds. There are alternative forms of temporary urbanism emerging too in response to the swathes of under-used land. These community-focused, if not always community-led, projects begin to move away from the economic rationality of redevelopment efforts in the city, which are geared towards marketization and investment, instead perhaps positing a bottom-up urbanism based in communality and a rationality of sharing and participation.

Within this Glaswegian context, the two case studies chosen represent two prominent examples of communal growing through which to explore communality. Representing two diverse approaches to intervening in the botanical life of the city, they offer a solid basis for comparing differing ways of growing in an urban context and differing styles of communal urbanism. They were chosen as sites with established communal dynamics, but also as sites that differed along a number of axes. First, only one is a community garden, the other an urban meadow. While the literature on community gardens is increasingly established, there is less work on wild urban spaces, which the meadow claims to be. Contrasting the two offers a window onto different forms of urban communal growing and a number of the different formal and organizational possibilities. The meadow in 2015–16 was not particularly formalized as a space, with two organizations working to save it and no formal permission to use the land. Growing holds a particular role within this as a form of protest, as well as an activity in itself. By 2022, when they finally got a formal lease on the land, a degree of formalization had occurred, shifting away from more obviously contentious positioning for the meadow.

By contrast, the community garden is much more formalized, as part of a community development trust, has only one overarching organization, and no battle to save it. Woodlands also own their site, rather than to all intents and purposes squatting it. Thus, the two sites differ along important organizational and formal axes, positioned differently within the broader field of communal growing within Glasgow. In this, they offer the opportunity to think through two different ways in which communal growing emerges, and in their contrast highlight the variability of communal growing. Nevertheless, what emerged was also a great deal of congruence, as will be explored in the substantive chapters.

A burnt-out tenement gap site

The first case study is the Woodlands Community Garden. It is part of a wider charity, the Woodlands Community Development Trust (WCDT), with aims broader than growing vegetables and the funding to do so. Its distinctive position in the Glasgow community gardening scene has produced many connections with other sites. Its distinctiveness derives not only from its longevity (surviving since 2008, with the community garden officially opening in 2010) but also the scale of interventions carried out by the WCDT. Some visitors to the garden expect it to be a large professional affair and are surprised that it is only the size of a tenement block, and primarily consists of raised beds for individuals and families, and some communal plots and fruit trees. It is neighbourly in scale and in focus.

Woodlands, the area the garden and trust is named after, is an interstitial area – on its eastern side bordered by the M8 motorway and beyond that the city centre, and with the affluent West End proper to its west. The M8 motorway, largely built between 1965 and 1980, is strongly associated with the demolition of 'grand 19th-century buildings' that would have been minutes' walk from Woodlands (Docherty, 2019). The effect of the major road is to carve a hard border between the city centre and the West End, with pedestrian and cycling access between the two forced to navigate major junctions or intermittent bridges. It is in many ways a transitory space, with a large number of temporary residents and a disproportionate number of houses of multiple occupancy and privately rented accommodation (to students to some degree because of the proximity to the university). This has been made particularly obvious by research commissioned in 2016 by the WCDT. The garden sits in an area of middling deprivation, neither greatly affluent nor home to great deprivation. It is in this sense mixed and ordinary as Scottish neighbourhoods go.

The Woodlands Community Garden emerged from a gap site that, by the time it was turned over to the WCDT, had been vacant for decades. The Trust built on the other sites given to them, but not the site of the garden. Nevertheless, the garden's previous life as a tenement is obviated in the landscape of the garden, where the path from the road has been built up to street level, and slopes down on either side to the level of the foundations. The garden emerged from a collaboration between the Trust, which emerged from a period of dormancy in 2008, and an activist organization, Garden Revolutions of the West End (or GROW), who seemed to shortly after disappear entirely. Despite such apparently radical emergence, the mature garden is principally a space of everyday growing and sociality within the city.

Areas of the garden sit much below the street, and the process of creating the garden involved sculpting its current shape from the rubble. After a house fire in the 1970s, the site lay vacant until 2010. Alongside the garden, the WCDT also runs a community café and built a community meeting room between 2016 and 2017, from which it now manages a number of outreach and education projects. While the garden is the main concern of this research, its entanglement and sympathy with the other projects means considering gardening alongside these other activities made sense. The garden lends legitimacy and support to the other projects, as well as sharing volunteers and sometimes physical space with them. The garden as a social phenomenon does not stop at the physical or formal boundaries of the site itself. It encroaches onto the lane behind the garden, growing in raised beds along the lane, and onto the street in hand-painted signs and wooden planters hung off fences.

Woodlands provides an interesting case here not just because it has physically intervened – reshaping the physical fabric of the city – but because it does so with a specific ideological mandate, invoking the idea of community as a basis for locally driven development. In this is a reification of the local and the communal that raises questions about for whom cities are made and using whose ideas. It also in its valorization of the community idea recalls the question of whether local is automatically progressive, what Purcell (2006) called the 'local trap'. Who is local to Woodlands however is of specific interest, since it is not a stable nor homogeneous group. The garden sits in a less valorized area with a high turnover of students and temporary tenants. This leads to tensions around whether or not Woodlands as a neighbourhood is properly cared for, something the WCDT are directly engaged with trying to change, including with hand-painted street signs that encourage people not to 'waste Woodlands'. They are actively changing the area, attempting to 'green' it and providing opportunities for communal behaviour to emerge. Exploring their engagement with development, justice and politics shines a light on city-making at a local level, their claim to a 'right to the city' (Lefebvre, 1996) through planters, painted signs and taking up space predicated on a vision of inclusive localism, imperfectly actualized (see Featherstone et al, 2012).

An abandoned council playing field

The second case study is colloquially known as the North Kelvin Meadow, and the Children's Wood. Fondly, people refer to the meadow and wood interchangeably. The settled terms by which people refer to the space belies the contestation behind the name of the space itself. Although signs carved in wood or printed on paper and laminated appear on the site declaring it as the North Kelvin Meadow and Children's Wood, the council in 2016 was still referring to the space as 'the former Clouston Street pitches'. This nominative contest is part of a broader challenge around the possible development of the space into housing, over which a campaign emerged to save the space and what it has become.

Its local names refer to what has happened since it was last used as pitches. The green space on the northern edge of Glasgow's West End is largely grassy now, with well-established shrubbery and many trees. Some are naturally occurring birch and buddleia, others have been deliberately cultivated, such as the cherry and apple trees. It has also gained human-built structures from tree houses, to raised beds and children's play equipment. The North Kelvin Meadow is generally taken to refer to the whole site, and it is a name that is encompassed by the campaign of the same name to save the site from being developed into flats. The whole space can also be called the Children's Wood, although this name more often refers to a wooded section of the green space where birch trees proliferate, that has been populated with a small wooden tepee structure and a mud kitchen. Besides referring to the physical space of the site, the Children's Wood also refers to a splinter group from the North Kelvin Meadow campaign that emerged in 2011. Its nominative focus on children belies a much broader concern with community building and campaigning to save the space. They also in later years began to develop the meadow into an asset for locals. What is of interest here is not just the space itself but the relationship between the various charitable organizations, networks of people, and the practices they engage in.

The trajectory of contestation dates back to the 1990s when plans to develop the site for housing faced local dissent. A charity called the Compendium Trust was created to turn the site into a sports facility, instead of turning it over for housing. This campaign to some extent succeeded: the housing plans failed to gain planning permission. Years later, after the sport facility plans fell through due to a funding shortfall, activists and organizers disbanded. That was in 2006–7. In 2008, plans emerged to develop meadow again, and the plans were highly contested by local groups. Out of dissent to this phase emerged the North Kelvin Meadow campaign and latterly the

Children's Wood organization. Both names refer to charitable organizations as well as spaces within the site in Glasgow, and both groups organize activities from growing sessions to protests and gala days. Both have fought to keep the meadow as a wild space, as communal land, rather than turn it into housing. Along the way, they have turned the space from under-used sports pitches (overgrown with grass) to the green haven that it is now. Questions arise however as to whom gets to share in the abundance of green space in this particularly green area of Glasgow. The meadow is equidistant from Byres Road, the affluent shopping street in the West End, and Maryhill Road, the latter often shorthand for deprivation. The space is associated with both, and the tensions arising from different claims to the land are explored in later chapters. These dynamics are worked out around the main activities on site: through dog walking, vegetable growing, orchard maintaining and child's play, and tensions between these.

At the North Kelvin Meadow, things are organizationally fluid. There are two campaigning organizations and a loose collection of parents, dog walkers, growers and other meadow users who are engaged in the space, some more than others. The North Kelvin Meadow organization has been around since 2008, with the Children's Wood starting some years later, and the combined activities present a miscellaneous picture of communal activity. The meadow was not usually called a community garden, although people have actively grown on the site since the first trees were planted (without permission) in the 1990s. Since 2016 a more regular programme of growing has emerged, with a related increase in garden-related activities on site, especially good cultivation and composting. There is also an orchard planted by local people and much work has gone on upon the land to improve it, such as wildflower planting, laying down woodchip and managing tree pruning. In its nomenclature, both locally used names for the site, the North Kelvin Meadow and the Children's Wood, reference the space as a wilder, less tended space than a garden, even if the space requires more management than this suggests.

The case study is of interest in a number of ways, not least in its tensions around who gets to be community. The site is well known for its long campaign to save the meadow from development. This is part of a long trajectory of collective action to invest energy in the space to transform it. It raises questions about who shapes the city and what kinds of sacrifices and compromises are necessary along the way. This is of particular note because of the Glaswegian inflection: the staunchly held notion of inclusion, the strong vein of social inclusion and a deep suspicion of those in power. These are arguably Glaswegian in that they are tied to a sense of place and identity, to questions of Scottish independence and whether the meadow sits in North Kelvinside (arguably a marketing term) or indeed in Maryhill (see Madden, 2017). Contestations around who names, shapes and owns the city refract through this site, making it an excellent place to ask what community means in relation to urban development, exclusion and politics.

The contrast between the sites was a fruitful way to explore dynamics of communality in relation to organizational differences, and the ways in which communal behaviours vary in different formations. Further, when considering the political aspects of communal growing, it seems important to keep a broad notion of what that encompasses in order to think through the different forms and frames, the hindrances and the flourishing, that can be highlighted in a broad comparison of urban communal growing.

From Glasgow to the world

Woodlands Community Garden and the North Kelvin Meadow offer distinct vantage points from which to talk about urban land politics, justice and community. This chapter has taken a broad overview of Glasgow and the case studies in order to situate the following chapters in historical and geographical context. In short, it matters for how we talk about justice, inclusion and community, that the repeated redevelopments of Glasgow have displaced certain residents and focused on certain spectacular, car-driven and event-related regenerations. Comparing the specific Glaswegian context to that of the predominant stream of community gardening work that emerges out of North America opens up why it is important to think outside of that terrain, not least to enrich the discussion of the politics of community gardening. The Glaswegian context's distinctive politics allows the possibility of thinking about the ways in which claiming a 'right to the city' can be an everyday, ordinary activity, not bound up in struggle but reproduced in everyday life (see Eizenberg, 2016).

Much of the community gardening literature has emerged out of North America, with a particular focus on New York's community gardens after they were threatened with mass eviction in the 1990s. A great deal of useful work has come out of this scholarship, but a literature that has a large emphasis on New York is likely to be skewed by its contemporarily high land prices and rampant real estate speculation. This is not to say there is not community gardening literature based outside of New York and the US more broadly: gardens in Milwaukee (for example, Ghose and Pettygrove, 2014), cities across Australia (for example, Nettle, 2014), Berlin (for example, Rosol, 2010, 2012), Manchester (for example, St Clair et al, 2018, 2020) and Singapore (for example, Tan and Neo, 2009; Neo and Chua, 2017) have been studied. Increasing attention is being paid to understudied global south contexts such as Peru (Cody, 2019), metro Manila (Saguin, 2020) and gardens across China (Ding et al, 2022), though a persistent critique of the literature is its Western focus and US dominance (Raneng et al, 2023). What has been interesting in this is that there are important connections between these sites, particularly around questions of co-option, health, community development and neoliberal governance, although in each case inflected with the specificities of its locale.

What makes Glasgow interesting in contrast to New York, Singapore and indeed the cities across Australia is the particular post-industrial situation in Glasgow, with high rates of derelict land and a permissive, even encouraging, local authority who encourage temporary uses of land to combat the high rates of empty and unused lots in the city (Cumbers et al, 2018). The cases studied here also reflect the specificity of the broader UK and Scottish context, including the impacts of decades of austerity, leading to heightened competition and precarity within the third sector (St Clair et al, 2020; Strong, 2020). As such, communal growing as a practice in Glasgow is shaped in distinct ways by the political economy not only of the already discussed regenerations and reimagination of the city, but also by this austerity context.

Calls have more recently been made to expand beyond the Euro-American focus of this literature, and I would echo this (Ginn and Ascensão, 2018; Raneng et al, 2023). But it remains that community gardening in its culture and structures should not be assumed to mean the same thing in different places even within an Anglo-American context, and that such a conversation should not assume that there is a straight line from the sometimes politicized, but often anodyne, practices of urban gardening in the global north, and collective growing practices in places of distinct land politics in the so-called global south. Work that has fruitfully explored, for example, unstable land tenure in South Africa (Kanosvamhira and Tevera, 2022) and health and food insecurity in the Phillipines (Matejowsky, 2013) point to both continuities and different local priorities; how translatable urban agriculture is as a practice, however, would require genuinely comparative research.

Perhaps the most obvious comparative point for Glasgow would be the writings on urban agriculture in Detroit, Michigan. In Detroit perhaps most notably, a problematized relationship with urban dereliction and concerns about the way the city was shrinking has shaped narratives around post-industrial urban growing (Peck and Whiteside, 2016; Paddeu, 2017). The role of urban agriculture within the policy landscape of Detroit has been problematized in relation to gentrification and particularly the erasure of communities of colour in the language of dereliction and emptiness (Safransky, 2014; Walker, 2016; Fraser, 2018; Draus et al, 2019). Glasgow here again is something else: neither dominated by the real estate pressures of New York or London (or to an increasingly extent its near-neighbour Edinburgh) nor heavily influenced by the narratives around the rust belt cities (Peck and Whiteside, 2016). Glasgow is however experiencing brutal and continuing austerity, like much of the rest of the UK, and this is particularly evident in shrinking local authority budgets. The city council are also particularly hampered financially by a recent court case around historical gender pay gaps, requiring a settlement deal worth over £500 million. In this context, there is pressure on the council to sell off assets and cut services, notably in 2021 threatening to close public libraries, to public consternation and campaigning to save them. An application to the Scottish Government post-COVID fund dedicated to public libraries was enough to reopen the libraries in the short term. The Scottish national devolved government publicly sets agendas around land-use legislation, most notably the Community Empowerment Act (Scotland) 2015 which extended community right to buy to urban areas, but the actual enactment of planning legislation sits at a local authority level, causing a degree of complexity to navigating disputes, as the meadow case study highlights. In this sense, to talk about growing in Glasgow is to look at post-industrial possibilities within a complex terrain of austerity governance and limited municipal authority capacity. This is a terrain of opportunity and of potential difficulty, and it is the backdrop and setting against which the action of this book unfolds.

3

The Rhythms of Urban Escape

'A depressurizing chamber'

In the mornings, on the way to school drop off, Natalie and her daughter cut across the meadow. As her daughter gets older, Natalie finds the encouragement onto the site can get rid of a certain funk associated with the morning drudge. No matter how stressed everyone is – getting lunches together, has the homework been done, where are the shoes – the space of the meadow provides what Natalie calls a "depressurizing chamber". It allows for the evaporation of the pressures of getting to school or work, and creates a brief period of quiet, green, social time in an otherwise hurried day. The idea of seeing the dogs and their owners acts too as an incentive to Natalie's daughter to get out the door. Natalie, laughing, admits to me as we talk in the woods that this works on her too. In this way, the meadow provides an important escape, however temporary and mundane, from the pressures of everyday life.

Both projects create time and space for alternative ways of living the city, opening up the possibility of alternative urban rhythms. In attempting to move beyond the pressures of everyday life, the case studies carve out spaces of autonomy and solidarity in the city. I characterize such action as escapist, although the experiences within each space vary between projects and participants, shaping how each place is understood. There are differences between the sites around how structured the rhythms are; but there are also many similarities, especially around reconnection with others and the natural world. In this, escape is a multiplicitous lens for considering communal growing projects.

Rhythm as a heuristic

Natalie's account highlights the everyday rhythms of the space; how the intersection of her school run with the lives of dog walkers creates a social moment in the mornings. In exploring how escape is lived, I draw on the work of Lefebvre, which provides a theoretical grounding for understanding the texture of escape within communal growing. Lefebvre (2004) noted that rhythm was everywhere, constructed at every juncture where place, time and action combine. An understanding of rhythm, he expected, would deepen our understanding of urban life and its various characteristics and structurings, extending his work on the production of space (Lefebvre, 1991, 1996). What rhythm offers is a way to think time and space together (see also Massey, 1994). Rhythm thus offers 'a localised time, or if one wishes, a temporalized place' (Lefebvre, 1996, p 230). In exploring the interconnection of times and places, the notion of rhythm captures the work that goes into producing stability, as well as the possibility of change (Edensor, 2010). Rhythm then is historically inclined, in a consideration of repetitions and layers of rhythm alongside changes.

Here, I approach rhythm as an explanatory concept rather than as a methodology. While rhythms have informed methodological innovation, including visual ethnography (Lyon, 2016) and walking methods (Chen, 2013), I want to stay with the analytical aspect of rhythms here. This does not disavow the importantly embodied aspects of rhythms, but finds that embodiment in ethnographic exploration of field sites rather than in explicitly designed rhythmic interventions. Edensor argues that '[s]paces and places ... possess distinctive characteristics according to the ensemble of rhythms that interweave in and across place to produce a particular temporal mixity of events of varying regularity' (Edensor, 2010, p 69). Here, I argue that the specific 'mixity' of communal growing produces the possibility of escape.

What rhythm lends here is a language for understanding some of the affective characteristics of collective growing practices and particularly a way to understand some of the urban difference posed in growing. The way that time and space *feel* within growing projects, particularly how they can feel slow, and how they can be spaces of possibility, are intimately tied to the rhythms of those places. That the projects both deliberately produced an alternative rhythm to the wider city connects to the idea of producing autonomous space within the urban: establishing a right to produce the kind of city they long for, often a slow city (see Harvey, 2003). Before coming to the politics of escape, however, it is worth setting out its characteristics in practice as they emerged empirically. In this, rhythm lends a heuristic for considering what escape looks like in practice and how it might be cultivated.

Escaping into valued labour

Adam came to the Woodlands Community Garden as something gentle he could do while in physical rehabilitation from a serious accident a few years previously. In the accident, which made national news, he broke both legs in multiple places and his back, and he has been in a lot of pain. Being involved in the garden for him is a useful form of keeping moving, of light exercise which is good for him, although he does have to be careful of his back that is full of metal pins. He has been off work since the accident, which unfortunately happened eight weeks into a new job, just after moving back to Glasgow. Now, instead of being a skilled professional with a nine-to-five job, he does some volunteering, some physiotherapy and is still trying to make sense of how his life is now. He told his story to me over a few afternoons while we worked near each other in the garden. We had been volunteering together for a few weeks, but as another gardener, a friend of his, Lizzie, said to me in a little pointed joke within earshot of Adam, he is not shy of telling his story.

For Adam, as with others, there are a number of reasons to value the Woodlands Community Garden. It does not deliberately try to rehabilitate him or make him useful, but it does give him a sense of purpose and has made him rethink what work should be like. As a practice that relies often on volunteer labour, questions often arise in relation to broader systemic dynamics of neoliberal responsibilization within communal growing projects. Particularly, questions have been asked about the tacit support in communal growing for urban green spaces in the context of reduced state funding for things like local green space upkeep. Rich analyses by those such as Rosol (2012) and Pudup (2008) offer key critiques of the way a neoliberal agenda can be supported (in complex, indirect ways) by the behaviour of communal growers, through becoming entrepreneurial citizens who fix problems for themselves (Rosol, 2012), or in Pudup's (2008) account through learning appropriate (organic) consumer behaviour.

In Adam's case, however, something else is visible: it opens up the notion of labour without exchange – a proto-Marxist imagining of labour as a fundamental action of humans, disembedded in a way from wage or productivity. While talking to me, Adam notes his relationship with work has shifted since spending time at the community garden. Since the accident, he has had to find ways of recreating his life. Being in the garden has meant he has found new things that he enjoys doing – ways of being that are not dictated by a nine-to-five schedule, that benefit others and connect him to new people. He tells me he would like to work in a similar project, although he recognizes the way this is so dependent on often quite variable and unreliable funding.

Skeggs' (2014) important work on the interrelation of economic value with a world of other values is useful for understanding how this reimagination of labour has its own structure of value, within a moral economy of volunteering. In valuing socially oriented work and labouring for a project he believes in, Adam resituates his own values away from a previously 'professional' career towards a more service-oriented position. Adam's transformation demonstrates a reorientation of what matters that can occur within Woodlands. Hanmer's (2021) work on self-valorization and the production of autonomous value by retired urban gardeners in Wales echoes here as gardeners come to define their own value structures.

Adam notes, in his quiet way, how Woodlands is important to him in terms of having things to do and having people around to work with and talk to. In the space of a few hours in the garden, Adam builds things from recycled scrap wood like a flyer holder that he paints with chalkboard paint. He says that it is a good-sized project and that he likes to have these things to do: things to make with your hands that you can complete fairly easily. Being useful and practically employed is something valuable to Adam, yet the timbre of this is distinct: it is socially oriented, collective.

Thus, while the work that is central to the maintenance of communal green space is voluntary, and therefore unpaid except in tea and biscuits, which raises questions about the mismatch between the value of the work to broader society and the lack of economic value attributed to it through pay, Adam's experience complicates this. The way participants themselves experience the growing projects and their social relations are as a phenomenon of value, social contact and often enjoyment. When carried out by those out of work, there may be uncomfortable resonances with compulsory work-programmes (or work-fare). Yet the idea of preparing people for employment (for the first time, or after illness or a break) that can and does occur in community gardens discomforts some community gardeners I spoke to across Glasgow, many of whom would privately condemn explicit programmes in some gardens tailored in this way. For the Woodlands Community Garden, seeing work in such governmentality terms does not account for the subjective experiences that the garden offers respite from: specifically the benefits systems, and difficult physical and emotional recoveries. In this context, Woodlands can be subjectively transformative. In remaking Adam's vulnerability and his physical limitations, Woodlands offers a space in which to rethink what limitations he has, and to work within and beyond a sense of being limited. It undoes and reimagines what it means to be capable, by accepting people as they are.

Thus, despite engaging Adam in volunteer labour that improves the local area for free, Woodlands Community Garden has also shifted in his relationship to labour itself. Adam now wants to work socially, he wants to be outside more, he recognizes the value of the communal way of organizing things he has found at the garden. Volunteering labour is clearly subjectively important in terms of how Woodlands helps people value themselves and their time, but it is crucial to its autonomous and transformative potential that they do so regardless of employment situation. Adam's value to the garden is not weighted by how much he does or does not do, but rather in his continued commitment to the project and its social environment. Whether perhaps in recovery, unemployed (long- or short-term), part-time or heavily pregnant, Woodlands Community Garden is a place where people can feel valued and make a difference. For many, this is a vital aspect of the garden and speaks to a different circuit of valuation within the space, a reordering of what matters in relation to labour (see Skeggs, 2014). Woodlands is a haven for those outside of nine-to-five employment conditions, particularly during its weekday openings. In this way, the space of collective growing is an escape for Adam (and others like him) from thinking only of labour through the idea of work: and it opens up a space for reimagining value, and what work could or should look like.

Spaces of urban escape – here, communal growing spaces – are imagined as distinct from the rest of the city, and performed differently to the rest of the city. In many ways, the escapism of this book rests on the production of autonomous space by participants of communal growing projects *against* the rest of the city, and a consideration therefore of the contrasts and similarities between growing spaces and other spaces traversed by participants in their everyday lives. Thus, an orientation to escape figures as a rejection of the time-space pressures of the contemporary city (usually imagined somewhat homogeneously). But it also figures as a relationship of the space of growing to the world of work and a vision of valued labour. In this way, escape is a practice of justice in that it offers reprieve and a space for re-evaluating current relations, a space of care where care can be felt to be lacking. While Adam experiences this at an important, pivotal moment of transition due to an important life event, others find in the garden a respite to a much slower crisis.

Against, in and beyond work

When I began the fieldwork in early 2015, Mark's position on the staff was unclear, as he was only funded for an eight-hour contract. Before that, he was a casual odd-job man who would be paid for a set number of hours to cover certain tasks. As a long-term volunteer who had spent a great deal of time at Woodlands, he was a valued project member and raised bedder known for his growing experience and practical skills in fixing and maintaining the garden. Mark had no job outside of the occasional work he picked up at Woodlands and had not worked formally for years. He was unwell for many years and attempting to return to work has been hard for him, he told me during one garden session. He worked for a while for a charity in administration but having been away from work, he told me he found it utterly mind-numbing to be behind a desk again 10–4, watching the time go by. He is grateful then for the Woodlands Community Garden finding some funding for him to be able to work, even if it is only for eight hours a week. This also gets the Jobcentre off his back for a few months, since he has an income this way. He sounds bitter as he tells me this, recounting the ways getting work has been tough but that even temporary administrative work has been difficult because he finds it deeply boring.

That spring I also spoke with the garden development worker, Jen, about Mark's employment situation, and was told that he was also going to be paid for some of his work this summer – beyond his eight-hour contract. According to Jen, though, there were concerns over what this might mean for his benefits that needed to be addressed. In this, Woodlands demonstrate their approach to employment – which tries in a difficult funding climate to value project members monetarily for their work, and to maintain a boundary between volunteering and employment, however fuzzy. It also shows the consideration not only for the organization's needs but for the staff as people.

In this, Woodlands offers a reimagination of paid work and its relations, though it does so in a situated way. It operates very much within the capitalist economy and the various systems in place to work alongside and mitigate its harms, as a third sector organization funded primarily by state and private grants. John Holloway (2002, p 88) offered a way of thinking about resistance to capitalism that argued it could work 'against-in-and-beyond a closed, predetermined world'. In many ways, this triad works to explain how Woodlands fits into and culturally pushes back against expectations around work. Adam's example, discussed previously, demonstrates a way of thinking about labour through involvement at Woodlands that situates it against a certain vision of work – reimagining perhaps what work looks like. But as an employer and provider of space to escape from work, Woodlands work both within and against work, navigating at times awkward dynamics such as those faced by Mark.

Woodlands practice a realistic and sensitive approach to their employees and volunteers that tries to take account of different income levels and needs, as well as offer employment when they can. In simple ways, this context-sensitivity expresses itself in the tiered prices for a raised bed for those in employment and those without (usually the figure is about half, but it depends on the size of the bed – some cost as little as £5 for the year for someone unwaged). It is also demonstrated in the sensitivity that the garden has shown towards employees' benefits and financial situations, like that of Mark.

Working within the austere state

The deleterious effects of the recent welfare reforms in the UK have been well-documented, particularly fitness to work interviews and sanction regimes (for example, Moffatt et al [2014], and in films such as *I, Daniel Blake* [2016]). Adam and Mark both had to deal with the benefits system. Adam openly talked about trying to get benefits, but not being able to get past the fitness to work interview. Being denied benefits put greater strain both on Adam and on his parents, who he then had to turn to for money to simply pay the rent. The garden in relation to these struggles for dignity, employment and time to heal, for both Adam and for Mark, is a place to be slow, to be outside of the world of work, and importantly to be valued without needing to be economically active. This has value for participants who are outside of the normal work pattern, a salve against systems like fitness to work interviews and Jobcentres that put pressure on people to not 'scrounge'.

Beyond providing a space of alternative value, the Woodlands Community Development Trust (WCDT) is importantly an employer. But the work it creates, it does in a specific way. For the right person, the WCDT can find funding, as Mark discovered. A certain amount of creativity in funding applications and fund designation keeps core costs covered (the least glamorous and hardest to fund aspect of the community project, including things like insurance and staffing costs). The WCDT work to keep staff like Mark employed. From the eight hours per week contract in 2015, by May 2016, this was a 16-hour contract, split over whenever he can or wants to do the labour, maintaining the physical space of the community garden. He remained steadily employed, and in the pandemic years between 2020 and 2022, he was found fixing things around the garden most afternoons. The funding the WCDT do find lives up to high standards too, as a Glasgow Living Wage Employer, meaning that everyone was paid over £8.25 an hour, as of 1st April 2016. Minimum wage at this point was £7.20 an hour (GOV.UK, nd). The Glasgow Living Wage Employer scheme is one which pre-dates the UK Government's introduction of the so-called living wage, and one that the WCDT have been proud to support.

What is notable in this, and it is a theme to return to later, is that Woodlands create jobs and support those with whom they have a connection. They value and actively work to keep insiders in work. As another member of staff at the Trust put it, trying to keep people on and pay them well is "about trying to honour relationships and networks that we've already established" (interview, May 2016). In a context that is in almost constant flux due to uncertain cycles of grant funding, the WCDT responds by keeping people who have committed time and effort to the cause in their employ where possible. In doing so, it does its best to provide some protection from the precarity of the project members' lives, the broader austerity context and indeed the instability of third sector funding.

Thus, the garden offers refuge for those outside of the working system, and cushions some too within relatively well-paid and sustained jobs. Alongside this, it also bears mention that it offers time away – for some, from the desk; for others, from the loneliness of part-time, freelance work. Particularly, these spaces offer escape from the emotional violence of the fringes of employment. Samantha's experience speaks to this.

She joined the garden as I started the research in 2015, first as a volunteer and later as a raised bedder. Samantha joined the garden as a way of finding connection with others, after going freelance at work made her miss the everyday sociality of having office colleagues. At Woodlands, Samantha met others in a similarly liminal position: mothers and carers, retirees, unemployed people with sundry backstories, and those working irregular hours. She jokingly, even affectionately, called this motley collection of people "waifs and strays". She was speaking of those who were able to attend the Wednesday sessions, which practically excludes those working office-hour, nine-to-five jobs. What Woodlands offers these people is a world of connection outwith traditional working structures. In this, communal growing can open up solidarities beyond work, and a space to think of value against work – indeed, about what else we might value. Woodlands demonstrably tries to work ethically within, but also culturally offers a space to think differently against and beyond work (see Holloway, 2002). In reordering structures of value, and offering spaces for those working irregularly or not at all to find connection and meaning, Woodlands enact a vision of inclusion and justice that sees the value in everyone, regardless of their position in society. Those "waifs and strays" find a place they can gather and belong, where they can be involved in something that feels socially valuable.

Autonomy is a helpful idea here to state in positive terms what is cultivated in urban growing (see Wilson, 2013; Ginn and Ascensão, 2018; Hanmer, 2021). Autonomy is a useful heuristic for making sense of the different kinds of alterity produced in interstitial urban spaces, defined broadly as 'a desire for freedom, self-organization and mutual aid' (Chatterton, 2005, p 545; see also Chatterton and Pickerill, 2010). It helps frame what is at stake. This is about who makes the city and what values are embedded in it, even as it is focused on two very specific places within Glasgow. In this sense, it localizes the right to the city, which is itself too abstract really to speak to the highly specific place-attachment that underpins the action described here.

Thus, communal growing offers an autonomous and escapist way of living the city through creating space for rhythmic disruption and reimagining social relations. It offers a degree of temporal sovereignty to participants, creating or indeed curating a different way of inhabiting space in time. Through this different experience of urban rhythms, the possibility of communality itself emerges. In an iterative, self-fulfilling relationship, reimagined rhythms and communal behaviours co-emerge, brought together under the idea of community itself.

Getting beyond consumption at the meadow

As Natalie's story at the start of the chapter demonstrates, the place the North Kelvin Meadow holds in people's imaginations of the city is primarily as a place of respite. Yet what kind of respite is needed varies naturally among those who use the place. It reflects a sense of different experiences of the rest of the city and what can be difficult in it. What is notable in this is the flexibility of communal growing spaces to accommodate varying visions and needs within escape; in this the meadow can be a salve for many wounds.

For some, the escape posed by the meadow is as a place of decommodified leisure. This often came up for parents, as the idea of the meadow as a free and stimulating place for children to come meant that it was a valuable resource. One home-educator (their preferred term for keeping their children at home to learn, rather than sending their children to school) noted the benefit of the meadow as a place for "not being a consumer". Toni and her three children were often down at the meadow; and I interviewed her while she babysat a friend's young child and kept an eye on two of her own and their dog. The interview meandered as we sat among the trees of the meadow, but she explained that she felt:

> 'Actually doing things is really important. Not just being a consumer or a passive recipient because I think in the botanic gardens you can meet someone there but you very much feel like you're in someone else's place and they're orchestrating everything, whereas here I really enjoy just planting seeds randomly and doing things and that makes me feel connected in another way that is almost beyond, sort of, I can't really articulate it properly.' (Toni, interview, July 2016)

In this, there is an importantly non-commodified element to the meadow, a space away from consumption, where creativity is valued. Intervention in space, Toni's "planting seeds randomly", are not circumscribed and there is an exploratory freedom that Toni feels is beyond her capacity to explain.

Mothers in particular were quick to point out the value of the meadow as a place to simply be, and indeed one can often find parents, alone with children or in smaller groups. Another home-educator, Diana, also acknowledged that the meadow was a place it was possible to be for hours at a time, and reckoned that she spent 8–10 hours there, sometimes, in a way not possible in a formal play park or place you are expected to pay for activities. Those who do not home-educate also recognize this: local parent, Lorna, noted in an interview that her kids "can be entertained for a long time". As we spoke, she was there after school with her sons for the second day in a row, pottering about the raised beds and enjoying the space.

Another mother, Caitlin, was involved in the campaign to save the space, and often volunteered at events and with the toddler group. Reflecting on her son's relationship with the space, she noted that "it didn't matter if we spent six hours here", her son would always be upset when they have to leave, noting a shared love of the place. This is perhaps more notable in Caitlin's case because her son is in the state school system, so she does not have long days to fill with her child as the home-educators often do. Nevertheless, instead of having to move on (like in the parallel situations often described involving play parks or cafés instead of the meadow), the meadow is a space where a temporary stasis, a lingering, is possible, for often incredibly long periods of time. Thus, the experience of periods of nominally unproductive time within the city is a relief for many, whether of a long duration, or as a brief release from everyday pressures. The parents on the North Kelvin Meadow value it as a place for unquestioned long plays, away from the pressure to buy things and as a space of creativity. It is an escape then from compulsory consumption behaviours, and a place to grow and learn slowly.

Yet the meadow is not simply a place to be slow, nor a place of valorizing slowness. Indeed, it has been recognized that the Slow movement and ideas about slowness as socially good are potentially elitist and exclusionary (Parkins, 2004). The escape of the meadow goes beyond this notion of slowness, as each escape is in its own way idiosyncratic. Time spools out differently for those who are not experiencing the hustle and bustle of time-pressured normative urban life. Sarah Sharma's (2014, 2016) work emphasizes the temporal as a category of relational difference – not merely a description of socially neutral physics. To this end, the escape at the meadow is more interesting: because it can also be a place of speeding time up.

Consider Tom, who sits on the edge of the Children's Wood, away from the mud kitchen and the children's play. When I met him by chance one day, he had found a good spot where the difference in surface level between the meadow and the wood creates a natural step, a bench of sorts formed of bridge edgework. It is a comfortable spot among the trees in which to read his copy of the *Sun* newspaper. A regular fixture in the meadow, Tom has no interest in joining the campaign to save the meadow, but he likes the space. His fondness for the meadow stems from the change of scenery it affords him from his home, and the fresh air. We sit and talk one sunny morning, and he tells me: "[I]t is nice to get out the house. You get sick of staring at the same wallpaper down in Wyndford."

Tom's mention of the Wyndford estate, his home, and his choice of newspaper highlight a different class positionality to perhaps Natalie, a working professional who lives on the wealthier side of the meadow. Tom's home estate is known for being statistically deprived, sitting in the most deprived 5 per cent of Scottish data zones, according to the Scottish Index of Multiple Deprivation (2016). But Tom's narrative is mostly notable for its boredom: swapping the wallpaper's unchanging façade for the openness of the meadow. Tom's use of the meadow is about moving time on, instead of being "sick of" sitting at home. This use of the meadow is not about taking a pause from hectic life, but about injecting some pace into an otherwise uneventful older age. Seeing the meadow as a place of escape opens up these different vectors of experience – not just the slowing down to appreciate nature and neighbours, but using the space to inspire pace, to inspire creativity and as a place of active learning for home-educators.

A different rhythm in the city

As such, communal growing projects become recognized as places of reconnection in part because of a sense of disconnect inherent in other city rhythms. The previous examples across the two case studies suggest not only the idiosyncrasy of urban escape, but that places of comfort, connection and peace are sought by those across class and age differences. Tom escapes the boredom of older age and his home; Natalie escapes the hectic daily life of a working mum. Samantha escapes the isolation of working from home; Adam finds a place to escape the difficulty of the benefits system, and a place to imagine recovery and his new life in. Across the board, communal growing projects provide havens that are as heterogeneous as their participants, but share commonality in offering space to reimagine daily life and find new rhythms.

This reconnection is an explicit rejection of urban disconnection, often associated with the pace of contemporary life but spanning a much deeper rhythmic disconnect in various forms. Theoretically, the city has been positioned as a place of speed (Crang, 2001; Prior, 2009; Wajcman and Dodd, 2016). The sense of reconnection available in urban growing is also prescient in the context of the acceleration hypothesis. Rosa's argument is that modernity can be seen as a long process of acceleration: 'an increase in the speed and ease with which space can be traversed or bracketed' (Rosa, 2005, p 447). Indeed, for some, communal growing is a place to be slow and within this slowness there is an often implicit criticism of the rush of the contemporary city. This returns to the Slow movement, which takes a politicized approach to slowness. Honoré notes that being 'slow' is akin to different 'ways of being, or philosophies of life. ... It is about making real and meaningful connections – with people, culture, work, food, everything' (2004, pp 4–5).

However, as Rosa (2003, p 5) notes, acceleration also implies a 'flipside' in that it itself produces a great deal of slowness and indeed stasis, from the traffic jam to the End of History. Thus, while speed might be ideologically linked to urbanization and modernity, it is not uniformly nor universally experienced as such (Sharma, 2016). In this context, communal growing's escape is a response to the multiple vicissitudes of contemporary urban life.

As Southerton (2009) argues, time pressure as a psychosocial experience does not map well on to the amount of free time available to contemporary people (see also Sullivan and Gershunny, 2018). Instead, it relates to a cultural acceleration – to the experience Erickson and Mazmanian describe as 'circumscribed time' (2016), a sense of time pressure and a culture of busyness. In reaction to circumscribed time, communal growing offers a place to escape, embodying slowness (when needed) and offering a space outwith the need for productivity. This goes beyond slow as a pathway to productivity (cf concerns raised by Michelle Bastian [2014] that slowness is an alibi for capitalist accumulation). Thus, escape can mean alleviating the time-space pressures of the capitalist city beyond a simple acceleration narrative. This is to emphasize the polyrhythmia of the city in everyday lives, and to recognize both the psychosocial pressures and cultural dominance of 'circumscribed time' and the slowness of those outwith valorized circuits of capital who are often left waiting (Auyero, 2011; Sharma, 2016).

Both sites in this respect give time outside of the pressures of the capitalist system – where vegetables can be grown rather than bought, where people talk to their neighbours, where children play freely for hours and parents breathe in the trees and the seasons. This has precedent across much of the literature in communal growing, which tends to emphasize the potential for urban social sustainability, cohesion and the like (Ferris et al, 2001; Tan and Neo, 2009; Crossan et al, 2015), although the more radical aspects of this, its externality to norms of consumption and work, are less often directly engaged with (a good exception is McKay, 2011).

Of course, urban growing cannot offer total escape, both projects recognize this, and being involved can strain time as much as lessen its pressures. The community grower hired at the Meadow in 2016, Ivan, was quick to point out how difficult it can be to get new people involved because of their work and family time commitments. He noted that while locals might like to get involved, we often "don't have time for stuff that interests us". In this critique, and accounts of the projects as spaces apart from capitalist production and consumption, the meadow and garden are offered as oases away from capitalist pressures though they cannot offer systematic change. Among the few who espouse these critiques, such as Ivan and his partner Toni, the colonization of everyday life by the capitalist productivist model of time is notably presented as restricting their ability to engage with that which we might otherwise wish to. Temporal control is something that is carved out from the city. It should, however, be noted that a radical anti-capitalist critique is uncommon, rather than central to understanding the spaces. Instead, a milder notion of the projects as depressurizing, therapeutic or simply peaceful was far more common.

Gardening is increasingly recognized as a therapeutic activity (Ferris et al, 2001; Sempik et al, 2005; Pitt, 2014), and the associations at both projects of slowness and peace with mental healthiness are suggestive of this. Armstrong (2000) summarizes research suggesting the dietary benefits of community gardening and increased levels of exercise, and her own research suggests gardening has a positive impact on the mental health of participants. The rhythms of communal growing projects are a potential pathway for this impact; participants in both projects talked of the improvement in their own mental health from their involvement in growing. This is suggestive too in references Hartmut Rosa makes to the German literature on the psychological pressures of acceleration in the work of Baier and others (Rosa, 2003, 2005). Alternative temporality is akin to a form of therapy, and it is valued by participants. Some having 'existential crises' find their way to the Woodlands Community Garden, seeking a different kind of place to be. As Mark noted, after saying how "valued" he felt in this garden: "I think the garden's really good for that – if you're suffering mentally or physically, it's a good place to come and be, really good" (Mark, interview, July 2016).

As a place to thrive and recover, the image of the escape emerges as a pertinent metaphor for the potentials of communal growing. It is of course suggestive, rather than clear, what the relation of slowness, plants, trees, other people and mental healthiness is precisely. Perhaps it is notable that since 2020, Woodlands have been offering 'Nurture in Nature' sessions, which with a local trained therapist allows small groups to interact with nature as a stress-reduction tool, as well as offering one-to-one support. That nature and company so often come up as a solutions or salves for mental ill-health suggests a powerful interaction of people, places and time. It recalls Lefebvre's (1996) notion of 'eurhythmia': of harmonic rhythms of health. In this, it also highlights the sense of the disturbed or arrhythmic quality of life against which the slowness of the meadow and garden are distinguished.

Seasonality

The complexities of escapism as an urban practice emerge through the relation of growing projects to seasonality – particularly in the experience of downtime in the year. In Scotland, winter is a dormant season for food growers, a period really of 'overwintering': of mulching tender perennial plants for a season, of simply surviving as growth slows. It can be used as a time for improving soil quality through green compost or leaving seaweed on a raised bed. In Glasgow, winter can be a little unforgiving in terms of the weather. Getting outdoor learners into appropriate rain gear and warm clothes is the bane of the meadow organizers' lives, as Rachel – who works closely with local schools and nurseries to get them to use the space – put it:

> 'Getting a Scottish person into a half decent rain jacket and get out when it's wet. … So just put decent clothes on! So that's one big, just huge, huge effort we just make people realize, use the outdoors but be smart about it. You need to put the right clothes on! You won't be happy!' (Rachel, interview, July 2016)

When they manage to entice people down to the meadow in winter, they light fires to keep warm and toast their lunches. They put down tarpaulins and the dense birch trees stop some of the rain reaching toddlers in the woods. The casual use of the meadow declines, however, as the weather becomes less clement for dawdling. It takes on a more austere look, too, with the leaves gone from the deciduous trees and the grass slow in its growth.

But the limited amount of growing that can occur outside during a Scottish winter mean that spring is a particularly important time of year. April becomes a renewal in the traditional symbolic sense, the beginning of the year far more than January. Many begin regularly visiting the Woodlands Community Garden again in April. This seasonality brings an annual pattern of decay and rebirth to the lives of communal growers, each spring marked by a reconnection to the garden and an efflorescence of activity at the meadow. But it also marks the partiality in temporal terms of any form of urban life that might be situated in communal growing. As primarily outdoor occurrences, social growing is limited in its capacity to offer a year-round escape from the capitalist city for all but the hardiest of escapees.

The annual repetition brings with it ebbs in the flow of people, and the rebirth of the garden, often bringing in new volunteers. This was particularly notable when as a researcher I returned to the garden in late March 2016 and the volunteers who began coming along were mostly new. There was still significant overlap, particularly among the longer-standing raised bedders, but volunteers shifted during the second season of the research. Those still connected to the garden in spring carry forward the ideals and culture of the garden, but its fluidity, its change year on year, is in part a reflection of this period of dormancy, during which people's commitment wanes and attention is dropped. This also tends to be when Woodlands allocate new beds and invite in new gardeners, early in the calendar year in preparation for the growing season. In this way, the temporality of the garden is determined to some extent by its connection to the seasons itself – a reflection of the yearly shifts so often flattened out by the year-round availability of the same fruits and vegetables in many shops. As communal and organized projects, the meadow and the garden both were often engaged with seasonality and indeed the celebration of seasonal change, encapsulated by harvest festivals, Halloween carnivals and mid-summer events.

Engagement with annual planetary rhythms offered to participants a notable discontinuity with capitalist time. Communal growing's way of living the urban does not simply sit inside a flatter temporality without problematizing it. The rhythm of food growing collides with the rhythms of food shopping, making obvious the flatness of consumer temporalities. In growing, one must work with the seasons and with the weather. Gardeners with less experience need to learn to think differently about time's relationship to food. This means learning to think seasonally, as Tracy, one of the more established growers, pointed out to me during my time at Woodlands. Discussing her raised bed one day in the hub, Tracy talked me through how planning her bed involved a long-term kind of thinking. She told me she was harvesting a lot at that moment; there seemed at that time to be a lot of broccoli ready for eating. The question then arose as to what to plant up next. She made a comparison between the different ways of thinking about time that exist for her, drawing a distinction between the time of supermarket food buying and the time of seasonal growing. In an age of going to the supermarket to buy what you are having for tea, she told me, it is a bit harder to think in terms of growing seasons, since you have to start planting now what you are going to want later in the year. It is a slower, longer-term skill.

This sense of thinking in a longer timeframe, rather than the foreshortened time of supermarket consumption, challenges raised bedders, although it ought to be foregrounded that no one relies solely on their raised bed for all sustenance. Even the larger beds are not big enough feed a gardener for a year, nor are they required to. Instead, gardening creates a contrast between the fast time of supermarket consumption – what do I want to eat today – and the slow time of growing – what might I like to eat in autumn. Having this contrast highlights the difference between them, creating for some – like Tracy – an awareness of the dislocated pace of supermarket shopping. We can see this latter as a kind of arrhythmia, which Lefebvre introduces as a moment when the general polyrhythmia of the social (its multiplicity of different rhythms) becomes 'discordant, there is suffering, a pathological state (of which arrhythmia is generally, at the same time, symptom, cause and effect)' (Lefebvre, 2004, p 25). In this, we can see arrhythmia as an embodied form of cognitive dissonance. The rhythms of communal growing, aligned as they are with seasons and growing, can highlight the accelerated and artificial speed of the supermarket and call into question its ease and simplicity.

Thus, the projects have a specific rhythm that can reconnect participants with the shifts of the calendar and the seasons. For experienced garden workers, like Ivan who worked for a period at the meadow, this is part of the impetus behind the community development aspects of gardening. Ivan and his partner Toni are both interested in permaculture methods, which explicitly connect nature and social connection within a holistic worldview. The three core principles of the permaculture method are: earth care, fair share and people care. Given that background, his opinions on the meadow as a place of connection are perhaps unsurprising, although clearly articulated:

> 'We're very disconnected from nature, we're disconnected from each other, we're disconnected from ourselves and the class system thing also ties in there somewhere I'm sure. But you know we're disconnected from all stuff so people can come down here and they can start to connect a little bit again with the land, and with the trees and with

the birds, and if they can also come down here and start to connect again with other humans within the area then that's a good thing as well. So I do really see [the meadow] as a connector.' (Ivan, interview, June 2015)

Ivan's clear sense of the meadow as a conduit for reconnecting with the land and with people comes partly from his own radicalism. But it also relates to the patterns of connection observable in both projects. Seeing the same people again and again, the rhythmic, repetitions of people in space creates for some a sense of continuity and community. Something that has been suggested to ground communality is a solid foundation of repetitions in time and space (Studdert and Walkerdine, 2016b). Repeated interactions build a foundation from which communality can grow, relationships can be built, and patterns of care can emerge.

Urgency versus longevity

A notable temporal contrast between the sites is the presentism that arises from the historical situation of the North Kelvin Meadow. At the meadow, the temporalities possible there are restricted by the sense of possible destruction and produce a way of being that is focused on the now, on the present tense. Between 2008 and 2016, the North Kelvin Meadow was under threat of demolition due to the council's agreement to sell the land to developers, pending planning permission. The planning process was significantly stalled by the global financial crisis, and the campaigns and on-site activism that flourished in the eight years that followed led to the rejection of the planning permission and the zoning of the space as open green space in the city plan. Nevertheless, during the fieldwork, this led to a distinct kind of temporality associated with the existential threat the space experienced during this time. This was emphasized by the presentist attitudes that are represented by people like the Conservation Volunteers who work with the Children's Wood. Talking to them, it was notable that they emphasized what they were doing as something that would benefit people in that moment – "something they can use now".

This was in contrast to the position of the campaign organization that, trying to build historicity, tend to emphasize the position of the pitches as historically leisure space and never before built upon. Campaigners drew on the historical use of the site to house Polish soldiers during the Second World War, and its prior use as a sports pitch to claim a sense of pristine space. For example, on the website of the North Kelvin Meadow campaign, they show a 'timeline', which begins: '*[P]re-1939* – Records show there were never any buildings on this land'. An older campaigner, Alasdair, who lived directly adjacent to the meadow, reflected on the hubris of the council in moving to sell the land off: "I've thought about [Glasgow City Council's] arrogance in just deciding that they were going to set all this for building. And we've, the old committee established beyond doubt that *this land is for leisure use only*, and they've just ignored it" (Alasdair interview, December 2014, emphasis added). Alasdair's invocation of the "old committee" reflects previous periods of campaigning to save the space, which he was also involved in, that fought another attempt to put housing on the meadow.

Nonetheless, the lack of longer-term security foregrounds a present tense in the space, underpinning its use for some. Certainly it did for Caitlin, a parent on the Children's Wood committee, who often brought her child down and volunteered both supporting the playgroup and at public events. Her closeness to the meadow campaign fostered in her a sense of urgency. In recent years, she says, it has become so apparent that using the space is important. She told me she likes to come and use it because she knows it might not always be there. Even unwell, she felt the need to turn up to protests and site visits saying, "I have to because it just means so much to me". Knowing it might soon be gone leads her to reflect that "if it gets taken away, I will be one chained to the railings". This threat to the land creates a certain ephemerality and urgency to using the meadow. During the period of this research in particular, this sense of urgency brought the space into the foreground, and also brought its users into focus to each other, highlighting their intertwining lives within the meadow.

The question of collective rhythm

The differences in rhythmic quality between the two spaces point to how rhythm is collectively created, maintained and experienced (Lefebvre, 2004). As should be readily apparent, the rhythmic qualities of the projects discussed here are not uniform. They are the result of different rhythmic markers – different determinants of experience. The rhythms of these spaces limit and shape the urban escapism of the different projects and through this their transformative potential.

The Woodlands Community Garden presents an alternative space that is structured in its escapology and focused on active gardening. Its form of escape is curated towards evasion from capitalist work, from consumption and the extenuated, anonymized food chain. But it also presents as an opportunity for leisure – indeed, besides being a site for growing, people come down to read, to enjoy their lunch outdoors, to escape for a little while into the garden, although primarily in the warmer summer months. The garden has visitors who come not to garden but simply to be in the space – and the illicit use of the space by youths at night, to gather, to smoke and drink, is no exception to this. Yet its organization to a purposive end (growing vegetables and other plants) nevertheless gives it a more structured time and a reduced sense of the time-freedom associated with the North Kelvin Meadow. Particularly having two set time periods during which the hub and the storage container are open, when there are definitely people about, structures these possibilities and temporally limits escapism in its more communal aspects.

Although the meadow has events, regular toddler groups and schools sessions, there is a sense in which the wider space is underdetermined and fruitfully so. In not being a garden, the use of the space for dog walking, reading, picnicking, and so on, is far more possible, and in this the construction of the space is important. The wildness of the meadow in contrast with the formalized raised beds; tree houses rather than potting benches. The physical space itself is important in shaping this experience of temporality. The space is underdetermined and remains liminal: being between specified urban functions opens up its possibility. However, there are limits to how well this functions as a *communal* exercise. As noted with participants across both projects who could not or did not emotionally connect with their limited experiences of temporary contact, a sense of community is often bounded by and created through a rhythmic propulsion, repeated sequences of events across time producing a historicized social bond. In this sense, underdetermination can lead to a loss of the cultural aspects of communal organization upon which much of the transformative capacity of projects of this ilk is based. In this respect, although freedom might be found as a less determined project, it is questionable how collectively oriented this might be able to be, without anchoring in rhythmic repetitions and organization.

The specific cultures of the case studies emerge from a particular lived time and place. Understanding this as escapist is by no means the only possible way of interpreting this. But taking the lens of escape illuminates the spaces as spaces of alterity: as slow places within otherwise fast lives (or vice versa), as connective tissue in otherwise lonely lives, as changes of scenery, and as spaces in which to be, without judgement, for long periods of time. As the next chapters will illustrate, this is rooted in concrete practices of autonomy but these are not experienced universally. There are cultural barriers to participation in escapism, although these too shift with the seasons. In this sense, while communal growing might open up space for "waifs and strays", it isn't equally open. Sharma (2016) situates the temporal as 'lived time', and she argues it 'operates as a form of social power and a type of social difference' (Sharma, 2016, p 132). In claiming an autonomous and at times antagonistic culture of escape in communal growing, a politics of the temporal emerges, a bounding of who does and does not belong. Thus, as Williams (2016) notes, actually existing practices of justice are uneven and messy, always becoming.

4

Who Gets to Escape?

Boundary work

'In Woodlands is there not a bit of a, slight race thing?'
Howard (interview, June 2016)

'Some of [the meadow organizers] don't really know how to talk to people outwith their own social demographic.'
Craig (interview, December 2014)

Although the spaces created at the North Kelvin Meadow and within the Woodlands Community Garden offer respite to some extent from a wide variety of pressures, this relies on boundary work. What makes escapist rhythms possible is a set of community practices that establish the collective basis for such rhythms. Reflecting on such practices foregrounds the uneasy payoffs central to communal growing projects; and thus makes space to consider the ways escape is an imperfect attempt to create just urban space. To do so, I begin from the ideology of inclusion and being 'open' that underpins the projects, taking it not as a fact or frame, but as a question. To whom are the projects open? Taking the case studies as contrasting organizations responding to specific sets of local dynamics, this demonstrates the vicissitudes of community as a practice of closure, indeed as a practice of boundary making and maintenance that reproduces class, race and gendered boundaries.

Community in sociological literature, though vexed and deeply fluid, has often spoken to the symbolic boundaries that emerge in the process of group formation across a variety of levels (see, for example, Cohen, 1985; Brint, 2001; Anderson, 2006; Belton, 2013). In discussions of belonging, which tend to focus rather more on the affective dimensions of communal life, identities emerge through contradistinction, as Benson and Jackson (2013) amply demonstrate. If community is situated then as something that is done, as a verb (Walkerdine and Studdert, 2015; Rogaly, 2016), then boundary making and maintenance are central to these social practices. Community is not a neutral thing that exists, but a set of dynamic practices that are replete with conflicting tensions. Situating communality as a central process and idea within urban growing (Traill, 2021), I argue that it is not an anodyne concept but a fluid boundary-making process with social and political ramifications for justice.

Taking justice as an everyday horizon towards which actors strive, the work of Fraser (2008) and Young (1990), although not entirely compatible, provoke the consideration not only of the distribution of resources, but also of recognition and process. For Fraser (2008), approaching justice in practice is an iterative process and, as the following sections explore in a limited way through considering shifts over time, there are ongoing considerations of exclusion and attempts to overcome these within the case studies. In this, we can see reflections on justice from the organizations as it emerges in considerations of who uses and accesses these spaces, who is involved in organizing and who might be targeted for outreach. It implicitly, however, also emerges as an analytical consideration when the language of inclusion runs against existing cultural exclusions. In this, I argue we can see the failure of inclusivity as a narrative to encompass the potential fullness of justice. In so doing, it questions the inclusivity narrative but recognizes the difficulty and perhaps inevitability of closure within communal practices within the urban, and their emergence from concrete conditions on the ground despite commonalities across national borders. Yet it remains attentive to how the production of an inside makes possible the connections within these spaces. As Samanani's (2022) work suggests, boundaries can themselves be generative of conviviality and connecting across difference. Thus, reflecting, prompted by the work of Iris Marion Young (1990), on the possibilities of a specifically urban vision of justice opens up the possibility of conviviality as a horizon for justice, however paradoxical, iterative and limited it might be in its everyday emergence.

Grassroots and questions of representation

The Woodlands Community Garden, ensconced as it is within the Woodlands Community Development Trust (WCDT), tries to encourage participation, belonging and inclusion, particularly aiming to reach out to those experiencing mental ill-health, those from Black and minority ethnic backgrounds, and other underrepresented groups like young people or the elderly. Inclusion practices take a number of forms, including educational programmes run with local schools and partnership work with organizations such as the Glasgow Old People's Welfare Association, whose offices they shared between 2016 and 2019. In 2020, new offices in the premises of Visibility Scotland, a visual impairment charity, opened up new collaborative possibilities, and ongoing work with a mental health charity, again very local to the garden, speak to a willingness to work with local organizations aiming to further social inclusion.

A mantra often repeated by management and staff is that they put 'community' at the centre of their work. Arguably, the structure of the WCDT lends itself to this. The board are local people, and the manager follows their lead: "We are community led, and that is where our priorities remain … it's still quite grassroots-ish in terms of our management board are all local residents, our volunteers are all predominantly local residents" (Oliver, interview, July 2015). Oliver, the manager of the Trust, takes pride in the connection the WCDT has to the 'grassroots', which is to say local people from whom it takes its 'priorities'. This connection is established through their board of directors, alongside a volunteer base formed by local people. There is a two-fold movement of ideas here: upward from local residents through meetings with growers and volunteers where possibilities can be mooted; and, similarly, downward from the board, although as Oliver notes, the board are also in some sense local, making this a 'grassroots-ish' dynamic on both sides. The WCDT take, in this instance, a loosely geographically based notion of what community is, perhaps unsurprisingly given their specific local focus. In so doing, they rely on active participation and it is here that the gap between the Trust and the neighbourhood emerges, through non-participation. Those who live in the Woodlands area and yet do not engage with the Trust's activities become a lacuna in the way that the Trust claim to represent a community, in the putatively singular, unified sense.

Nonetheless, as Oliver suggests, the Trust and the community garden itself are closely interwoven into the fabric of the social life of the neighbourhood. As such, the Woodlands Community Garden should not be simply understood as a group of people working in a local garden; instead shaping and engaging with the wider environment and changing how it is lived. This moves across terrains, from the produce of the garden to its collaborations and interventions.

Herbs and salad leaves from the garden went to the Woodlands Community Café, also under the umbrella of the Trust, in 2015 and 2016, and were used in free-to-access community meals once a week. Although by 2020, this practice had died out due mostly to an increase in numbers at the café making it practically impossible to utilize garden produce there, Woodlands had by then set up a veg box scheme, delivered by staff with varying ways for people to 'pay it forward' to allow those who could not afford it to access fresh fruit and vegetables. WCDT have also worked closely with Glasgow Old People's Welfare Association's Fred Paton Centre and local schools to educate people about growing, and they look at many ways to create inclusive settings and learning opportunities. In 2020, they responded to the waves of international fury and activism emerging from the Black Lives

Matter movement, and particularly the deaths of George Floyd, Ahmaud Arbery and Breonna Taylor. It also engaged with the outpourings of grief and anger around the death of Sarah Everard, and later the rape and murder of a local woman involved in the garden, to create discussion groups and take local action around issues of gender and racialized exclusion and violence, including support and discussion groups and an anti-racist library that in 2022 celebrated its first birthday.

Yet despite these later interventions, in the initial period of fieldwork in 2015–16, inclusion was predominantly discussed as an issue of welcoming people who came through the gate. There are no formal barriers to entry to the garden or community café – volunteering is easy and open. This latter is valued by a great many volunteers and raised bed gardeners who speak of the ease of getting involved. When speaking of inclusion at the Woodlands Community Garden in 2015, however, an interesting thing would happen. The focus would immediately become one gardener whose story had received attention in local media.

The recurring inclusion narrative is the story of John, whose autism and speech and learning disabilities create difficulties in communication between himself and others. After 15 months volunteering at Woodlands Community Garden, John showed a radical improvement in his speech, an excitement in gardening and a willingness to share his stories when he got home. John's brother, who is not greatly involved in the garden but visits from time to time, has spoken publicly about how transformative it has been for John to be part of the garden. John's progress resulted from the structure and activities provided twice weekly at sessions at Woodlands Community Garden and it garnered the garden accolades for being inclusive, culminating in an award and press coverage. During the first period of research in 2015, when I asked about inclusion, gardeners and staff would all mention John, proud of the garden's inclusive stance.

John himself is enthusiastic about the garden, but reticent. His enthusiasm is demonstrated best by his constancy and his willingness to work. The obvious pride held by gardeners over John's improvement is touching and they want to share the story, often. John's case is highly visible, making it into the media as well as the minds of those involved in the garden. It is a positional good too: it helps the garden gain funding to have a success story like John's to tell.

After a while, I began to find it uncomfortable how quickly the idea of inclusion was linked to John. Consistent singling out of his case as one that exemplifies how open the garden is highlighted his difference from others, confirming in some ways that association of John with the idea of being inclusive, rather than him being just another gardener. In John's case, there is an unmaking and a remaking of his disability. Although not uncontested, the 'social model' of disability suggests that vulnerability is socially constructed (Oliver and Barnes, 2010; von Benzon, 2017). In the space of the garden vulnerability can be seen to be deconstructed. John is a valued worker and he labours alongside others during the sessions, with small adjustments for his needs such as regular prompts to take toilet breaks. Given the context in which he labours: alongside pregnant women and people in recovery, among others, his needs are catered to along with everyone else's. Nevertheless, because of his specific, visible role as a success story, his vulnerability is remade as a marketing tool and as a badge of honour, repositioning John as different, as *the* story of inclusion. Thus while in practice John can be a gardener among others, discursively he gets repositioned as vulnerable and different. This highlights a problematic aspect of inclusion as a by-word, particularly as used to promote the garden in the media online and off. It also implicitly emphasizes the conceived similarities of the other gardeners, and renders inclusion as something related to disability. For much of the fieldwork, he remained the touchstone – the glowing paradoxical principle of inclusivity. Nevertheless, while John was a highly visible case of integrated practice, not all users are equally integrated into the communality of the garden.

Much of the outreach activity at Woodlands happens outwith normal gardening hours and does not involve integration into the regular gardening. The school programme and work with older adults falls generally outside of gardening sessions. Indeed, Common Knowledge UK – an organization who work with adults with learning disabilities – for a while were working with a group of men on a Thursday in the garden, separate from regular gardening days. Their funding ran out in late 2015 and was not renewed, so their involvement ceased. Nevertheless, for a period of time a parallel workshop would run weekly at the garden, leaving artworks in their wake. However, their separation from gardening sessions demonstrates how inclusion does not always mean integration. In the case of Common Knowledge UK, it meant being allowed to use the garden, to get the benefits (often cited) of gardening (see Armstrong, 2000) and being outside in nature, but without engaging with local residents. Similar but more individualized uses of these therapeutic elements of the garden led to the use of the space by one former volunteer to support local people during the pandemic in one-to-one outdoor therapy sessions. This relates to parallel ideas found in horticultural therapy, which is a distinct and specific approach to growing (Sempik et al, 2005; FCFCG, 2016). Thus, the wellbeing uses of the garden are not always synonymous with the communal aspects of the garden, in this case producing separate groupings, and different solidarities in the same space but at different times. This separation of different populations into silos reflects the structure of funding into projects, something to be discussed in depth later. It also highlights a sense that inclusion is about access to growing and the garden, rather than about access to communality.

Commitment to the idea of inclusion is something that can be seen in growers' concern around mental health, but it prompts critical reflection on other axes of difference like ethnic diversity and class. Spending time in the garden often prompted conversations explaining the garden and its culture to me. It was Mark, who sometimes works for Woodlands, who pointed out to me what he considered to be the diversity of gardeners found at the site. Mark asked first, if I have noticed, perhaps, how many 'foreign' people get involved in the garden: more so than native Scottish or British people. Mark reckoned they are just more into nature as a rule and, as Adam comes in at this point, Mark looks to him for back-up. Adam agrees and begins talking about a cousin of his who owns a Christmas tree farm in Denmark where he raises chickens and other animals, entirely self-sufficiently. Mark and Adam (two White, British men) talking through foreignness as associated with the garden, raises an interesting point: Eloise is continental European, as is another woman who has been along on this particular day, but everyone else who was there is British. It is curious that Mark's impression of the garden is as such a 'foreign' project. To back up his point, perhaps in response to a sceptical expression on my face, Mark goes on to list a number of nationalities of growers to emphasize this aspect of growing. European is how I would group the nationalities he lists – Icelandic, Danish, French – but he does seem to think they are more involved, more likely to come along and want to garden. It figures as attitudinal – those deemed 'foreign' in this context are seen as more likely to want to be involved. It is in many ways a critique of fellow Scots who are *not* involved, a sense really of their lack. However, there is a persistent Whiteness among gardeners that sits across this perceived difference and does so uncomfortably, given the diverse neighbourhood in which Woodlands Community Garden is situated.

'Not a race thing, but a class divide'

Questions around how inclusion figures at the Woodlands Garden are most obvious when considering the ethnic make-up of Woodlands as a neighbourhood against that of the garden. This was highlighted in research carried out by Yellow Book, a consultancy company, on behalf of Woodlands Community Garden. They found a mismatch between the ethnic diversity of the area compared to the organization, something I noted too during fieldwork. The diversity that exists in the garden is largely European, but the local area has a substantial non-White population. Census results from 2011 show a significant number of people in the Woodlands neighbourhood categorize themselves as 'Scottish Asian' or 'Asian' (23 per cent versus the Glasgow average of 8 per cent; National Records of Scotland, 2014), with a small minority considering themselves 'other' (6 per cent versus a Glasgow average of 3.5 per cent). Yet ethnic diversity is limited among those engaged with the garden. The proximity of a local mosque around the corner from the garden might seem to lend itself to working in partnership, but there is little connection.

Instead, there are hints of local friction. Howard, a rare volunteer at both case studies in the research, had heard rumours of a disagreement over a gap site the WCDT have recently taken over for their Workspace project, which he claimed the mosque had wanted for a car park. In describing it, however, he was not sure if it represented a "race thing" or a "class thing":

Howard: In Woodlands is there not a bit of a, slight race thing. Not a race thing, but a class divide between the garden which is mostly White people, not only, but then there the – I heard there was a conflict with that space next door? Someone wanted to turn that into, the mosque wanted to, the Imam from the mosque wanted that turned into a car park for the mosque apparently.
Helen: Really?
Howard: Yeah, that's what [a staff member] told me. And the garden wanted to turn it into another garden, so it's like there is some community there and it's contrasting with the White community. (Howard interview, June 2016)

In moving between class and ethnicity, and suggesting that there is an elision between "a race thing" and "a class divide", Howard makes an interesting point. He is trying to establish that there is a serious gap, but is wary of what to call it – moving through the ideas of race, class and coming back to the "White community". It is notable that Howard struggles to decide whether class or race is the appropriate frame for this social distinction: an elision between the two suggestive of the intersection of these signifiers. This difficulty in discussing difference recurs through both field sites and there is not an easy language for it. It makes people uncomfortable, as a rule. Nonetheless, as Howard points out, there is a gap between the Woodlands constituency and another putative community based around the mosque (with a problematic assumed cohesion due to religion and ethnicity). What his narrative emphasizes above all else are the boundaries around the garden and its practices, and the intersection of class and ethnic difference. This boundary is observable in everyday life on West Princes Street, upon which the Woodlands Community Garden sits.

Raised bed gardener, Samantha, who also went on to work for the WCDT, also remarked on this absence in an interview, saying she felt there was a difference in levels of involvement between those of different ethnic backgrounds. Having carried out research with the consultant on behalf of the Woodlands Community Garden, Samantha reflected on that discrepancy:

'But doing the surveys, people of certain ethnicities in this area, they're not interested in the garden ... I suppose there's that guy who comes, the guy who grows the artichokes, I don't remember his name. ... He's an exception isn't he? But in some of the Asian supermarkets and things, they're not really that interested.' (Samantha, interview, April 2016)

This sense of a lack of interest speaks in part to the methods of the research, based around asking local businesses about the WCDT. Yet it also speaks to a sense of boundary that maps disinterest onto local minority populations. The gardener here mentioned as an exception is a useful point of tension around this however. Mr Abdul was most often referred to not by first name, but in this more formal way, again pointing to the distance between him and other gardeners; though it was often a politeness masking a simmering tension, particularly on my return in 2020. Mark in particular in later years had issues with Mr Abdul's multiple raised beds and inconsiderate behaviour around the compost, taking more than his fair share (according at least to Mark) and using it in plants outwith the garden, such as his houseplants. Originally from Algeria and with limited English, but excellent artichoke-growing skills, Mr Abdul himself often offered tips and opinions on my gardening when I was volunteering in 2015 and 2016, and had a tendency to come over and simply intervene, showing me how to earth up onions "properly". He noted that he felt part of a community at Woodlands, telling me that to him this meant "knowing each other, it's being known"; but being known in this case also means being known as someone who takes more than others think they should.

Without deeper ethnographic work in later years, I cannot here speak to how racial boundaries had or had not shifted. That said, small everyday frictions such as tensions around the proper use of compost that prompt regular, uncomfortable conversations about rather than with Mr Abdul speak to some of the ways an inclusive narrative is not always met by inclusive practice.

This complicated relationship to inclusion limits the ability of the WCDT to say they represent the entire community if it is imagined simply as a geographical unit. From the perspective of the trust, it raises the question of whether there is much the WCDT can do about that: how can you engage a group of people who it appears are not interested in being engaged? Yet given the versatility of community gardening as a form that in some cases has been suggested to bridge ethnic differences (Langegger, 2013; Aptekar, 2015; Crossan et al, 2016), the distance between the growing project and the broader neighbourhood constituency seems suggestive of a boundary that excludes those who do not easily fall into the White, educated profile of the average gardener. It echoes, uncomfortably, Schmelzkopf's (1995) assertion that 90 per cent of volunteers in the community growing networks in New York in the 1990s were white, which raised race and class tensions as they tried to encourage gardens in predominantly Latino Loisaida. Notably, the organizations Schmelzkopf discusses promoted self-determination among neighbourhoods to try to ameliorate social tensions. Similarly, the recommendations of the consultants mentioned previously suggested a need to diversify the board at the WCDT to increase representativeness, including tapping into different social groups to engage them in the work of the trust. This concern to broaden the board suggests an engagement with the Whiteness of Woodlands as a potential problem, since the board themselves predominantly consist of older White professionals, although there is usually at least one gardener or volunteer involved. The WCDT have worked in later years to broaden the board and actively welcome in racialized people, hosting discussions around race and developing an anti-racist library, with the involvement of a radical bookshop.

Thus there are distinctive dynamics of difference at Woodlands. The racial boundaries are not deliberately cultivated perhaps, but they exist. The garden is physically open, but it is also predominantly White, a handful of gardeners aside. In a particularly ethnically diverse locality this is an awkward situation for Woodlands – especially as they try to work to challenge some of the issues in the area through, for example, the greening West Princes Street project. This latter project aims to involve local residents in improving the planters and the environment more generally along the street the garden is on. This project, however – rooted as it is within a sense of neighbourhood – seems destined to the same partiality unless Woodlands can overcome its cultural Whiteness. As noted in the literature, if Woodlands could overcome this partiality, the benefits can indeed be socially transformative (Langegger, 2013; Aptekar, 2015; Crossan et al, 2016).

'Everybody's space'

> 'Community groups change and grow and move around. It's a very fluid format. I think the bottom line is does it work or not, are you representative, and I think we are here.'
>
> (Terry, interview, July 2015)

This language of representation as a way to assess fundamental moral claims – not connection or belonging – relates to the context in which the North Kelvin Meadow campaign emerged. It was a reaction to a planning application on the land and the campaign tends to focus heavily on the land itself and its innate value to people. The North Kelvin Meadow campaign does not generally work to deliberately promote connection or belonging. They work often with practical things – fixing fences, painting, picking up litter – and encourage people to engage with these activities. The language of representation, rather than say belonging, as being central to community relates to how the North Kelvin Meadow campaign is positioned – as a campaigning body rather than a deliberate means to grow communal feeling. When discussing who participates at the meadow then, the question to some extent becomes understood as: who is represented in this campaign, and how that relates to its successes. In this context, class becomes an important but difficult topic to explore.

Class talk has been positioned as a difficult terrain in and of itself. While Savage et al (2001) found class to be a topic of ambivalence for their research participants, discussing class in the context of an interview is *itself* an ambivalent and tricky interaction, and some scholars claim class talk is prone to 'sub-articulation' (Payne and Grew, 2005, p 909). This has implications for the possibility of situating class purely by self-ascription and deliberate articulation, yet the interpretive and contextual work required to position people otherwise is open to contest and politically volatile. Nevertheless, sifting through the complexity of class talk and how aspects of social class affect communal growing and organizing is important for understanding the dynamics of belonging at the meadow.

The position of many participants as highly educated and middle class benefits the campaign, despite claims the meadow is 'everybody's space'. Class is discursively reproduced through dualisms of middle and non-middle class, verbal constructs that appear in discussing patterns of involvement with participants. The movement to protect North Kelvin Meadow and Children's Wood is based in a largely affluent, professional area. While the housing is dense and parking is difficult, the houses are well maintained and there is little unemployment, at least in the immediate streets surrounding the plot. Some within the movement recognize that there are arguments that stand against what they are trying to do that are perhaps perfectly valid. One respondent, an economically poor, but culturally affluent mother of three, was self-consciously aware of this. She told me that the council's argument for developing the space was that this area is already so green and relatively affluent – they do not need more. To Toni, the meadow is still unique and worth saving, but she admits the resonance of the argument. Similarly Joan, a committee member, noted that her friends say to her, "It's all too much, the people are all smug marrieds and you know people with children, that kind of thing" (Joan, interview, July 2015). There is an anecdotal conception of the meadow users as privileged families who do not need, or perhaps deserve, more green space (and "smug" with it).

Campaigners at the meadow find discomfort in this image. It echoes Sayer (2002), who highlights the discomfort and indeed embarrassment of talking about class as a topic associated with guilt and moral judgement. Class is 'not an innocent descriptive term but is a loaded moral signifier' (Savage et al, 2001, p 889; see also Sayer, 2005). Instead of class talk, participants often preferred a language of relative economic position, of 'poorer' people. Considering the meadow in the context of social class challenges the openness suggested by many participants in relation to the space: as if class should not matter, because everyone is welcome. Nevertheless, class has shaped the campaign to save the space as well as affecting the way the meadow is received, raising distinctive questions around who gets to shape urban space, and who simply to inhabit it.

The middle class and the other

A dualism arises in the discourse around the meadow between the middle class and the other. This latter is referred to either by references either to local working-class areas, Maryhill and the Wyndford, that connote nearby deprivation, areas of deep stigma; or by more contentious terms like the "bams" that Howard refers to, or as Alasdair calls them, the "polite thugs". Colloquial references to slang terms like "bams" highlight a discursive connection of working-class youth with criminality or illicit behaviour in the meadow and wood. This is a form of what Imogen Tyler (2013) has called 'social abjection'. Tyler argues that 'the abject is a spatializing politics of disgust' (Tyler, 2013, p 41) that creates political others outside of normative political citizenship. The abject other at the meadow is counterposed against the middle-class locals housed in old tenement blocks, symbolized by Clouston Street which runs along the southern side of the meadow. Howard, an interviewee who had lived in the area for much of his young life, reflected on the way that different users of the meadow relate to it:

> 'The police used to come here every weekend, or very regularly, and there used to be a lot of mess, a lot of late nights and rowdy bams here. The bams have sort of stopped coming. I feel bad saying bams. ... But it was basically people from this side of Maryhill come here, and there are people from over there who come here [gestures to Clouston Street]. From over there [Maryhill] they come and can be rowdy, but from over there [Clouston Street] they tend to be a bit more respectful, probably just because they're *from the community* but mainly because it's the community from this side that's using the space, that've got more engagement with it.' (Howard, interview, June 2016, emphasis added)

Howard was very aware of the way that people from working-class Maryhill had been slowly pushed out of the meadow by increasing middle-class use of it. His language of community distinguishes the middle-class residents as being a community in themselves – distinct from people from Maryhill or further north. This echoes work that situates middle-class claims to space as positioned against less desirable neighbourhoods as a discursive and performative practice (Watt, 2009; Benson and Jackson, 2013). The juxtaposition between North Kelvinside and Maryhill becomes an articulation of class and neighbourhood boundary as synonymous. It is a contrast built over time, with the shift in the activities and class significance of the meadow.

Before much of the campaigning activity took off, many locals associated the space with criminal activities. This atmosphere of criminality, and regular police presence, has been blamed on the poor and the marginalized: the homeless, alcoholics and drug addicts, or the poorer youth (the "bams" to which Howard refers). The meadow is still used by teenagers, but one participant, an older Scottish resident of Clouston Street, Oonagh, described how they would now wait to one side: "Quite a lot of boom box holding teenage guys with huge amounts of really strong beer. ... They still come but they quite often sit on the steps of the scout hall until the, you know, the families have wandered off, gone away themselves" (Oonagh, interview, July 2016). This temporal slicing of the meadow into use by families and use by teenagers (usually boys) is suggestive of the way that middle-class use of the site has pushed previous users to the temporal and spatial edges of the site. This highlights the contingency of middle-class spatial claims as they are negotiated and struggled over in the everyday; and it sits uncomfortably against their narratives of putative inclusion.

In the context of their agenda of inclusion, it troubles the Children's Wood committee that attendance at their events does seem to be largely middle class. From the playgroups to the gala days, this tends to be parents and a particular subgroup at that. These are, for the meadow, the 'easiest' people to engage:

'The easiest groups were middle-class families to get involved, the hardest group was, well there were two harder groups. One was the schools. ... Another category has been sort of the socio-economically poorer areas around the meadow.' (Phil, interview, June 2016)

'I think that we have a tendency to be a little bit middle class and whilst we have very strong wishes to work with perhaps the likes of the Wyndford and things, we don't necessarily achieve it.' (David, interview, July 2016)

Both Phil and David, highly educated, middle-class dads from the Children's Wood committee, were keen to emphasize that the organization was trying to address the gap between themselves and those from "socioeconomically poorer areas". Their efforts to include more people from Maryhill and the Wyndford usually worked through deliberate outreach to organizations like Maryhill Integration Network, who work with asylum seekers, and

Home Start, both of whom work with racialized families in poor north Glasgow. This work, however, is heavily mediated by staff members and volunteers who invite in those 'other' people that the Children's Wood deem to be missing.

In its most successful form, inclusion work is practised through the everyday work of one man in particular. Ivan would often gain praise from others involved in the campaigns for his ability to ignore difference and engage those who some in the Children's Wood find difficult to talk to. Part of Ivan's ability to engage with people in the meadow is to do with his own sense of being unreadable in the context of the class system. Ivan is not from the UK. His accent places him as other, and his distinctive look makes him easily noticeable and recognizable. He stands out, but not in a readily classifiable way, neither in class nor racial terms. Reflecting on this, Ivan notes not only his externality but also his wilful ignorance of British class hierarchies.

> 'Maybe that's part of the reason that I've been able to connect with all different parts of the community here because I'm just oblivious to that class system thing, you know? People I talk to might not be oblivious but then eventually they just have to forget about it mate because I'm not going to take any notice am I? … I'm not going around thinking oh I can't talk to that person because they're from that side of town and then oh, I shouldn't be seen talking to them because they come from there. I guess I do transcend that a bit, I think partly I am actually probably completely ignorant of the rules that you're supposed to do, I'm ignorant of those rules so. Ignorance is bliss! [Laughs].' (Ivan, interview, June 2015)

What Ivan highlighted was his sense of the absurdity of the class system and his ability to stand outside because of his otherness. His personal difference, as well as his very open and sociable personality, led him to break down some of the barriers to entry. He did particularly well during his time working for the Children's Wood in engaging teenagers, a feat that impressed many who were involved in the organization, and those who simply used the space. His ease with those that others find dangerous or difficult, such as drunk men and teenagers, made it possible for others to encounter each other across the divide created by difference. Ivan's refusal of complicity in the class system allowed him to overlook cultural barriers that others see and cannot, or do not know how to, cross. In this sense, through Ivan, it was possible at the meadow to unmake differences of social class: but only under condition of contact, and often only through the work of Ivan. Because of the lack of formalized growing sessions, and the limited cross-class appeal of the outdoor toddler group, these moments of contact were limited at the meadow.

The other main conduit for inclusion in the Children's Wood's agenda is through work with over 20 schools and nurseries who by 2016 were either coming to use the space themselves as part of a Scottish curriculum requirement of outdoor education or joining sessions organized by the Children's Wood. Through this, the aim is to get children involved and through them reach out to multiple generations of families:

> 'The kids will bring their parents and the parents'll be like "Oh I don't want to be here" but they'll bring the parents along *so you're getting the kids to change the values of the parents.* And that, that's something that we've noticed has been really quite a big thing and actually what we realized quite soon was that it wasn't just nature that was the thing that, a lot of the schools were saying to us, well the parents are saying it's actually the community that they really, that seems to be the thing that they really, really like, so it's not just the nature, it's actually being part of the wider community, so that's from working with 14 schools and nurseries.' (Polly, interview, July 2015, emphasis added)

Attempts to reach out and include those from poorer backgrounds (who are usually assumed to be somewhat outdoor-shy) take on this paternalistic tone. But the disconnection runs deeper than a slightly patronizing assumption of the universality of middle-class ideas and values. The disconnection emerges most clearly through a sense of externality expressed by those, like Jack, who regularly used the meadow but were not involved in either organization or the broader campaign.

I met Jack on the meadow one morning as he sat on the edge of a raised bed in the sun. He had a long history with the space going back many years. I asked him how he felt about the way the space has changed recently and he told me he thinks some of the things the organizations have done are a bit "twee" – waving in the general direction of the part of the land known as the Children's Wood. But he makes clear this is not something he is against, he is happy for "them" to do "their thing" – it is just not *his* thing. What becomes clear when talking to Jack is that the cultural shift at the meadow, the taming of its more wild (and less child-friendly) aspects, has a potent exclusionary facet. Positioning himself against a "them" illuminated Jack's sense of being outside of the organizations. Jack did not feel that there was anything wrong with what the Children's Wood were doing, yet he did not feel like it was anything to do with him. There is room here for disengagement and an unwillingness to participate, not simply exclusion from campaigning and organizing.

Others are more forthright about their feelings of classed externality. Craig is a local father and activist. Known for being militantly against the organizational aspects of the Children's Wood, as well as disliking the increased use of the space that the actions of that organization created, Craig is however very aware of the class-aggravated nature of this. He highlights the gap between the committee culture and some of the users of the space:

> 'There's different demographics that come down here, there's different folk with like large incomes and there's folk with like wee tiny incomes and everything in between, and eh some folk who have got themselves in position of eh responsibility we'll call it due to their organizational talents, some of them don't really know how to talk to people outwith their own social demographic.' (Craig, interview, December 2014)

This echoes Terry's concerns about representing the community, but Craig's more antagonistic position sees nothing in the attempts to include all, instead finding them too distant from those who use the space who are not of "their own social demographic". Although the Children's Wood – with their committees, events and protests – are reflective about trying to 'include' everyone, there is a sense in which this doesn't always play well to those who sit outside the official organization and campaign. Craig has disagreed with much of what they have done in terms of bringing people on to the site, because he feels it has lost its ecological character, he more closely aligns with the North Kelvin Meadow campaign, but he is deeply critical of them too. The complex dynamic of inclusion and building social connection also rubs against competing visions of what the meadow should be, complicating an already difficult issue. Part of Craig's vehemence is also about his feeling of being ignored and dismissed by the campaigns who have struggled to find common ground with him as a working-class environmentalist. This connects to a cultural difficulty within the organizations at the meadow: a difficulty dealing with difference, and perhaps a naivety regarding the impact the physical changes to the meadow might have on feelings of belonging among those who have a long-standing connection to the meadow. It emphasizes too the reproduction of class in this context. Despite the potential space of connection and deconstruction inherent in the contact between people of difference class positions that emerge in Ivan's effect on the meadow, this seems to be limited by a lack of continuity in collective moments that are simply that: ephemeral situations of contact, rather than repeating communality.

The assumed universality of the outdoors

The limited backgrounds of the campaigners, for all the efforts to reduce barriers to accessing the meadow, lends itself to a specific approach. In emphasizing the benefits for mental health and child development, and the 'magic' of the meadow that will work on people who come along, campaigners take a highly professionalized and research-based approach. Wild play and the importance of children being outdoors are core ideas in the Children's Wood as an organization. Yet through it runs an assumption of universal benefit of the idea of wild play, but not much consideration of its cultural embeddedness as a value, nor of the particular assumptions and tenor of these arguments.

But in taking such a universalist position (even while recognizing that it is not, in fact, widely taken up at present), the Children's Wood in particular do not engage with how wild, muddy play and the 'Great Outdoors' are culturally specific ideas. At times, staff and volunteers will bemoan the failure of Scottish people to own sufficient waterproofs, and yet at the same time not note this as an economic barrier (and a question perhaps of priorities). Children's waterproof trousers are not something everyone can afford, although a nearby budget supermarket about once a year stocks cheaper ones. One of the dads on the Children's Wood committee thought that the culture of being 'outdoors' would trickle down, seeing it as a fashion, a cultural turn en masse, that would affect the working class eventually. This echoes a point Lawler (2012) makes in regards to seeing middle-class Whiteness as associated with progress, counterposed against the backwards notion of the White working class. In the context of the meadow, the middle-class organizers position themselves as a cultural vanguard. In this, there is an implicit sense of class separatism that is suggestive of why much of the outreach of the Children's Wood only works in limited ways: they are culturally middle class and the activities they are promoting are seen in this way too.

Although resisting the destruction of a community amenity for further (high-end) housing runs contrary to the economic logic of value extraction from land, the meadow as imagined by the Children's Wood in particular has a different kind of value structure. Valuing children's education and particularly outdoor education is a way of reordering the value of the land. Thus, in elevating the use value of the land, they do so from a position of wishing everyone to adopt their research- (and class-) based notion of what is best for locals and their kids. When discussing where the Children's Wood project came from, it is possible to see this research-based approach in Polly's description of her early work persuading teachers and others to come on the land: "[I] just started making documents saying this is the educational value of the space, this is the value of the space for your child, come to this event, just basically trying to build a community around the space" (Polly, interview, July 2015). Polly's campaign to persuade people into the space began with compiling research documents and disseminating them, which is a remarkably research-based way of "trying to build a community" based partly in rational debate. The Children's Wood also post lots of research on their website, including studies showing the impact of nature on children, referring to 'Attention Restorative Theory' and being 'Nature smart'. This leads unavoidably back to the high levels of education associated with the meadow campaign.

As such, the dynamics of difference reflect a specific idea and approach to inclusion and representation as a way of imagining what a just movement to save the meadow looks like. That there is a certain class positionality associated with the Children's Wood committee, the North Kelvin Meadow campaign, and the protest more generally seems clear. The space itself however is utilized by a whole cross-section of people from the surrounding areas and, much like that geographical spread, offers a much wider range of people than would be suggested by simply taking the committee as metonym for the aggregated users of the space. This lack of reflection is something that the Children's Wood are interested in ameliorating it would seem, but the way they do so (with committees, events and bringing people in) is potentially alienating to those precise individuals they are trying to reach out to. This is also inflected in specifically gendered ways, which I turn to now, before providing a similarly gendered set of practices within the Woodlands Community Garden that offers a distinctive line of continuity between the projects.

Female labour and the mothers' campaign

Parenting, and indeed mothering, can be seen as central to the fight to save the meadow. The centremost point of the Children's Wood is a mother of two, and she has committees of women and men helping her craft children's and community activities, many of them parents too. The most recent organization formed nominally foregrounds children, thereby centring the campaign on families. But it is also importantly about mothers. Evie was attending a community event held by the Children's Wood, when she spoke at length with me about her perceptions of the campaign. One of its most salient facets to Evie is it is such a "mothers' campaign". For Evie, who connected the meadow to her experience in Hastings working with immigrants and refugees, there was something important and valuable about the contributions and knowledge that different women can bring to these spaces – particularly in the use of produce, cooking dishes that were different and using things in novel and interesting ways. The way women could be experts was for her an important part of the value of the space itself. Thus emerges a perspective on valuing women's expertise in community gardens and campaigns like the Children's Wood and North Kelvin Meadow as a radical revision of gendered labour, a remaking of mothers as campaigners and experts, as active citizens. Yet how contrary is promoting a highly normalized conception of childbearing as a key female behaviour? Or, indeed, having women at the forefront of organizing caring, children's activities and feeding hungry people (see, for example, Tronto [1987] for how care and 'women's morality' come to be problematically dovetailed)?

Nevertheless, in valorizing caring and its flexibility to the needs of participants, both spaces offer the freedom to embrace care in the manner proposed by radical calls for a politics of interdependence (see, for example, Care Collective, 2020; Graziano et al, 2020; Hobart and Kneese, 2020). The meadow and the garden are both spaces in which parents are explicitly welcome, with activities put on for children in toddler groups and the outdoor learning club. It is a place where people feel they can stay for long periods of time, where indeed parents and carers spend hours letting children run free and feeling connected, like this is a space they are allowed to take up. This was reflected in people's narratives around the long hours they could spend on the meadow. Yet because of this welcome and the focus particularly on the Children's Wood nominatively and practically on children, this implicitly offers a narrow role for women as mothers and can feel exclusionary to those who are not. Indeed, Joan noted that her friends struggle to see the meadow as she does, since they see it as for 'smug marrieds' and kids, rather than for those outwith family units. Normative parenthood can be exclusionary (a situation not unknown in academic spaces; see Jackson, 2017).

For the North Kelvin Meadow's part, although they are not predominantly parents, Terry's persistent attitude that if you want something done in the space, you ask a single mother rather than a professional banker (implied as male), is again telling. Playing on the assumption of a busy but efficient mother, as opposed to an interested-in-principle but terribly busy banker, reinforces the sense that these are spaces in many ways run and cared for by women. This is itself an interestingly positioned critique, as Terry himself works in a bank. The weight of organizing communally (and organizing communality) then becomes one that is principally borne by women, and particularly mothers. They are also perhaps those who benefit most from it: from a free space to entertain children, from a sense of connection and from building solidaristic networks from whom support can be forthcoming.

In moments of public representation, however, this labour can become invisible. Men often stand in for the campaign as metonyms for community, in press and in public. At the crux of campaigning, a public hearing was held with a reporter to the Scottish Government, the civil servant appointed to compile a report on the planning objections. Present for the developers and the council, on one side of the table, were five men. On the other, however, the only woman was Polly. The audience, such as they were positioned physically, was made up of supporters for the meadow, primarily an audience of women.

The imbalance was not lost on activists. During the proceedings, other members of the campaign felt the council representatives treated Polly unfairly. En route to the meadow for an accompanied site visit, Elaine and Natalie (campaigners and mothers) talked with me about how Polly was treated on the panel, particularly by the main council representative. Natalie expresses a wish that the council's man would stop "mansplaining" (following the conversation that followed Rebecca Solnit's [2014] essay, *Men Explain Things To Me*) and presents her frustrations with the way he disregarded "the community". This builds upon the sense of the campaign as gendered, and blurs the line between "the community", here represented in the way that comments from the audience were diminished and undervalued, and the very female turnout, reaffirming that elision of campaign into parenthood.

But the question of representation is not a simple erasure, it was also a question of tactics. Representing the North Kelvin Meadow campaign – who put in a separate objection – as well as the North Kelvin Community Council, are Terry and Alasdair. As head, and pretty much the only long-standing member, of the former organization, Terry was the obvious choice. But Polly's husband – a professor and supporter of the campaign – was on the panel, whereas all the outspoken women involved in running schools sessions, lobbying MPs and handing out cups of tea were in the audience. Long-term committee member, Michael, whose contributions have been more strategic rather than practical, also joined Polly around the table. This reliance on White middle-class, middle-aged men of professional status (a professor, an ex-professor, an architect) is provocative and raises questions. Is it just playing the system, presenting a familiar face to the council and developers (who were consistently White men, and mostly middle-aged)? Does it diminish the 'community' to represent it not as a 'mothers' campaign' but as a panel of White professional men? Side-lining the femininity of the meadow in an official set up seems important, not least because it symbolically devalues the contribution of these women who have actively campaigned for the space and engage in the reproduction of community daily. Instead, and presumably as a tactical decision, they put forward a series of men, while on a daily basis, the spaces researched were by and large spaces where women predominate. The spaces may offer an opportunity to value care and social connection, remaking structures of value. However, they also reproduce a conservative, procreation-centric sense of being female, and leave that face unrepresented in public life. While this can be read problematically alongside the predominance of caring work, this has implications for how being male figures in the meadow.

The spaces offer the potential for a different kind of space for the development of masculinity, although at best it is nascent. In growing and the more caring aspects of the garden and associated projects, is there room for an expanded way of thinking about masculinity? Michael is one of the older members of the Children's Wood committee and he has many years' experience in social work. Reflecting on what has changed during his lifetime, he made suggestive comments about the potential of the space for reimagining masculinity:

> 'With young people growing up, and getting the right balance and not feeling emasculated, and knowing it's good to do things which in yesteryear [mutters] you know, pushing prams, dyeing your hair, doing what you want, letting young people develop the way they want to develop. It gives them identity. I think guys have lost their identity or are trying to shrug off their previous identity. Saying, no, no, I don't want to be like this, in a very small way, I think this kind of project can help with this kind of thing.' (Michael, interview, July 2016)

What Michael is suggesting is the meadow as a space for doing masculinity differently, or perhaps for even undoing masculinity in Deutsch's (2007) sense of undoing gender: the potential for a shift in ways of being male and what it means to include caring. In this broadened sense of a caring masculinity is a sense of undoing heteronormative assumptions of a division of labour that places the burden of care on women as a kind of innately feminine trait (a good critique of the domestication of care as women's sphere can be found in Green and Lawson [2011]). Perhaps then there is room for more flexible explorations of masculinity in these spaces, or to even go beyond an understanding of caring as part of a binary gendered characteristic. This involves seeing caring as universally *human*.

On 'garden babies' and defensive masculinity

A remarkably similar pattern emerges around gender in the Woodlands Community Garden, although it is inflected differently in a space less defined by protest. A noticeable aspect of the garden and particularly in relation to the community café is the predominance of female volunteers in areas that are traditionally female (that is, childcare, early years education, cooking and crafting). The gardening itself tends to be more balanced, which in many ways reinforces this pattern. Consider attendance at a craft workshop held by Woodlands Community Garden during a gardening session. In a discussion on who was coming along to a weaving workshop, it became clear that the workshop was going to be predominantly, if not solely, female. One woman who was intending to attend, Mona, says in reference to this gender imbalance that she could not get her boyfriend to come and check out the garden that day, let alone come weaving. We fall to discussing the day's session, and discover that actually there were not that many men involved in the gardening session that day either. There are about five men to 14 women, and I suspect our rough count might have missed some more female participants. This is not an unusual set up, and a suggestive link might be made between this female-heavy context and the previous discussion on the garden being a place of haven for those who are outwith normal, valorized labour arrangements. That women should be overrepresented in such a section of the labour force recalls the overrepresentation of women in part-time work (Bates, 2015).[1]

Equally, most of the volunteers at the community café during the period I was involved were female. This was made most obvious by the exceptions. Two women run the community café's kitchen, directing the actions of a handful of volunteers (from around five up to sometimes ten or more). Primarily, café activities involve chopping things up and occasionally some supervised stirring, but some volunteers spend a large amount of their time doing washing up. In this context, one male volunteer, Roger, would regularly joke about how strong and masculine he was, despite not conforming to hyper-masculine standards. In the years between 2016 and when I returned to the area in 2020, he also lost a leg to the health implications of his previous lifestyle and addictions.

The discontinuity of Roger's behaviour with the otherwise supportive (rather than competitive) atmosphere could be disconcerting. When he was asked to open a jar of olives for me, he happily acquiesced, easily shifting the lid and then joking about his strength again. In the context of the café, this behaviour is knowing, and is so often Roger's modus operandi as he does this caring work. It is suggestive when read alongside Michael's comments regarding the meadow and its potential to open up new ways of being a man. Roger's behaviour creates instead a tension between loud jocular vocalizations of masculinity while carrying out caring work, almost explicitly linking the two, in this jarring, humorous way. This behaviour is particularly notable in contrast with the otherwise female surrounds.

The relation of gender to volunteer labour can be positioned as problematic in relation to the reproduction of hierarchies of valuation. The café makes use of volunteer labour, relying on the availability of the "waifs and strays" that are free in the late afternoon on a Monday, as one participant puts it. That women should be heavily represented in these spaces suggests a strong relation between women, an ethic of care, and flexible working patterns (Green and Lawson, 2011).

The outward facing 'goodness' of volunteering may account for its validity as a non-work activity for women, yet it is not – at either the Children's Wood or the Woodlands café – perhaps as equally valid for men as for women. Certainly, this is the comparison Terry at the meadow makes between the busy banker and the busy single mum: only the latter gets things done, only the latter makes time for volunteering. Perhaps this is women's third shift: not just working at a job and in the home, but also in civic life (Gerstel, 2000).

For pregnant women in the community garden, traditional gender roles also mean a certain kind of body-policing. This often figures through the practice of care, through looking out for the mother-to-be. How agile and active Eloise, for example, remains late into her pregnancy surprises people, to the point of commentary. It is also noted how small she is, how neat the baby bump is. Her body is watched and commented upon as an object of collective fascination. This has elements of care threaded too with elements of watchfulness, of keeping her in line, of care taken to remind her not to do too much. This continues after birth, through the notion of 'garden babies'.

A garden baby is a baby born into the garden, whose mother was pregnant while involved in the garden (or near enough, the boundaries are perhaps more flexible than this and it is, after all, a term of endearment). Eloise, after having her daughter Therese, brings her by the garden often. Therese is very much a garden baby. She is babysat by another in the garden, and while very small is passed around the room for cuddles. Other mothers – such as myself – who were involved in the garden while pregnant have their children claimed under this title too. During one visit, when Therese is being passed around, conversations abound about how many mothers come to the garden, and how the garden has a number of these garden babies. Eloise and I have talked before about the number of pregnant women who visit, though we were at the time pregnant ourselves and prone to noticing. The sight of Samantha with Therese provokes a different conversation: the 'who is next' conversation. It has a gossipy tone, light and joking. Mona says that the garden is making her more broody. We laugh and discuss whether Mona or Samantha (the most obvious candidates) will be next to have a baby. A year or so later, Samantha does indeed have a child. Though I expect the conversations at Woodlands had little to do with it, exposure to a greater number of babies does influence her decision. Parent-talk is not necessarily used to police people. Mona is not chastised for not procreating. But the predominance of families and of traditional gendered roles is heteronormative and leaves little space for discomfort, disavowal or alternative models of kin.

In one telling incident, Adam is told he cannot possibly know or understand what is being discussed, when he dares to offer an opinion about the need to stay fit while pregnant. He offers this during a conversation about what 'garden babies' are like in the womb, usually producing only small bumps that do not show very much (a slightly wild generalization). Adam's input into a conversation about pregnancy among women who are either pregnant or have been pregnant is reacted to with humour, but also with a pointed comment. In response, Lizzie asks, rhetorically: "what would you know about that"? In an implicit way, this reinforces gendered imaginations, particularly around who has the right to talk about pregnancy and pregnant bodies. Incidents such as these reinforce the idea that caring is a gendered issue (see, for example, Tronto, 1987). It also asks whether masculinities are being reinterpreted in the space, or whether this is too rosy a future to imagine for the projects.

The promise is of a field (sometimes literally) of utopian potential, where caring and feminine labour is valued. But there is also a clear sense in which a heteronormative sense of White, straight parenthood permeates the projects. This can translate into limited appeal to those outwith those traditional institutions. Approaching this through the lens of inclusion, it is possible to see how tensions arise between creating a space for parents and families as an inclusive focus, and a restricted sense of whom the space then becomes for. (Un)doing gender in these case studies was intertwined with care, and motherhood is a central and celebrated role within this context. This also involves the potential (but empirically limited) reinterpretation of masculinity along caring lines. Considering the way gender figures in the projects also raises questions around the representation of the projects, which are not always represented as female-dominated.

In this way, gender emerges through the projects as ambivalent, both celebrating caring practices but also reaffirming gendered roles and heteronormative family patterns. Similarly to how inclusion in general figures, there's an imperfect reimagining of an alternative set of values. While, again, this can be seen as an attempt to articulate a more just space in the city, with inclusion so often standing for a better, more just vision of communal life, it is often uncritical and tends to the exclusionary.

The limits of inclusion

This clearly points to the ways in which practices of community at the meadow and at the community garden reproduce class, race and gendered boundaries, despite cleaving to ideologies of inclusion. Thus, despite an imaginary of justice and being 'welcoming', grassroots or somehow representative, there is within these practices definite limits to the ways escapist spaces are inclusive. As such, the politics of accessing and using escapist spaces are shot through with dynamics of social power.

At Woodlands, this most prominently emerges around a tension in the neighbourhood between its predominantly White gardeners, and the neighbourhood's diverse, though often deprived, ethnic population. However at the meadow there is a more distinctive classed pattern of exclusion, though it intersects there with age and motherhood too.

These patterns matter not only in terms of the way they perpetuate social hierarchies of class and race in everyday life, but also because of the partiality they bring to claims to represent a putative community within governance processes, whether in consultation, shaping a neighbourhood or staking a claim to an alternative future for a piece of land. They also, however, are the boundaries that make possible some of the more prosaic rhythms of escape described in the previous chapter. In this way, they offer not only a vision of an alternative way of doing things, but also a clear picture of how they might fail – and need to try again, to fail better (with sympathy to Fraser's [2008] sense of iterative attempts at justice). Indeed, as later chapters more fully explicate, this would seem to be the direction of travel of both projects, though their paths are to some extent divergent.

5

Ownership, Autonomy and the Commons

Staking claim to history

> *Pre-1939* – Records show there were never any buildings on this land.
>
> North Kelvin Meadow website

> 'It'd always been used as historically by kids because the land was sort of connected with the school originally and obviously you know hasn't been built on, *you probably know a lot of the history* you know, playing fields and so forth.'
>
> Polly (interview, July 2015, emphasis added)

> 'I've thought about [Glasgow City Council's] arrogance in just deciding that they were going to set all this for building. And we've, the old committee established beyond doubt that *this land is for leisure use only*, and they've just ignored it.'
>
> Alasdair (interview, December 2014, emphasis added)

In building a claim to the space of the meadow, activists often called on a history of the site that situated it as a pristine space of leisure. It is important for the way the campaigns have portrayed this land that it was never 'built' on before, although the surface of the pitches was artificial and it at one time had two changing room buildings on the site. Only one of those now remains, crumbling on the Clouston Street side of the meadow. The lack of historical building on the land is written on laminated posters on the site itself, as well as on the website. In making claims to 'history' and the idea that this is 'established', Polly and Alasdair, as well as the posters around the site, make knowledge claims about the site and position it as a local community good: as playing fields, as for 'leisure use'. In invoking history they are also making claims to precedent and legitimacy, to shift what could be seen as an argument for a change of use, to an argument for continuity of use.

This historical perspective, however, was part of a framing of the site that sat awkwardly against earlier periods of activism. Sean, who was active from the mid-1990s until around 2007, took some umbrage with this pristine vision, noting to me in 2016: "They're talking as if this site has never been developed, never been put forward for any kind of community scheme whatsoever. ... But that's not true." As part of an earlier wave of activism, he was involved in the development of an organization called the Compendium Trust, who worked to try and develop the space as a sports complex for the community from the late 1990s. Sean, an older man who still had a strong emotional connection to the space, showed me plans and newsletters from that period that spoke directly to an alternative (though still leisure-oriented) vision of the space. Sean's issue was the elision of an entire phase of the space's history into a more convenient narrative arc: the space as undeveloped, as wild remainder in the city.

Sean's irritation points to the contestation over what the idea of *developing the meadow* means and how different definitions and meanings within that idea come to impact the site. It also highlights the specific and partial narrative of the campaigns. The most formalized narrative of the space, from the activist perspective, lies in the coalescence of both the North Kelvin Meadow and Children's Wood's discourse around the history and development of the space. The idea of the meadow as pristine and never built on is important as a way of framing the meadow as a place of pre-existing commons, a place which has been used solely for the common good. Although they do not speak of it in terms of commons, it is implicit in the way activists, particularly older ones, discuss it as part of the 'war effort'. Campaigners publicize how the meadow hosted barrage balloons to protect the nearby regional BBC buildings, as well as foreign soldiers during both world wars. Sometimes empty bullet cartridges are still found on the site, according to participants and local history enthusiasts.

Seeing the meadow as a commons in this sense underpins much of their argument to 'keep' it in community use. Activists thus do not say 'turn it over to community use', even though from the council's perspective it was never formally in community use. In this way, particularly the key campaigning participants in the two organizations shape a specific narrative about the meadow as a way of staking a claim to the space. Through positioning themselves as *the* community, and arguing that the space has always been a community asset, they argue for their right to determine the space and develop it how they see fit.

In this way, the meadow campaign makes explicit the urban intervention inherent in communal growing. In reinventing a small part of the time and space of the city, communal growing projects project their right to the city – to its determination and to its future development (Schmelzkopf, 2002; Eizenberg, 2016). This is done on a decidedly local scale – the imaginary invoked is not of Glasgow, so much as of the neighbourhood. In this, it nonetheless recalls the 'right to urban life' as imagined by Lefebvre (1996, p 158), where urban life is situated as encounter, creation and the primacy of use value. As Harvey (2003) argues, the right to the city is 'not merely a right of access to what the property speculators and state planners define, but an active right to *make the city different*, to shape it more in accord with our heart's desire, and to re-make ourselves thereby in a different image' (Harvey, 2003, p 3). As Chapter 3 set out, communal growing in a mundane way does precisely this: reshaping the urban fabric and its rhythms to reflect an often slower, more connected way of being. In this, participants are reclaiming the right to time sovereignty, the right to set one's own pace in the city and to tell a different, collective story about land use and common good. In carrying forward such interventions, the projects engage with questions of legitimacy and authority, and actively shaping an alternative vision of the city. Who shapes the city, and how they navigate the power dynamics involved in staking a claim to doing so, are inherently questions of justice.

Reimagining the city

Both case studies explored here reimagine the city in the face of an expressed injustice, a sense that they should and could be more involved in shaping the city. At both sites, they engage in 'the dirty, real work of activism that expresses a pragmatic "get on with it", an antagonistic "no", and a hopeful "yes"' (Chatterton and Pickerill, 2010, p 476). While neither case study always positions itself as activist per se, this spirit of 'get on with it' and trying to sculpt a new way of living the city resonates clearly with both the Woodlands Community Garden and the North Kelvin Meadow. Justice thus is enacted through projects of involvement and revitalization, of bringing people in to enacting the city.

Through their campaigns, the meadow organizations make a claim to their right to determine the city. In contrast to local attempts to establish a historical narrative around common use, the council refer to the site as 'the site of the former Clouston Street pitches', emphasizing its loss of function, having had no official purpose since its iteration as academic sports space. During the public hearing to assess the development's planning application, the council's representative consistently emphasized the importance in planning terms of the 'last established use'. In this, they mean as sports pitches. Critical here is how use is or is not established, and by whom. The council also emphasized the lack of permission the people who use the site have to be there, mentioning the injunction they took out against two campaigners for trespass.

Contrary to this council narrative around 'last established use', the campaigns have created an alternative narrative about what the land is and what the land could be. The gap between these visions leads to a sense from locals of the distance between the bureaucracy and local life, and a sense that councillors are 'out of touch', as activists often put it during the planning process. Instead of developing it for housing, they argue – as Schmelzkopf (2002) argued the community gardens under threat in New York in the 1990s did – that the *use* of the land is the important facet and that it is 'incommensurable' with the economic benefits that the council gain either through the initial sale of the site to developers, or through council tax gains. This is explicitly a clash of visions of whom the city is for, or what indeed the logic behind its development is.

This recalls James Scott's (1998) work on the modernist state, particularly how legibility emerges as a problem. Being illegible to the state for Scott creates what he calls 'hidden transcripts', things that are unknowable and untranslatable into the perspective of the state. A similar logic is at play here: one issue for campaigners is the opacity of their claims, and their non-economic valuation of the space. They attempt to overcome this through not only campaigning and lobbying but through taking on recognized forms of organization (the non-profit). In this sense, the meadow campaigners are engaged in a specific struggle: trying to rewrite and reframe its history as being one of shared use, to recode the space as communal, and themselves as legitimate actors. In doing so they run into the issue Scott's (1998) legibility ultimately presents: the bureaucratically limited definitions of process, and of prior and legitimate use. The power dynamic inherent in this, where the meadow campaigners were fighting against a decision in theory already taken by the council on terms they have no control over ('last established use') highlights some of the difficulties in staking a claim to the city. It also returns us to the question of autonomy and control as a positive statement of what communal growing aims for: in local issues, a voice and the right to be involved.

Contested neighbourhoods, diverging narratives

The Woodlands Community Development Trust (WCDT) stake a claim to their involvement in the city rather differently, as a result of a very different landscape in which they work. While the campaigns around the meadow sought to stall housing development in favour of local ecological, educational and leisure uses, the *raison d'être* of the WCDT is nominally 'development'. The WCDT own the site of the community garden because of their practice in the 1980s of renovating and rebuilding housing in the area. They were gifted a number of gap sites by the council that they built on, all except the site that is currently the community garden. This phase in the WCDT's history ended in the late 1980s, as the trust was mothballed. It was dormant until 2008, when at the behest of local activists looking to grow on the site, the WCDT renovated the gap site that had sat empty since a house fire necessitated the controlled demolition of a tenement building that had sat there until the 1970s.

Development, in the current phase of the WCDT since 2008, is very specifically understood: "We are community-led ... so it has a different feel from maybe different projects where you might have a larger organization, and this is a satellite project that they run but they're not a local organization" (Oliver, interview, July 2015). Woodlands thus stake a claim to authenticity: to being 'community-led', and therefore promoting local voices and their rights to determine the city. They promote such voices in their work rejuvenating gap sites into the community garden, developing the community café, and more recently engaging in beautifying local planters and building a local community meeting room on a second gap site leased from the city council.

Woodlands anchor their legitimacy as actors in the city in representing the local area, claiming to work on their behalf. When looking specifically to increase the valorization of the space, they work to reduce what might be seen as the environmental degradation of the space through small interventions such as the community garden and the work they have done with schools and residents to put up signs asking people not to fly tip, cleaning up rubbish from back lanes and asking residents to take on the maintenance of the neglected concrete planters which line West Princes Street, the road on which the garden sits. The planters were given paint jobs to cover graffiti, each given a number and small signs saying things like 'Don't waste Woodlands'.

Thus the narrative of the WCDT, particularly with regards to the garden, is about providing for the local area – allowing Woodlands to become a better, nicer place through environmental interventions. It claims to be *for* the community. In this, there is the potential to see a locally empowered version of what development might mean. In the critical literature, urban development can figure as a problematic process, producing gentrification or fixing problem places (Paton et al, 2012). Against this, the community development trust envisions a different way of doing development: oriented specifically around the idea of community itself. In this, an autonomous vision of the city is posited, and indeed a right to develop the city towards the values of community, inclusion and localism.

Land use, land value, land use value

As this suggests, the garden and the meadow both produce a specific kind of narrative which positions each project as part of a temporal trajectory, emerging from disrepair and disregard, and revaluing the spaces. The concurrencies between the narratives of the projects are notable. First, both sites have had periods of limited use, where they have been considered derelict. This is a key part of the way community gardens and other interstitial projects often emerge – from dereliction, or vacancy, in the gaps of what has been before (Loukaitou-Sideris, 1996; Andres and Grésillon, 2013; Drake and Lawson, 2014). The notion that community gardens turn vacant land into thriving green havens bears similarity to dominant narratives around urban development more generally.

In critical terms, dereliction can be an alibi for creative destruction and neoliberal regeneration. Weber (2002) explores this at length regarding the use of 'blight' metaphors as a means of denigrating neighbourhoods. She argues that this produces conditions for a large rent gap. After the demolition of the extant buildings, the spaces they held become narratively positioned as diseased and in need of remediation, as a biological necessity (Weber, 2002). The growing projects studied here reproduced a level of stigmatization in their own narratives about the sites: noting rubble, criminality and waste as associated with sites prior to interventions by the projects. Yet the echoes of the dereliction story arc within the narratives of the WCDT and the organizations fighting to save the meadow should be seen against their work to reframe the value of the land in a specifically communal way. This collectivism is central to the way the projects position themselves ideologically.

Further, this collective revitalization is itself one aspect of justice as practised in these spaces: by engaging in practices of care and valuation, these projects emerge as reparative solutions to injustice. In the case of the meadow, this is the proposed injustice of loss of the commons, of a public amenity; for the garden, it is years of neglect and disrepair in the wider neighbourhood. Through tidying up derelict spaces and making oft-ignored interstitial plots beautiful, communal growing can rejuvenate neighbourhoods, and reinterpret notions of dereliction and devaluation (Drake and Lawson, 2014). Communal growing as a practice thus interferes in the way that land is valued, reinterpreting it and valuing use of exchange.

This temporal arc of improvement echoes dominant narratives of urban development as fixing problem places (Polletta, 1998; Paton et al, 2012). Beyond the symbolic violence of categorizing past places as needing fixed, this narration also calls into question the relation of the projects to local urban dynamics. There is a tendency for such improvements to be pathways towards gentrification. Loughran (2014) has written of the effects of the development of the High Line park in New York on local spaces, increasing rents, supporting the continued suppression of the homeless population and curating middle-class businesses around access points to the elevated park. Similar work around community gardens by Voicu and Been (2008), also in New York, suggests that communal growing has an effect on surrounding house prices.

In Glasgow, the city council make this explicit in their promotion of meantime uses of derelict spaces through the Stalled Spaces programme. On their website, Glasgow City Council tout increased land prices as a potential benefit for landowners leasing out plots on a temporary basis as part of Stalled Spaces (Glasgow City Council, nd). Stalled Spaces has also been a small but widespread funder of community gardens in Glasgow. Naturally, there is a tension between this potential land value increase and the ways communal growing values the use rather than the exchange of land (Schmelzkopf, 2002; Drake and Lawson, 2014).

This research was not explicitly positioned to address what effects the communal growing practices were having on processes of rent increase and associated displacement. Nonetheless, local dynamics of exclusion highlighted in the previous chapter might be seen to reflect some critical urban scholars' concerns regarding gardening as potentially gentrifying as it is primarily engaged in by the White middle classes. Yet as an emerging and iterative phenomenon, practices of urban justice are not reducible to questions only of representation. They must be situated against the explicit and intentional actions to welcome in and empower participants, practices that prefigure an alternative, and more autonomous, relationship with the city.

Common ownership, open ground

> 'Aye its communal, everyone's entitled to use it, which is the kind of thing I've been encouraging for quite a long time now, and I think it has actually caught on. I think people have got the idea that it's theirs ... and that is one of the things that the corporation[1] [Glasgow City Council] is desperately afraid of that the peop- we, I use the term we loosely, that we now feel as if we own it and if we do we have a right in law to say this is ours ... you know, we've been on this land, we've taken it over, we've improved it, have you had a proper look round it. Have you had a good look round out there? I mean, there's an orchard out there. ... They have actually taken what I reckon was my idea to begin with of a communal ownership and they've, they've absorbed it, they've actually, they seem to me to have taken this idea on board, that, eh, they have a right to be on it.' (Alasdair, interview, December 2014)

As a long-time resident of Sanda Street, which bounds the meadow, Alasdair evokes the spirit of openness and common entitlement that weaves through the campaigns. At the core of this notion is inclusion; that all are welcome, that all are equally responsible for and welcome to the land. This is reflected particularly in unwillingness at either of the projects to close off entry to anyone. Ownership, however, goes further – not only are all welcome, but all have equal right to the space. This is the inclusive ideology at its most radical, but also at its most contestable, reflecting the limits of practices of inclusivity within the projects. Despite the critical question of whether all are truly common owners, as a political proposition the cases offer a potential alternative vision to private property: ownership imagined in common.

Yet this differs between the projects. At North Kelvin Meadow, common ownership is a meditation on openness and welcoming in all. It reflects a lack of centralization too. With two charities working in the space, and a sometimes-uneasy coalition of dog walkers, teenagers, parents and casual users regularly engaging in the space, access and ownership are part of the common cause, part of what brought everyone together under the umbrella of the campaign to save the space. At the meadow, ownership is an idealized projection. A subsidiary body of the city council, City Properties, owned the land. Since users of the meadow had no legal tenure in 2015–16, the idea of ownership here is imagined, although it is no less consequential. Indeed, the campaign's use of the land and claim-staking prefigured and preceded the legal use of the land that came about in 2022. By contrast, common ownership is a much less salient idea at Woodlands Community Garden. The gardeners are imagined as common, as communal, but the land of the garden is owned by the WCDT. This means that in effect gardeners are renters, rather than owners. Reflecting the structure of the garden organization, they are not without voice, but the garden (particularly in contrast with the meadow) is subject to hierarchical relationships, formalized in fees and agreements.

When the Children's Wood emerged in 2010 from an impulse to use the space for children's events, they continued and expanded the organization of what key campaigner Polly calls "guerrilla events". Using the space without formal permission, this has garnered what might be considered tacit consent over the years. It recalls an argument proposed by Adams and Hardman (2014), which suggests that although guerrilla gardening draws on radical histories (with guerrilla literally translating as little war), its transgressive aspects can be overplayed and it can be congruent with local authority plans and aesthetics. Utilizing this language seems to offer rather the veneer and thrill of radical action within a programme of otherwise acceptable and respectable practices. The Children's Wood and the North Kelvin Meadow have seen no eviction of activities or materials, the complicity of community police, and the use of the space by corporate volunteers through the Conservation Volunteers scheme, besides a minor fracas about bat boxes in 2009 that led to the indictment of campaigners for trespass. Nevertheless, the sense that this space became 'owned' by the community – recognized as theirs, or at least for their use – rather than by the council's subsidiary company (City Properties) – defined everyday relations with the space.

While Alasdair takes perhaps questionable responsibility for the ethic of communal ownership of the land, he also emphasized the anarchic idea at the heart of this imagined ownership of being "entitled to use" the land and to change it because "it's theirs". The implications when translated into action are equally anarchic: the freedom of all to construct what they wish within the space. As explored in the previous chapter, the construction of 'all' is imagined broadly but practically vexed, supported ambivalently at best by an open door policy. Nevertheless, this approach to ownership opens up possibilities for a kind of autonomous practice, embodied in creative approaches to the land itself whether in conservation, planting orchards or indeed in creating BMX runs. BMX runs appear on the site from time to time as young adults decide they want them. During 2016, heaps of earth were piled up along the usually fairly flat ground of one of the paths on the meadow. Howard, only a bit older than those building the runs, facilitated their activities: "I hang out here a lot as well and again I've got access to the shed, so I've given, I gave the guys down here on their bikes a spade, they were like 'Oh, can we get a spade out of that shed?'" (Howard, interview, July 2016). As Howard narrates, those involved feel a sense of entitlement to build the runs and are willing to ask those with access to tools for help to bring their ideas to fruition. Three heaps of earth may seem small as interventions go, but it is indicative of a broader theme at the meadow: the feeling of empowerment created by a culture of common ownership. This sense of freedom led to all kinds of interventions, such as when a sign appeared offering directions to fictional places such as Narnia, seemingly inspired by the imaginative capacity the meadow offers.

Nevertheless, this imaginative capacity has its practical limits, not only in terms of how inclusion figures within the meadow, but also in terms of running into state barriers to autonomy. Even after decades of local objection, the council remain more of a hindrance to community ownership and use than a help, despite legislation that came into effect in 2015 that explicitly set out provisions for community land ownership within urban areas in Scotland.[2] In 2009, Glasgow City Council indicted local campaigners Terry and another of his then committee for putting up bat boxes. They were taken to court for trespass, but the judge threw out the indictment, calling out the council for their actions, saying neither had done anything wrong. However, as Terry has regularly pointed out, you cannot take a community to court. So although he no longer has anything to do with bat boxes and is careful about the wording of emails asking people to, for example, trim the lime trees so it is possible to walk along Clouston Street without stooping, he still encourages others to do as they please in the site.

Where the common ownership ethic runs into contradiction is in the construction of raised beds that belong, ostensibly, to one individual or family. There are a number of these scattered about the meadow, some in advanced states of disrepair, although Terry spent the summer of 2016 fixing the worst of the rot. Ownership of the beds, known sometimes as 'allotments' but rarely big enough to qualify for this name, is through subscription. A small annual donation is made to the North Kelvin Meadow campaign of £5–10 in return for a raised bed. It is intended, according to Terry, to provoke consideration of whether the bed is still needed. What it creates is an ownership dilemma – to whom do the beds belong? As the few raised bed owners who were encountered during this research noted, one could not take a fully proprietorial attitude to the beds: food goes missing. Further, many are poorly tended, and they are often used as ad hoc seats, due to a lack of other appropriate structures in the meadow in 2015–16. By 2020, a greater attention to accessibility and the practicalities of running educational activities on site meant a proliferation of logs for sitting on, both in the wood near the mud kitchen and on the meadow proper too. A table appeared too, which facilitates children's parties and informal gatherings, and works as a high bench for those who are happy to repurpose it as such. None of the extra furniture, however, resolves the question of ownership that such interventions raise.

Despite perhaps a tendency from the campaigning organizations to narrate it as such, the meadow should not be seen as an entirely common space: the beds are technically rented to families; and the wood is often seen as the home of children's play. While ownership is imagined in common, in practice ownership is negotiated between users and often transgressed. Joan, who holds a somewhat in-between position in the Children's Wood committee as a 'dog walker' without kids, noted the tension this can provoke, with children telling people with dogs or adults there without offspring that they are not welcome as the wood is 'theirs'. However, the already questionable tenure of the organizations on the land would make it difficult to strictly enforce private ownership, and thus there tends to be equality of use – including to some extent of other people's produce – despite signage and loose agreements between growers and the North Kelvin Meadow. In this way, the imagination of ownership in common can come awkwardly to fruition, although more because of a lack of collective growing activities and an equal claim to trespass, than because of a shared orientation to the rules of the space. The terrain of common ownership then is not flat but full of emotional and economic claims on the landscape of the meadow, although a broad ethic of joint and open ownership has facilitated a broad range of creative practices in the space, bringing to life an imperfect everyday commons.

Transgressions of the collective imaginary

In Woodlands Community Garden, there is a rather different dynamic when it comes to expressing ownership and it relates to the spatial practices of parcelling up land (or raised beds more specifically) and renting them out. Although the communality of growing is central, the activity itself is quite individualized. There is a balance then between ethos (a sense of community, of doing things together) and the pseudo-allotments that people actually grow in. Woodlands Community Garden is home to around 40 raised beds, each of which is allocated to one individual or family. Although growing sessions bring people together, there is a sense in which the responsibility and joys of growing in that space are for that individual or family alone. As such, taking down a structure built by one gardener who had been neglecting his bed and had not paid for the year, became a strange point, something uncomfortable. The transgression of the private growing space of one gardener made obvious the background logic of the space: that the raised beds constitute pseudo-private space. Interfering in the raised bed of a now-absent grower was uncomfortable precisely as it foregrounded the property arrangement between grower and Woodlands as an organization. It also in that moment emphasized the power of land ownership, and the reversion of power to the organization to take back that which is deemed neglected.

This transgression of previously private property occurred early in the growing season, in April. One of the large structures that dominated the eyeline in the garden was being removed. There were guarded conversations between Mark, there as a volunteer and taking the structure down, and Jen, the garden worker, about this. Enquiring afterwards, I learned that the construction that was being removed was on the bed of a gardener who had not been responding to emails about the construction, or his bed. Jen was deeply reluctant to remove the structure, but said that if he did not respond, she would have to offer his bed to someone else. "I don't want to", she said, "but if he doesn't talk to me, there's not much else I can do". The structure came down because he is blocking someone else from renting the bed and growing vegetables in it. Notably, the identity of the gardener who was being uncooperative was kept hidden from those who did not already know him, to protect him in a sense, as they considered the possibility of a return to mental ill-health.

As volunteers, Lucas and Mark, dismantled the structure with wire cutters and pliers, they saved as much as they could. Jen says that the plastic was actually the garden's and Mark was surprised. He blusters, "I thought he'd bought it himself! It's the good stuff, the stuff that lets air in and all that." In response, Jen says the plastic was 'ours', adding that he did not ask if he could use it either. Mark's eyebrows rise and he puffs out air as he continues to demolish the plastic and wood plant cover over the raised bed. This incident played on the tension between the communal and the individual – the sense that private beds and communal sensibilities are balanced against each other. The negative judgement of a gardener for unauthorized use of good quality, expensive materials, but still a concern for his wellbeing and a discomfort over removing his work from his bed, demonstrates how the balance is struck between these two ideas. While this can be seen in economic terms – of rent and private property versus communal ownership – there is also implicit in this a respect for the integrity of another grower's labour. In this the individual thus is not subsumed by the collective good but respected and held in balance against Woodlands as a communal enterprise. This is a careful tightrope balance between property relations and respect of individual labour. Out of it emerges this uneasy and anonymized intervention in the raised bed of a grower; an awkward realization negotiated and contextual in its enactment of its values.

The balance between individual and collective ownership is a tension that threads through Woodlands Community Garden. Individualized growing works against a sense of shared ownership, for although the space is ideationally and physically open all the time, it is emotionally and culturally quite closed. For example, gardeners bring items of their own down to grow in and find it upsetting if they go missing. Take Eloise, a raised bed gardener originally from France, who got upset when she discovered someone had made use of one of *her* pots. She had planned to use it for marigolds, to have some colour in the autumn. She tries to find out who this was, roaming around the garden asking other growers, in order perhaps to correct them, but to no avail. She does say that she thinks the person who has taken them should have *known* the pots were hers – they were next to her bed after all! Even if they were empty. Eloise was later persuaded by other gardeners to admit that her pots were in a communal space and therefore to understand how someone else appropriated them. This process was at once a consolation and a reiteration of collective space and its culture of openness.

Nonetheless, this event highlights the tension between that which is communal and that which is not, which is so often a question not only of material relations but of emotional connection. The idea of communal ownership here is predicated on the formal relationship of the WCDT and growers themselves; an agreement that the land owned by the former can be used by the latter. As a practical arrangement, there is a culture of sharing, but it starts from the grower as an individual. Communal ownership here is again imagined, yet in fact the growers are there as renters. This becomes obvious when transgressed – when the property of growers goes missing, or is used differently than intended. The language of inclusion and communality, the way sharing is central to the garden, overlays awkwardly at times the actual rental arrangements at the garden. As Cathy, a raised bed gardener, noted, tellingly perhaps: during community events, there is a need to work to accept people sitting on the side of your bed, a need to try not to feel 'territorial'.

What remains, however, despite this restricted sense of communal ownership, is still an orientation to openness and an idea of freedom. Without the full sense of the commons, there is still a remarkable sense of enabling: that is, the sense that one can do things in the community garden which one could not in another public space. Thus, talking about the ethos of the garden in the hub building one day with a few of the gardeners, Cathy pointed out how a kind of anarchy is possible in the garden, and how that is facilitated by the garden worker, Jen. Cathy says, "there aren't really committees saying how you can and can't go about things". The implicit comparison with allotments and their committees is favourable to the community garden. Cathy suggested that there are no power structures that stop you from simply "going out and growing". Eloise agrees – she illustrates the point with her own sense of "bumbling about" and getting on with things, and says that the relationship with Jen is important in this. Jen is not there to shout at you and tell you what you cannot do. She will guide and if there is some plan for a piece of wood, she will stop you from using it, but she isn't there to direct or control gardeners. In this way, the freedom of the garden, much like the ownership in common, is cultural, but predicated on a set of rules: rules about what is shared and what is not.

Practically, curating collectivity and common ownership exists through delineating what is and is not collectively held, and transgressions of this are uncomfortable. Particularly, the use of the garden by groups of youths tends to transgress organizational conduct rules around littering and acceptable behaviour. Further, the distribution of collective goods (wood, plastic coverings) is mediated through the organization of the garden where, regardless of the sense of Jen as a hands-off guide rather than a dictator, the garden development worker (and ultimately the WCDT) is the arbiter of what is and is not common property. Despite its utopian imaginings, then, there remains a power asymmetry built around land ownership.

Ownership at Woodlands is thus present in a different way to the meadow. The relationship to property, and the associated rules of propriety, are closer to classic individual ownership at Woodlands, although it is always in tension with the communal ethic. The struggle to balance these comes across as an emotional tension – of loss, of trying to share. At the meadow, the loss of sovereignty over property, whether food grown or emotional ownership over a play site, is eroded daily, and although this produces intergroup tensions, it also produces a relaxed sense of property-rights and blind sharing. It is this attitude, this openness to sharing the space, and often produce, with anyone that some newer participants take a while to get used to, but which allows the culture of DIY and creativity to flourish.

It is worth returning to how the space of the garden and meadow are counterposed *against* the rest of the city, and how this collective ownership ethic is known to run contrary to the standard rules of property in the city. As explored earlier, Woodlands Community Garden and the North Kelvin Meadow and Children's Wood are often put in direct contrast with the broader urban environment (usually favourably) and part of that stems from the capacity of the spaces to provide the freedom to do, to produce and to be. Arguably, this derives from communal ownership as imagined, although this is obviously more complicated in the community garden where personal rent relationships create territorial claims and emotional ties to specific raised beds. Communal ownership is thus mediated through property relationships and organizational structures at both sites, with the centralization of both ownership and organizational capacity at Woodlands pushing back against a more anarchic, liberated practice.

Considering commoning

Given the sense – across both case studies – of a 'for everyone, belongs to no one' attitude, it is possible to see each as an 'actually existing commons', as Eizenberg (2012) has done regarding community gardens in New York. Eizenberg sees the commons as an always imperfect, sometimes contradictory way of organizing, a position that finds echoes in Cooper's (2013) insistence on the partial, continuous processes of actualizing concepts in everyday life. Both sites could be considered in this light: they clearly have a strong sense of common ownership, but neither utilized the idea of a commons. This is not uncommon among projects with a commoning ethic, which is often a category of analysis rather than of practice (de Angelis, 2017; Hanmer, 2021). At both sites, communality had to be explained and learned as a cultural facet of the projects. At the same time, it was limited. Rather than repeat that discussion and its connection to social division, I want to suggest here that the incipient commoning at the meadow and the community garden offer the possibility of urban communality in all its messiness. As Stavrides (2016, p 262) puts it, common space is 'a network of contested, reinterpreted and re-evaluated social relations' as it comes to encompass new individuals within its form, and thus is theorized in ways that are fluid and emergent. Thinking with the idea of commoning foregrounds processes and practices in which it is possible to see the ongoing imperfect aspect of making urban commons. It further highlights the work and deliberate designation of spaces as collective that goes into producing spaces for communality; the process of making the urban common (Linebaugh, 2010; Bresnihan and Byrne, 2015).

Seeing communal growing projects as sites of commoning demonstrates the resonance within such projects, not only of common land and relations of joint responsibility, but also with the sense of precarity and possibility which are conjoined in the notion of the commons (Ostrom, 1990). In particular, the projects show the workings of joint ownership and collaboration within the urban environment. This connects with Cooper's (2013) notion of everyday utopias, particularly in the sense that it has limits and messiness in the actualization of ideas, but presents the potential in the cracks of capitalist society (Loukaitou-Sideris, 1996; Holloway, 2010). What is created in such cracks can be spaces where autonomy is possible (Stavrides, 2016), articulated through alternative rhythms to capital-centric visions of economic productivity and through practices of autonomous production, away from direct imperatives of need and productivity for economic gain. In this, escape is a kind of prefigurative moment, a reimagination of urban social and land relations oriented towards a vision of collective life.

One further point of resonance between the idea of the commons and communal growing projects is a certain attitude towards self-governance. Pervasive attitudes at both sites talk about *getting things done*. There are few practical barriers to trying things out, exploring a kind of experimental way of growing and building. Aesthetically, this means that, across both sites, there is a specific style, which is reproduced in other gardens and allotments. It is based on simplicity: ease of assembly and upkeep, based around materials that are not hard to come by or are cheap, with a preference for wood over plastic (for environmental grounds, mostly) and a general cheerful air. Some of the Glasgow gardens that have been designed by the arts organization, NVA, who set up a number as part of their Sow And Grow Everywhere project, are sleeker, modular builds that have a uniformity to their look with a strong design identity. Woodlands and the meadow err towards a more handmade look, with things sometimes crumbling a little, a little muddy and homespun. This often means accepting a lower standard of precision around edges or finishes, and a sense of the spaces as constantly shifting. Over my time at both sites, the project's aesthetics shifted in mundane ways as structures went up and down, tree houses came and went, and things were painted or weathered. This has continued since 2016 at the meadow, embodied in a rustic looking bee-dovecot, a structure for elevating beehives to an enclosed elevated platform with a periscope to allow distant proximity; new planters and a bath reimagined as a raised bed in the communal growing area at the meadow. In the garden, things are slowly replaced, grass put down in lieu of woodchip; beds rebuilt and a new plastic recycling hub emerging, all with a somewhat thrown-together aesthetic.

Aesthetic decisions are partly driven by funding: building and maintenance are often done as cheaply as possible due to limited funds. This aesthetic also has ramifications beyond the visual: the point here is that in adopting a homespun aesthetic, the spaces require less skill, continuity or professionalism in their upkeep and this enables a broader range of people to engage in their production.

In light of considering the spaces as commons, this might take on a slightly tragic sense – a lack of care. Certainly, discussions of the commons are often forced to deal with Hardin's (1968) tragedy at some point; a vision of the depletion of natural resources through individual incentive structures. The discursive constructions of 'good enough' might seem to lead in this direction. When discussing DIY projects around the garden, Mark talks about decorating and building as something that need only be "good enough", because it is for the community garden rather than in his own, or anyone's own, house. It might lead to the conclusion that because it is common, because it is no one's and everyone's, there is no incentive to do the job well. When we are decorating the office at Woodlands, this becomes important in terms of the approach and Mark makes the comparison between doing the office and what you would do if you were in your own home. Things like multiple coats on the wall, carefully catching the ceiling and getting it all perfect, filling in the holes in the walls and the panelling are all discussed in this way. Decisions are usually taken to minimize effort and time. It is part of a rationale that underpins the whole endeavour, this idea that because it is the office, we were not aiming for perfect, just 'good enough'.

Yet to see this as a tragic aspect of the commons overlooks the underlying value structure at play, the importance of seeing people's time as more valuable than having a perfectly painted wall. Woodlands (and indeed the meadow too) are usually in project work relying on one member of staff and an army of volunteers, whose time is valued above the aesthetic appearance of the final outcome. Thus, especially when painting the office, less care was taken with the outcome in favour of giving lots of breaks, cups of tea, lunches and making sure that everyone got home at a reasonable time. Thanks too, in abundance, were offered for helping to paint the office. Thus, 'good enough' actually illuminates a different weight of values in this case: valuing labour time over aesthetics. This recalls the liberatory effects of valuing participants as full people and escaping from logics and value systems that circulate elsewhere. Indeed, this is the transformative potential of commoning practices (Stavrides, 2016; de Angelis, 2017).

Thus, the DIY aesthetic is more than simply a visual intervention in the city, although it undoubtedly is that too. The aesthetic is also a marker of an attitude to production: that anyone can and should produce, whether vegetables, BMX runs or indeed tree houses. Drawing on the notion of commoning, this is about the autonomy of all within the common spaces to have an impact on that space, to indeed be architects of it. In this, it relates back to the self-direction inherent in staking a claim to the right to the city, as formulated by Harvey (2003, p 3) as the right to 'shape [the city] more in accord with our heart's desire'.

Yet it is worth connecting this rugged aesthetic to the distinct class positions of its enactors. It is illuminated to some extent through conceptions of the 'urban idyll' proposed by Hoskins and Tallon (2004), which as Harris (2012, p 237) writes, 'draws on idealised imaginaries of rural life seemingly removed from the complexities of contemporary Britain'. Hoskins and Tallon (2004) highlight that the urban idyll is a form of renewal specifically for and by the middle classes: 'a favoured kind of urban citizenry ... in a landscape informed by a bohemian aesthetic while other residents are rhetorically and materially recast as outsiders' (Hoskins and Tallon, 2004, p 36). Thus, the democratizing aspects of DIY spaces in Glasgow are also part of a socially situated aesthetic, recalling the person in Chapter 4 who felt distant from recent aesthetic developments on the meadow on account of them appearing to him as "twee". It is necessary to see the autonomy possible in communal growing in balance against the politics of difference that also play out in the space. In this light, autonomy can come to be seen as a socially situated and classed attempt to move outside of rather than against the logics of capital as they (unevenly) pervade the city. This remains political, but it has rather a different valence as an urban intervention than the contestation often associated with alternative urban practices and spaces.

The politics of alterity and autonomy

In the context of urban growing, alterity has been understood in a number of ways, from radical to co-opted, which raises the important question of how we should or could understand the politics inherent in urban growing's autonomy and escapism. Whether urban growing is political comes down to a debate around the potential of interstitial projects and their politics, about whether indeed a politics can be situated in what Iveson (2013) calls 'DIY urbanism'. Iveson himself is wary of this conclusion, arguing that '"appropriating" urban space for unintended uses does not in itself give birth to a new kind of city' (2013, p 942). This critique works at a holistic urban level, yet a politics can be located in the everyday, in the lived experience of the city. Beveridge and Koch (2019) argue this is an important aspect of what they term *urban everyday politics*; a politics at the level of everyday transformation in the lived experience of cities. Yet Beveridge and Koch are wary to note that not every mundane urban transgression is automatically political, but must meet minimal conditions of collectivity, strategy, conflictuality and organization. The question of what alterity can come to mean in communal growing remains open, inasmuch as these minimal conditions are barely met, or are met in ambivalent ways. One way of approaching this question lies in borrowing from Holloway (2002) the idea of 'against-in-and-beyond', which is to say that resistance can be understood as multiple and polyvalent, sitting within as well as struggling against and seeking a 'beyond'. This opens up a way of thinking disruptively against a vision of hegemonic, often overly coherent, economism (Gibson-Graham, 2008), to see the everyday resistances, politics and practices of justice of mundane local projects. In this context, escapism captures not only the complicity of working within funding cycles and volunteerist practices, while creating space for thinking differently about plural values. It also captures a sense of being 'beyond' that Holloway interjects, that Chatterton and Pickerill (2010, p 476) situate in autonomous geographies that 'simultaneously interweave "anti-", "post-" and "despite-" capitalisms'.

Due to its explicitly resistant character, the North Kelvin Meadow and Children's Wood are somewhat antagonistic organizations, pushing back against capitalist development oriented towards economic gain. It resists development, and Glasgow City Council's definition of it, and their educational practice supports alternative visions of what education can be.[3] By contrast, Woodlands resists little explicitly, but does create alternative kinds of food provision for those in need and reinterprets people's labour value. In mundane, subjective ways, Woodlands can be figured as resisting and reimagining one small piece of Glasgow. But this does not preclude either project working alongside development as usual, or tacitly supporting council cuts and so forth.

Arguments around the co-optation of community gardens are suggestive of this line of reasoning. Woodlands creates useful labour for those who are otherwise without labour, it trains them in useful skills. It also provides therapeutic spaces for those burnt out by capitalist wage-labour. The North Kelvin Meadow and Children's Wood could be framed along the same lines – providing children's play, inviting youths into 'useful' and socially productive activity (growing vegetables, moving woodchip around to protect tree roots). Meadow activists cleaned up a derelict site that the council had neglected and, in invigorating and beautifying it, created a space that allows them to continue their stressful jobs and schooling by spending time in it. Is it the therapeutic other to the capitalist city?

That it is possible to frame the projects each way, and that in doing so each seems partial and an exaggeration, suggests first that these ideal types may not necessarily be that useful on their own, and, second, that what appears to be most important in deciding which is more applicable is a relation to politics and to 'otherness'. This is where the argument about interstitiality returns because the perennial questions around whether and how small projects in the cracks of capitalism (Holloway, 2010) might make a difference seems to return to power relations, the question of how those interstitial moments of resistance come to have a broader effect (if at all). This is in part an empirical question which I turn to in the next chapter. It requires an exploration of the interconnection of projects with broader dynamics of power in Glasgow.

This is not to remain agnostic on the political question, but to consider it as to some extent polyvalent, much like community itself. Yet still there is some benefit in considering the everyday as the terrain of politics, as its eventual aim. Taking seriously the everyday as the point of political contest, a different question arises: what transformation of everyday occurs in these practices? What is demonstrated here is an escape in the everyday, a contravention that is less an opposition to capitalist urbanity, and more the creation of a haven and a retreat. In this, it sits *beyond* capitalist relations (as well as within and against them). Thus, escapist urban practices is a way of situating this aspect of communal organizing which turns away from the political system and outward contestation. This is not to figure communal growing projects as apolitical, but to situate the political aspect of such projects alongside their co-opted and evasive aspects. It is to pursue McClintock's (2014) notion of going beyond a bifurcated vision of neoliberal or radical growing, and embracing the projects' 'creative uncertainty against-in-and-beyond a closed, pre-determined world' (Holloway, 2002, p 88), and to think with the dynamics of these multiple politics.

From the commons to community

In this chapter, I have been concerned with the collective urban alternatives constructed by the projects of this research. First, this consists in building mythology, in narrating the projects in time and space. This has its silences, and although it brings use value to the fore, care should be taken in easy celebrations of this reconstitution of land use over land value. Although the projects reject commodification, they also represent the class bias of this process in the West End of Glasgow, which raises all sorts of questions about the relationship projects have to urban development and indeed what it means to engage in local development. The escapist rhythms and mundane communal boundaries the earlier chapters highlighted complicate claims to valuing slowness and the empowerment within the projects.

There is a concern from writers on the commons to argue for the transformative potential of urban commons, especially, as Stavrides hypothesizes, their ability to 'challenge situated identities as well as the fixity of boundaries of any pre-existing community from which individuals draw their own self-images' (Stavrides, 2016, p 262). Yet, the autonomy and alterity so valued in commoning is to some extend posited on boundary processes – the creation of an inside from which to reimagine social, property and land relationships (de Angelis, 2017). This paradoxical relationship to social boundaries belies to some extent a limited engagement with a more sociological vision of community itself.

De Angelis (2017) argues that commons are home to 'real communities' thus:

> Commons thus are not the place for imaginary communities (Anderson 2006), for those who feel they belong to the same nation, race, or football club without even leaving their private living rooms. Commons are instead made of real communities, in the sense that their practices reproduce not only a network of relations, but also a web of recognisable faces, names and characters and dispositions; the accidents of life also shape the web of affects, the mutual aid and the networks of reciprocity that constitute the web of solidarities and friendship. (de Angelis, 2017, p 125)

Yet his reliance on a sense of multiplicity (via Wikipedia and Delanty, 2003) on the one hand, and the work of Benedict Anderson (2006) on imagined communities on the other, leads to a false dichotomy between community as an imaginary (and therefore both utopian and non-existent) and a messy lived multiplicity. This leads to a thin sense of the social role of ideas in shaping what he calls 'real communities'. As I have argued elsewhere (Traill, 2021), community plays an important ideational role in creating space for the kinds of egalitarian, autonomous ethics valued by theorists of the commons.

Yet commons theory tends to start not with the collective per se but with the economic relation, leading it to undertheorize community in itself; though the parallels between recent re-theorizations of community (Studdert and Walkerdine, 2016a; especially Blokland, 2017) and the sense of community as emergent from collective orientations to property and social relations embedded in commoning are striking. To take one example, when Caffentzis and Federici (2014, p 102) write that '[c]ommons in fact entail obligations as much as entitlements', they implicitly echo of Esposito's (2010) writings on obligation as central to community. Equally, Caffentzis and Federici's concern that community is produced in relation to a specific set of practices and projects has deep sympathy with concerns to see community as verb, rather than noun (Walkerdine and Studdert, 2015; Rogaly, 2016). As such, a richer engagement between the commons literature and the sociology of community might find new grounds and interesting questions around how utopian visions interpolate with everyday social dynamics, such as those suggested when Stavrides (2016) writes of the capacity of some urban commons to perpetuate gendered hierarchies.

The next chapter takes this up more explicitly to unpack how practices of collective escape are predicated on the tension between communal responsibility and freedom from economistic structures of value. Thus, the centrality of escaping into obligation, of reaffirming interdependence, emerges as a core ethic in the projects.

6

Escape into Responsibility

Like 'littering in your back garden'

On a mild June evening, Terry, a couple of well-dressed visitors from the local Green Party branch and I spend a few hours wandering around the meadow. It is a tour of sorts, so Terry is in tour guide mode, explaining the history of the site and what the North Kelvin Meadow campaign stands for and how it is shared and managed. One story that he tells, pointing to the space around us, is of an absence – a notable lack of rubbish. Terry says, people do not tend to litter much and people often pick up anything they see on the ground. He goes on to say that the mindset of kids on the site is interesting: they pick up on "the community aspect" of it, and instead of dropping things, they hang on to them. Terry then points out that there is this sense that if they littered here they would be pissing off their parents. For them, Terry argues, it just would not make sense to litter here. One of the visitors nods along and makes the comparison to "littering in your back garden".

Terry agrees, and claims that at the nearby Glasgow Botanical Gardens they have eight or nine people employed to keep the space pristine and litter-free. Because of a shared relationship to the land and to the people who use it (implicitly absent in his account at the Botanical Gardens), Terry thus weaves a story about how people are inhibited from littering.

A sense of ownership is undoubtedly important in this specific iteration of community, but this also highlights the way community as a frame gets used to explain things at the meadow, in this case, a dearth of littering: the resonance of the idea of community, of being part of a collective, is argued to work against practices of misuse, like littering and arson. What is elided in Terry's account into a simply community ethic is that litter-picking is a common enough activity, especially before toddler groups. Someone usually checks the area for left-behind bottles, cigarette butts or other miscellaneous rubbish before toddlers use it. This is an important grounding to this otherwise glorious vision of communality: it might well inhibit littering, but it also involves an active practice of litter *removing*. This maintenance work – carried out not for pay but out of a sense of value – is also core to demonstrating how communal escape functions.

The symbolism of a space designated as communal produces care – in narratives of impeded littering and in tidying practices, care of the space itself and of those using it. This caretaking can be seen as a practical enactment of an idea of *responsibility* within communal behaviour. Sharing is a way of engaging with each other, part of a culture shaped by the expectations around the idea of community. While it remains a fuzzy and questionably descriptive object, community is the guiding idea around which these practices of sharing and caring circulate and it rationalizes and explains them to respondents. Nevertheless, practices of care are built on the interplay of being known and a level of non-intensive intimacy. It presupposes then a level of group formation that creates the *outsides* discussed earlier that map onto broader social dynamics of exclusion. As such, attending to care and responsibility allows us to gain a perspective on the positive (in the sense of productive) facets of group boundary creation, bringing into focus the interrelation in these spaces of escape and responsibility.

The idea of community

The escape made possible through the growing projects is predicated on connection. It acts as the bedrock for claims that community does or does not exist in these places. However, my purpose here is not to dwell on whether or not a community does or does not exist. As Jean-Luc Nancy (1991) argues, community at its fullest expression is philosophically impossible. More than this, it is probably undesirable socially to have a totalizing, all-encompassing community. Community, particularly the kind of urban community described in the work of Blokland (2017), as a way of being, a culture of knowing, can be found in all manner of fleeting and distant connections, not just the kind of intense merging imagined by Nancy to be impossible.

Still, the imagination of community shapes the practice of escape in important ways. Drawing on Davina Cooper's (2013) exploration of how everyday utopias exist as imperfect enactment of ideas, it is possible to trace the way that community is actualized, or practised, in communal growing. The idea of actualization reflects the limited and conflicted ways that ideas are expressed in everyday situations. In following the shape and complexities of interconnection as a practice of escape, the purpose here is to focus on how a more just world is imagined and brought into being through care, knowing and responsibility.

This responsibility within community can be seen theoretically in the work of Esposito (2010). In situating obligation (the *munis*) as linguistically and philosophically central to community, Esposito's work calls attention to community as rooted in responsibility. Echoes of this emerge in the field, where one community growing practitioner referred to community simply as "really annoying" – a tangle of sometimes awkward relationships and interdependencies. An understanding of community growing as a kind of commons, and as a means of staking a right to the city, raises a question: what kind of an escape is posited in such a collective process? Community can be an undertheorized element of commons writing, but it is crucial not only in expanding our understanding of commoning but in teasing out key tensions within community growing as a field of both politics and justice.

Turning first to how connection is embedded in practices, this chapter draws out the ways that escape figures as a kind of positive freedom – a freedom to, rather than a freedom from (Berlin, 1969). Thus responsibility emerges in practices of sharing and care. This positive freedom (to care, to connect) is crucial to understanding the ambivalence of community growing politically. The oxymoronic idea of escaping into responsibility is thus opened up through positive freedom. The limits of this are also explored – in particular, the way that the closure in Berlin's conceptualization mirrors a certain closure in communal practice, but one that is constantly in motion, and therefore incomplete and fractious.

Imagining community, practising care

The interconnection of care, connection and the social imagination of community is hardly surprising, though often only implicitly connected in theory. Tronto (1993) sees care as a 'species activity' carried out to make our world liveable, that Crossan et al (2015) connect to the learning and social connection found in community gardens. In this study, practices of care were demonstrated in an extension of a sense of 'we', and a willingness to spend time getting to know each other. Thus, imaginations of community were invested with ideas of care. At the North Kelvin Meadow, Lauren – a parent who regularly brings along her children to play in the space – exemplifies this: "It's about a connection. ... I very much feel a part of a local community that is reciprocal and supportive and respectful of difference, I guess" (Lauren, interview, July 2015). In being communal, participants can approach each other with needs, and expect them to be "reciprocal". Community organizes, or frames, this mutuality and responsibility (Goffman, 1975). Natalie, a local mother, activist and volunteer, found this in being able to ask people to do things for her. In her work with the Children's Wood around events, she found that she associated a "sense of community" with asking for help:

'What do I mean about the sense of community? [pause] I think quite often we're having to ask people to do things for us, so even just can you go and boil me some kettles of water. You're, I guess for me on some level it means just being forced out of myself and working more closely with your neighbours.' (Natalie, interview, June 2016)

The sense of giving and receiving support is a key part of both field sites, in that it enables this sense of "being forced out of myself" that Natalie describes. It ranges from the practical to the emotional, and covers different levels of need.

Supporting each other is in this way part of the ethic at the meadow. It goes beyond simply knowing people to what David called "collective-ness". This encompasses experiences that are shared: "It's about the larger-scale shared experience, yeah, I don't really know any other way to describe it. I think bringing all the different groups together. Now the disparate groups having a shared focus. ... I think that it's just the collective, the collective-ness" (David, interview, June 2016). This "collective-ness" allows connection without direct intimacy; it creates a culture of mutual attention to need, practically considered in Natalie's need for hot water at events. In this sense, it recalls the idea in work by Crossan et al (2015) that care is central to the functioning of community gardens. This draws on the work of Joan Tronto (1993) in suggesting that a caring activity is one that takes care of one's world, and in this what is important is the connection between people that this caring practice facilitates. It is the paying of attention, instead of the practice of anonymity, it is the creation of a 'we' and an inside.

As such, conceptualizing care collectively seems in tension with the broader trajectory of individualism and the commodification within economies of care, which crowds out the relational dimension of caring (Tronto, 2017). Care has been seen as domesticated, and situating it in this communal sphere begins to reimagine it beyond the dyadic, in a more socially embedded, relational context (Green and Lawson, 2011). As such, what the idea of 'communities of care' (Crossan et al, 2015) suggests is that connection and care can be found together in communal growing, though it seems germane to ask what a community without care might look like. Care thus is the flipside of obligation, its Janus-faced partner.

In creating a sense of commonality, sharing is a central practice. The space of the meadow and wood is shared by many groups of people using it for disparate things: dog walking, entertaining toddlers, growing vegetables, riding BMXs, having barbeques and other activities. The putative equality of all these activities makes it an inherently shared space, as discussed earlier – it is everyone's and nobody's. That it is defined as a community space, and thus a shared space, meant that practices of care extended to encompass a wide range of people. This is made particularly clear in the relation to littering, as Terry's version of events at the start of the chapter makes clear. While showing off the meadow, emphasizing these positive narratives about the space is a way to ground practices of care in the everyday. In this, Terry was attempting in some way to explain the physical space of the meadow to outsiders. That this required an understanding of collective feeling and care speaks to their importance at the meadow.

Common garden friendships

When Sukey and Samantha meet in Woodlands Community Garden, they talk about Samantha's dog training. The two of them see each other every morning around 7am when Samantha takes her dog to the park and Sukey goes to exercise. Before Samantha joined the garden, their daily rituals brought them to the park at the same time, but they remained strangers. The key difference, Samantha tells me, is the garden. There are lots of other people Samantha sees daily that she does not get talking to. Because of the connection with the garden, however, Sukey and Samantha have a reason to talk, a place in common to start from. That the community garden provides Sukey and Samantha with a reason to talk emphasizes how community gardening facilitates connection, and the keystone in this is the idea of community itself. Community as an idea organizes the garden into a space where connection is possible. Embodying practices of care, attention and non-committal friendship, the experience of community projects is in direct contrast with the lived experience of other parts of the city. Discursively, the community garden or meadow were often placed in contradistinction to formal parks or living conditions, as part of the 'rest of the city' where it is hard to get to know people. The garden offers a space in which this is overturned, especially during the growing sessions organized twice a week on Wednesday and Sunday afternoons.

Although gardening is oriented towards an overarching idea of community, there can be a great deal of variability in terms of the experience of intimacy, and indeed in the cases studied here there were quite diverse levels of contact and intimacy. This varied depending on what was sought, and how proximate to the projects participants were capable of being (whether in time or energy). It demonstrates the flexibility within community as a framing device, capable in its discursive fuzziness of encompassing a great deal of social meaning. For Fiona, a raised bed gardener who moved to Glasgow alone a few years ago from America, it is a "great wee community", where she made so many friends. For those like Fiona who sought deeper connections, it was often possible to make strong friendships. For others, however, part of the value of the garden is the shallowness of being known. Samantha appreciates the everyday chatter of the garden, like her connection with Sukey around a similar morning routine. She finds it soothing precisely because you get to talk to people but they do not know you intimately.

Helen:	What do you think you get from the garden?
Samantha:	More of it, more of the social aspect than the growing and the learning about gardening. I think what I get from it is some space and some time out and some fresh air and nice chats with people when it's needed. But sometimes I don't realize I need it and I go and it's almost like therapy for me? Not that I have a really tough life compared to some of the people who go but it is like a form of therapy for me.
Helen:	What do you think you value most about the social aspect of it?
Samantha:	I quite like that a lot of the people I don't even know their surnames and we're not friends on Facebook or they don't really know much about me and it's just like non-committal friendships that I have with people and meeting people when I'm there it's not like, so what university were you at? (Interview, April 2016)

There is a level within the garden of what Samantha calls "non-committal friendships" that refers to people you are co-present with regularly, but who aren't "friends on Facebook" or close friends. That friendly but not intense conversation can, as Samantha suggests, be a balm, when found alongside pleasant growing activities, especially in relation to a lack of status-seeking behaviour, suggested here in relation to university attendance. There is a specific tone that being known then has in the context of a community project. A lightness to the social activity which gives a sense of contact without emotional exposure or status seeking. Yet, despite the distance within this kind of intimacy, it is paralleled by everyday practices of care.

Care is embodied in a number of ways, not only attending to social but also physical elements of the garden. It emerges in the practices of slowing down and revaluing labour, as earlier chapters illustrated through stories like Adam's physical rehabilitation or the care taken over Mark's economic situation. It also emerges in material practices such as sharing, which extends the ownership imaginary discussed in the previous chapter. This materializes an orientation to community within growing as an urban practice. At Woodlands, this is most obvious in sharing surplus, whether seeds, seedlings or produce.

One day in May, Eloise turned up to the growing session with sunflower seedlings. She left some specifically for fellow gardener Ethel, but also placed some around the garden for others to take since, as she told me, she had too many herself. As with intimacy, sharing can be variable. It can be specifically between two gardeners, or it can be a more general orientation to surplus being for everyone. On the same day in May, Pete – another longer-term raised bedder – brought his excess seeds along, joining them with the existing Woodlands stash. It was thus common practice to share what one had in surplus.

Some of the gardeners are also enthusiastic sharers of produce. In conversation with Ethel, a few weeks later in June, she worries over her courgettes and how she has promised them to various people. She lists off both fellow gardeners and friends outside, concerned about the possibility of having over-committed herself. Despite the largely symbolic quantities of produce grown in the garden, sharing is a means growers have to invite others to be involved in their ethical labour, to reconnect themselves with ideas of land and community, to share in the joy of freshly grown food.

This sharing ethic is exemplified more formally at Woodlands in the community café. Unlike the direct peer-to-peer sharing exemplified by Ethel, this is at a much broader and more formalized neighbourhood level. Every week in Woodlands, people gather and eat a free or pay-as-you-feel vegetarian meal together. This has varied in format and location over the years, drawing in produce from the garden in the early years, though stopping once the café outgrew the productive capacity of the garden. By 2019, the café was feeding up to 80 people a night, with meditation sessions, music, advice from the Citizens Advice Bureau and usually at least a dozen volunteers. Although this has varied in location and number of people involved, varying in timings and complexity, there is a high level of continuity that runs through these different models. The food is always high quality, seasonal and where possible organic; the bar to entry is low and the emphasis is on eating *together*, something increasingly celebrated and understood as *more than* simply eating (Blake, 2019; Smith and Harvey, 2021).

Through eating together, boundaries between waged and unwaged, or mentally well and unwell, can be eroded. This can be difficult for some participants to get their heads around early on, but it becomes a practice of equality that allows them to embody the values of the project. Attending the café one week, I got talking to Cormac, who tells me how he originally came along to the café to support the homeless men he works with, making sure a familiar face would be there to make it easier for them to access the food and warmth. He reflected on how his attitude shifted after coming along a few times. Cormac used to come along but not eat, he told me, because "I have a wage, I can afford to eat". But he was cajoled by staff into eating and now understands that that is part of the point; that eating together is what makes this a nice place to be, that no one is outside of that, waged or otherwise. He talks about the way that he gets this real "community feeling" from the place and this stretches beyond the few hours that people are gathered here. In this way, sharing can be a way of connecting equally between people and broadening to a sense of welcome to everyone in attendance.

At both sites, then, communality is reproduced in relation to three things: practices of attention (or being known), non-committal friendship and practices of care. These are made sense of with reference to the overarching frame of community. It is through an understanding of communal space that people become more than strangers, yet because of the mundanity and intermittency of contact, intimacy need not be intense and a level of privacy can be maintained. Privacy does not preclude the extension of practices of care, extended as they are along ideological lines. Nonetheless, this interplay of communality and inclusion relies on the dynamics of group formation creating critical tensions within practices of care and responsibility.

In-group, out-group

The practices of care detailed previously arise from social connection and stability within projects. This is particularly important in creating the grounds for intimacy and care; but it is also how the exclusions detailed in previous chapters emerge in everyday settings, through implicit codes of conduct and practices of pragmatic stabilization within the projects. Thus, at both field sites there is a core group that might be considered at the centre of the organized practices. This is to some extent a relationship to the space-time, the rhythms, of the projects; it benefits those positioned as carers (mothers, care workers), and those out of work for a time or who work flexible or nonstandard hours. Despite their often undervalued position in the wider social milieu, at Woodlands it is easy to see them as forming a core of volunteers and regular gardeners who attend growing sessions. Entry into this group as a volunteer is straightforward, but to gain a raised bed, participants have highlighted how useful it is to have shown dedication to the project.

Samantha (a raised bed gardener occasionally given work by the garden and latterly employed by them) was quite open about the existence of a core group, as we sat outside a café near the garden in the sun:

> 'I dunno just because we only had a certain amount of spaces on [a course], it kind of felt quite like ooh I'm sort of *getting in there a bit*. ... I think they're not like emm rude to newcomers at all but yeah I think you need to give something to get something back from them. Definitely.' (Samantha, interview, April 2016, emphasis added)

The allocation of raised beds highlights the importance of this integration, of "getting in there" in Samantha's terms. Although there is a formal waiting list, the allocation of beds is not a straightforward process. In giving raised beds to people, it is not just about who is on the list. Woodlands value those who have given time to the garden and shown a willingness to come down and get involved. This was explained to me in conversation with a member of staff over an abandoned raised bed. When I asked who would get the bed, I was told by Jen, the garden worker, that there is a waiting list and a few people on it have already been contacted. "It is a delicate process", she tells me, "because you have a list for a reason, but some of these people have not been down to the garden before so it is weird to give them a raised bed". She tells me, too, that it is better to give them to people who have come down before at least, or better yet, volunteered for a while, because then you know they are likely to actually keep the bed up and use it, rather than leave it abandoned like this one has been. She adds: "Some people just take up space on the list – they put their name down and then you don't ever hear from them again."

Jen's account of the delicate process of raised bed allocation acknowledges a balance of different considerations at play. The unknown represented by outsiders who haven't been down before challenges the pragmatism of trying to keep beds in use. When Samantha gets a raised bed a month or so after my conversation with Jen, she relates this back to the work she has done in the garden, saying it was a combination of "nagging" and "consistent volunteering". It underlines this facet of the garden's culture: getting a raised bed is in part about putting work in, to those initiated.

There is a pragmatism in this insider dynamic that is intended to protect the longevity of the project by allowing raised beds to those who have shown commitment. This is not of course the only aspect of that "delicate process" but it is a nod to the need for some stability in the garden, in order for any kind of continuity. To some extent this need to prove yourself to enter the inner core reflects the common idea that raised bed gardeners are separate and more deeply committed to the garden.

Cathy, a raised bed gardener of many years and vocal member of the garden in garden meetings, tells me that the raised bedders (as they are often known) are a "community within a community". They have a vested interest in the garden in a more direct way, she tells me. For Cathy, the raised bedders *are* the garden. This sense of the raised bedders harks to an inner group that is reliable. They turn up to the garden and its events. It is a common phraseology that is used to designate a particular set of gardeners: those in a rental agreement with the Woodlands Community Development Trust. Notably for Cathy, this is a more concentrated version of the broader community. That this core is bounded and reliable suggests that replicable group formation is at the heart of community-as-imagined.

However, this core does not easily map onto raised bed gardeners directly. Those who are less able to regularly attend growing sessions and do not make it along to social gatherings are not really part of this group, though they still have a material proximity to the project (assuming they maintain their raised bed). As such, analytically there are two centres to the Woodlands Community Garden – one consisting of those who are there regularly, raised bed or otherwise, and one consisting of raised bed gardeners, a more imagined community (Anderson, 2006), who together represent those who are committed to the project materially.

As a result, at the Woodlands Community Garden, there is some closure within their practice of communality, the creation of the group closest to community conceptualized as an impossible stable object. It has a few in-groups, although the relations between people make this boundary fuzzy, not least the overlap between raised bed gardeners and regular users of the garden makes the distinction analytic as much as empirical. What the distinction really emphasizes is the peripheral status of some of the raised bed gardeners rather than the separation of the two cores. What this closure suggests is a limit: a boundary around who gets to be in that inner group, to maintain it as a more concentrated 'community within a community'. There is a logic of sustainability here, those who have proven themselves committed are more likely to get a raised bed, but it creates a tension against the idea that the community project is open to all. It recalls sociological works that emphasize the boundaries of community (Cohen, 1985; Belton, 2013; Fraser, 2013) but introduces a blurriness around not only the edges but also around whether there is one consistent group at the centre.

Fragmentary meadow boundaries

This boundary work echoes in a different way at the North Kelvin Meadow and Children's Wood. It is more fragmentary and distinct, and this suggestively mirrors the greater ambivalence on site about the existence of community. There is already a bifurcation when one considers the existence of two separate charities that are acting in the space, not always in exact concordance. While the North Kelvin Meadow group are interested in conservation of the space, growing and tending the meadow, composting and the raised beds, the Children's Wood has been more interested in developing community activities and children's events, although their interest in the raised beds and growing does often overlap with the North Kelvin Meadow campaign's. This bifurcation, however, can be overplayed: the North Kelvin Meadow group has been in slow decline in its presence in the space. People have left the campaign (some through simply leaving the area) and the rising momentum of the Children's Wood tended to draw in new activists. Nonetheless, there are a number of different centres to the Children's Wood, not only the committees and activities there, but also the playgroups. For committee member, David, community means parents of other children around his child's age, and then there are more peripheral aspects:

Helen: For you, who is the community?
David: There's kind of the social aspects, which is mainly with other parents who are mainly kind of [his daughter's] friends' age.

> So that's kind of the core of the community that I know but through that then, I've met other dog walkers, gardeners, all the other groups that kind of use the land. So I am aware of the wider community but I don't necessarily engage with it too much. (David, interview, June 2016)

Dog walkers (part of what David calls the "wider community") are regularly present in the space but are somewhat separate from the more formalized uses represented by the campaigns. They constitute a secondary core, less organized but highly present in the space. Dog walkers are often around at similar times and usually daily, giving a kind of structure around which their interactions fall. Early mornings and evenings around 5 to 6pm are times it is common to see many dog walkers, plus a smaller clustering around lunchtime. They also tend to stay out of the more densely wooded area where the mud kitchen is, especially while there are families there. A distance then presents itself between dog walkers and other users in the meadow.

As such, although dog shows usually feature at Children's Wood events, there is often a separation between the Children's Wood activities and the dog walkers despite their shared billing. It manifests in spatial practices. After a dog show at an event in summer 2016, the dog walkers move off to just past a small copse in the middle of the meadow, sitting themselves on sawn-off logs and chatting, still in the space but distinct from the rest of the Children's Wood event. Their physical distinction– sitting away from the gala day activities – demarcates an important sense of difference, although in very practical terms it also reflects the different needs of dogs and small excited children. Yet this distinction can extend to tensions between the groups. Joan is a member of the Children's Wood committee, often having a craft stall at events, but she also has a dog, putting her between these two putatively distinct camps. She explained that while both groups are present in the space, there is more tolerance than mixing:

> 'Certainly not most of the dog walkers I don't think are involved. I think one of Polly's neighbours' children helps out and she's one of the dog walkers. ... I wouldn't say there was tension between them, but you do sometimes get children saying to dog walkers, what are you doing here? This is our Children's Wood. ... And I think there are a couple of people that aren't into kids, so I'm not going to pretend it's a nice harmonious, but in general it works quite well. Different groups tolerate each other.' (Joan, interview, June 2015)

This sense that they "tolerate" each other, that they exist alongside but do not mingle, gives a second centre, alongside the official Children's Wood activities. This tolerance recalls work on urban conviviality, particularly as it highlights the tolerance of difference as critical social dynamic in cities (Neal et al, 2018), though it has often been related to urban multiculture more than the space between dog owners and parents. Since growing did not flourish as a communal activity at the meadow until the years after 2016, it didn't represent a focal point for the creation of an in-group during the main body of the research presented here, although this absence was noticed by participants and often bemoaned. For example, Dana, a raised bed grower and recent transplant to Glasgow, interviewed at the North Kelvin Meadow, was disappointed not to meet more fellow gardeners. She said, "[I was] hoping it would be like, you know, I'm gardening here, someone else is gardening there, we would start talking" (Dana, interview, July 2015). During trips back to the meadow in the intervening years, the gardening does seem to have formalized somewhat and could now plausibly be another anchor for communal behaviour, but without further ethnographic fieldwork I cannot speak with any certainty to that here. It does however pose an interesting question about how such spaces and activities coalesce as a way to anchor communal feeling. The employment of a member of staff at the meadow to coordinate gardening activities indicates perhaps that a degree of rhythmic fixity is helpful in establishing that, alongside the incidentally aligned dog-walking rhythms and the organized weekly toddler groups.

It is suggestive to compare the projects because although both had arguably two centres to their activities, they align differently. There was one central (if blurry) group at Woodlands made up of people that fall into at least one of two camps that greatly overlap – those who volunteer regularly and those who have a raised bed. At the North Kelvin Meadow, there were two separate activities that align people to at least two different centres, although there is overlap between the groups, friendships even. Perhaps more often, what exists is convivial coexistence and a shared interest in perpetuating the meadow. No one wants to see the space destroyed and it brings people into greater alignment as a result. But because the central orienting feature of the meadow is the space itself rather than a specific activity, the communal practices are more fluid, and less coherent than those at the Woodlands Community Garden.

This could lead to reflections on whether community exists at the meadow or not. Analytically, this would require an arbitrary set of minimal characteristics for the existence of community, a boundary of its own. Instead of creating or hypothesizing such a boundary, I suggest community's lack of replicable social form relates to the way that it refers to a socially constructed but practically impossible idea, and the ways in which community-as-idea is destabilized by other cross-cutting ideologies and practical conditions. This is critical for understanding communal growing as a social phenomenon, and these dynamics have ramifications for understanding growing as a site and practice of justice.

Responsibility and justice

Staying for now with the positive, or productive, element of communal growing projects illuminates a core intricacy within the practices of justice at the communal growing projects. To some extent, the production of insiders and outsiders is a basic function of creating a localized culture and set of shared norms. There are those who are more or less proximate to both projects, creating a group – whether this is a community or not is not an analytically useful question. The group creation is the groundwork for the rhythmic escapes and revaluations and the autonomist practices describes earlier, yet the boundaries created – the insides of collective processes – map onto social exclusions described in Chapter 4, which trouble attempts to be inclusive. There is in this a cleavage to an idea of being collective – and these impacts are the result of behaving in such a collective way.

There is perhaps something paradoxical in figuring such collective behaviour as an escape: particularly as communality has been associated with – and indeed, can easily be seen in these case studies as producing – a kind of closure and unfreedom (see a particularly clear case in Belton, 2013). The associations of communality (particularly the nosy neighbour and closed cultural norms tropes) can be rigid and stultifying; certainly when the counterpoint is the (negative) freedom of the urban to (re)create and immerse oneself in the novelty and flow of thrumming cityscape, it's 'magic, phantasmagoria, ritual and transcendent content' (Franklin, 2010, p 2). Yet this imaginary of the city-as-freedom, even as its flaws are obvious and its lived experience deeply uneven, is also a vision of deep individualization, even dislocation, from social connection.

As Blokland (2017) reminds the reader, living in a city is not as atomized an experience as this vision would attest. Recalling the way urban life creates frictions and anonymous patterns of knowing, Blokland reasserts the interconnections of social life, even within the otherwise individualized lifestyles of the typical Western city. It is the way lives brush past each other, the little rhythms and repetitions that build patterns of knowing, that are crucial to the functioning of communal feeling at the growing projects. It is this recurrent and rhythmic knowing that they explicitly encourage and facilitate – in many ways, this *is* the work of communal growing projects. The growing only functions as communal when collective knowing flourishes.

It is worth here noting the suggestive difference between the rhythms of the two case studies, because it has theoretical implications. The meadow has a greater degree of escape in the sense of freedom from structure, formally speaking, yet in so doing it has less of a collective character. The lack of formal gardening sessions during the 2015–16 period led to some disappointment and certainly a limited 'garden' feeling of collectivity. This leads to much lower possibility of connection with other people, although the natural rhythms of daily life and seasonality are still appreciable in abundance; and the children's activities produce their own node of connection. In the Woodlands garden, a greater regimentation around timings and repetitions produces a greater sense of communality to their escape, although it requires commitment. Thus although communal escape offers salvation from the atomizing aspects of capitalism, there appears to be a need to anchor this in delimitation and rhythmic inflexibility.

In this way, the comparison between the daily practices of escape in the two projects recall Esposito's (2010) articulation of community as derived from the *munis*: from collective obligation. Communality in this respect becomes something requiring work together, which restricts an abstract (negative) *freedom from* (here, obligation) but facilitates the possibility of connection. This recalls the categorical distinction that Berlin (1969) made between negative freedom (or freedom from) and a positive freedom (freedom to).

Negative freedom, in Berlin's conception of it, refers to the more intuitive sense of liberty as the 'absence of interference beyond the shifting, but always recognisable, frontier' (Berlin, 1969, p 174). He traces in the history of the philosophy of liberty, particularly in the work of J.S. Mill, a general trend that recognizes the need for a private realm beyond the interference of others and it is this that is centred in a negative concept of freedom. A positive liberty is something less intuitive, centred on self-governance and, as Berlin argues:

> The desire to be governed by myself, or at any rate to participate in the process by which my life is to be controlled, may be as deep a wish as that for a free area for action, and perhaps historically older. But it is not a desire for the same thing. (Berlin, 1969, p 178)

What Berlin traces in his foray into positive freedom is the ends to which a positive concept of liberty can slip, via a notion of 'true' or 'real' purpose, to coercion to the enlightened ends that they *would* desire should their 'true' or 'ideal' self be available. As such, positive freedom as self-mastery is in Berlin's telling a concept prone to manipulation for political ends – whether by the state, the church, or ideological ends: 'Enough manipulation of the definition of man, and freedom can be made to mean whatever the manipulator wishes' (Berlin, 1969, p 180).

The issue Berlin addresses at length is what translations these ideas of freedom take on at the level of the legislative state. But that is not my concern here, focused as this book is at the level of the small-scale social collective: the putative community. Rather than being concerned with what meaningful political philosophy emerges from a positive conception of self-direction and the need therein to produce a vision of true or real wishes and wants, I am concerned to think with what a localized vision of a positive freedom might entail.

A positive vision of freedom at the level of the everyday could be one defined by 'self-control' and 'self-direction' (Berlin, 1969, p 190), which gives more of a notion of liberation via reason. The everyday as a 'source, stake and site of struggle', where urban actors jostle for political authority and seek alliances (Beveridge and Koch, 2019, p 146), presents a different kind of space in which to situate a positive freedom. Here self-direction is more attuned to autonomy – to the anarchist notions which are clearly more relevant in the everyday. This is to retune politics more widely to the lived possibilities they inhabit, the radical everyday that is to some extent always illegible from the level of the state (something Scott [1998] parses as hidden transcripts).

Thus it is notable that Berlin concedes that a positive sense of freedom feeds the demands for social justice. The self-mastery inherent in joining community as a means of aligning oneself with what one respondent at the wood called a "common justice" is a way of articulating collective obligation and shared responsibility as a value – not an absence (a freedom from) – this is the freedom to belong. In this, the *munis* is not a burden but a recognition of collective and shared (and, to some extent, perhaps paradoxically, voluntary) obligation as the terms of association.

Yet Berlin's wariness of positive freedom, his sense that it tends towards a singular vision of the good life and is therefore prone to authoritarianism, also resonates here. As previous chapters noted, tensions emerge within the visions of collective justice and inclusion, and the values that are expressed within these communal spaces are often in conflict with one another. As such, collective escape is a kind of positive freedom – an immersion in obligation and responsibility – with the associated challenges that come with such a potentially totalizing vision. Jean-Luc Nancy's (1991) vision of community as potentially totalizing at its limit also resonates in interesting ways here.

This more positive, more directive vision within community growing resonates with Neo and Chua's (2017) discussion of the governmentalities of community garden, inasmuch as they situate community as an ethic, and guiding principle behind some community gardens. They position this against the gardens which are more oriented towards growing in itself, and are therefore less interested in creating strong social bonds. Though there are also important contextual differences between the Singaporean context of Neo and Chua's work and the Glaswegian context here, this emphasizes two things in relation to the case studies at hand. First, the spaces of escape here, as a practice of justice, are contextually specific and driven by the ideological framings of community and inclusion. Second, community growing, like many practices often written about in the vein of DIY urbanism, is not innately imbued with political inclinations or characteristics of justice or indeed exclusion, but is a literal and metaphorical space in which these dynamics play out.

The attitude of 'yes, we can'

How then to explain the distinctive patterns of inclusive rhetoric and bounded community behaviour that create the possibility of an escape into collective life? To some extent the generative potential of growing emerges in part from a framing of the potential to act: a decision taken simply to go ahead and stake a claim. The next chapter explores the external dynamics that come to foreclose a more public political framing in this particular pair of cases, but the possibility of transformation and radically reimagining everyday social life sits clearly within the scope of escapist practices in these sites. Polly at the Children's Wood had a clear insight into the necessity of framing community action as possible, and its challenges:

> 'I think it's just the general Scottish culture, I think that's what you're up against, it's just a can't do attitude. And I think here has been a can do attitude and I think that's what's made it so successful, it's just that thing of, we can do this and we will do this [laughs] and you know that's been one of the biggest barriers in the community is that can't do attitude. It's just like come on, no we can, let's just do that and move it over here and you know and it, it is something that I think has been quite bad in the general scheme of things because you always hear, oh you'll never succeed and oh they'll never win and often they don't, and it's often attitude. That's where I started to get involved, I was like, no we can. Everyone you talk to is so no, we don't, we can't, and it's just like well if you say that, and that's what the council is saying all the time, no one's going to help, no one's going to volunteer, who's going to bother getting involved? Och it's just going to get built on anyway, why bother, it's a done deal. So that was the biggest thing we worked on in the first couple of years was trying to get away from the done deal aspect that the council were spouting out because they would just say, oh it's a signed contract, it's basically done and so just trying to educate people and say, no we can.' (Polly, interview, July 2016)

Polly argues that the prevailing negativity of the Scottish mentality (as evidenced, she argues, in psychological studies) blocks action. The idea instead was to produce a 'can do' attitude, to shift away from this constant sense of disempowerment. In a report from 2016, the Glasgow Centre for Population Health suggested that a hangover from a democratic deficit in the 1980s was not only creating a sense of the inability to change things, as Polly is, but that it was also having negative health affects in contemporary Glasgow's early male mortality rate (Walsh et al, 2016). In this perhaps emerges a cultural mindset both unhealthy and disheartening at play in Scottish cities, yet it is not totalizing. Deliberately refusing a sense of 'can't do' is something the meadow campaigners attribute their success to. That is of course difficult to verify and should not be read outside of the campaign's capacity to leverage resources from media-savvy press contacts, educational levels, architectural skill, research knowledge and time to pursue their goals. Nonetheless, this kernel of radical hope – the can-do of the Children's Wood – is a utopian basis found across growing projects, the belief in a different way of doing things and a potent framing device. There is something inherently hopeful in planting seeds and nurturing connections between people, especially in the current moment of climate crisis and sense of impending apocalypse.

Yet this hope and potential connection, this escape, is clearly bounded, and paradoxical. The productive potential of urban communal growing is based in a set of prosaic exclusions. It is based in a set of boundary behaviours that on a micro-scale make possible cultures of connection and escape from a broader urban alienation in many forms. Because of the obligations at the heart of collective urban projects and on which they firmly rely, escape in such a context is a retreat in a positive sense. This sits uncomfortably against an understanding of the projects as practices of justice, particularly as it predominantly emerges through the themes of inclusivity and autonomy; reiterating the imperfections and challenges of creating spaces of urban alterneity.

7

Field Dynamics and Strategic Neutrality

Playing the field

> 'I mean I would love to get somebody to pay us to have a full-time gardeners who could just do the garden, just do what they want. So but that's not really going to happen.'
>
> Oliver (interview, July 2015)

As Oliver and the other staff at the Woodlands Community Development Trust (WCDT) noted, funding the garden itself, as a garden, independent of any kind of agenda, is a deeply unlikely prospect. Like many community organizations, then, WCDT play the game of funding, becoming a legible organization, playing by the rules and applying to carrying out projects that meet the aims of funders while trying to balance this against their own goals. This is a precarious balance, and one made harder by the increased competition and declining funding within the sector (St Clair et al, 2020). This game, however, what we might call the field of social relations in which the WCDT act, shapes in important ways the daily activities of the organization and the broader political possibilities inherent within it. To understand how politics and justice are curtailed within a collective context such as community growing requires a foray into the practicalities of community organizations and funding context. The contrast between the organizations in terms of their position within this field of action is particularly illustrative here. Their contrasting levels of formalization and the struggle over the meadow highlight the complicities of organizations in depoliticizing community growing as a phenomenon, despite the internal dynamics of autonomy and revaluation described in previous chapters. In this, escape is limited by the context from which it is attempting to turn away, but in which it is still embedded.

WCDT place a strong emphasis on finding funders whose aims align as closely as possible with those of the Trust. This is one of the main teachings of a seminar that Oliver, the manager and main fundraiser at the Trust, expounds to a room of charity colleagues in Glasgow in September 2016. The seminar is itself a fundraising exercise for Woodlands, explored for its capacity to bring in extra funds not earmarked for anything else (known as 'unrestricted funds'). Oliver's learning emerged from years of practice and missteps along the way, including a brief foray into eco-driving lessons in the early years of the garden. Oliver would not, however, offer something that sits outside their remit anymore, but centring the aims of the organization was learned the hard way.

The tactics of the organization reflect an understanding of the difficulties of working alongside the state, local authorities and other funders. It reflects similar strategic moves carried out within the South African Anti-Eviction campaigns that see remaining critical and autonomous as more important than funding opportunities with non-governmental organizations that come with strings attached (Miraftab, 2009). The similarity lies in aiming for independence and a reflexivity about how funding shapes what occurs at an organizational level. It also suggests that goal displacement, the replacement of an organization's own goals with that of a funder or set of elites, can be mitigated by cultural factors such as a strong orientation to values (Osterman, 2006). At Woodlands, valuing independence leads to a will to find funding that suits the aims of the organization, although this has been a learning process for the Trust that has included, in previous years, funding for giving eco-driving lessons, before a balance was struck between funder aims and garden aims.

The danger in this balance is always that of changing the nature of the project to suit funders' aims. This is often translated in the community garden literature into ideas of co-option into neoliberal governance (Rosol, 2012; Ghose and Pettygrove, 2014), but the idea of institutional channelling – the directing of organizations towards less challenging action – is a perhaps more apt way of viewing this. Developed in relation to social movements, the idea of institutional channelling suggests the potential for funding to push social movements towards less contentious claims (McCarthy et al, 1991). This is part of a dynamic of challenge and response between those in power and those who would see the city arranged differently. Nevertheless, restrictions in charity funding also help produce this precarity, and that indeed can be linked back to austerity governance (Williams et al, 2014). In this, the field of community growing practice is shaped by broader neoliberal policies as the local particularity through which governance is experienced (Peck et al, 2009).

Subtler ways of shaping communal growing exist too, through the tendency of funders to ask for applications to delineate clearly set goals, end-points and measurable outputs for each funding application. This is what Holly describes as making everything a 'project'. While packaging up activities neatly is part of the funding process, it reduces a sense of continuity and can be itself problematic:

> 'Funding is usually project kind of orientated so things get badged up as projects. Then Oliver goes for funding and if we're successful, we roll with it. That's kind of the pattern it takes really at the moment. ... [Unrestricted funding] certainly would take, it'd take the pressure off doing things in set time scales. ... I think it would give a bit of breathing space to really get to the root of what people are interested in and what they need and how to go around solving that, without having the pressure of having to get something finished in a year.' (Holly, interview, May 2016)

Holly notes that the timelines of grant funding are relatively short, meaning that in her position, trying to develop relationships with schools and locals, it is difficult to 'get to the root' of what is needed and there is a distinct pressure wrapped up in this. The intensity of the funding cycle and its short-term imagination (projects rarely last longer than a year) attracts organizational attention to funding applications, taking up a large part of the WCDT's managers' time and administrative energy.

At the Woodlands Community Garden, this has particular ramifications regarding the capacity of the project to be a source of a dissenting political voice. Despite taking publicly oppositional positions regarding food poverty[1] or cycling infrastructure, there is pressure on the WCDT to remain neutral in some sense. This is evident in the criteria from funders themselves. Guidance notes from previous funders of the WCDT, the Robertson Trust, suggest they do not fund 'activities which incorporate the promotion of political or religious beliefs' (Robertson Trust, nd). Equally, the Climate Challenge Fund (a Scottish Government fund often used to support community gardening) state that 'political or religious activities' are 'ineligible' for funding (Keep Scotland Beautiful, nd). In funding criteria at least, political activity is compartmentalized from community action. There is a sense in which political activities are left undefined in these criteria, yet it hangs as a warning away from more obviously political work.

This separation of community and political action is less widely debated at the WCDT than it might otherwise be due to the professionalization of the organization. Most decisions are taken on behalf of the whole community by the board of directors or by Oliver himself, then latterly rubber-stamped. This means that questions around funding are not part of the everyday talk of the garden or café, except when it gets short, and worries circulate that the projects might stop. One interesting lack of debate occurred as the Big Lottery funding ceased in 2015 and the community café was due to run out of funds. Despite several conversations around whether there might be more funding, or if it was going to be possible to keep going without, most of the stress and conversation was to be found among staff members who were likely to lose jobs and who struggled to maintain business as usual under those conditions. Roxana, one of the café workers, noted that it was harder to maintain any kind of progressive thematic programme when you did not know whether half the programme would even happen. Yet the direction of events, or where funding came from, was not usually debated. This was notable especially when funding came through from a mainstream bank. As such, professionalization at the WCDT abstracts funding questions from volunteers and participants, bracketing them off as practical concerns and closing off questions of funding sources or other ways of working.

The escapist tendencies of WCDT translate sometimes into outward-looking programmes, aiming at dietary shifts for climate change or supporting anti-racist work, but they are not framed politically. Local interventions, despite staking a right to the city, are framed largely as responses to local distaste for, among other things, fly tipping. Long-running clean-up work exemplifies this. The efflorescence of signs saying 'Don't Dump Here' and 'Don't Waste Woodlands', and advertising 'Community Clean-ups', are an unmistakeable visual reminder as one walks West Princes Street that WCDT claim some responsibility as a local body. Litter-picks are an activity that Woodlands have engaged in before but in 2016 the focus on cleaning up around the local area increased after some research commissioned by the Trust suggested that it was a major concern for residents and businesses alike. It has continued, under the stewardship of one of the board members, throughout the pandemic and gained a mention at the 2021 annual general meeting as a continuing positive force in the neighbourhood.

In recent years, a more prominent theme on climate action has emerged, including encouraging cycling, mending workshops, veganism support, and supporting advocacy for reusable nappies. As Oliver noted in 2021, however, this stream of climate funding remains separate from their anti-poverty work. For the café, this can be galling because it separates the veganism and climate action of the broader organization from the equality work around the café. This speaks to the way that politics emerges as an idea in the field; and the ways things are framed in distinctly apolitical ways.

Because of the organizational need to remain neutral, the work at WCDT in cleaning up the neighbourhood and addressing climate issues has not been actively framed as political work. Thus, the community clean-ups are not described as engaging with a politics of local administration or as questioning the capacity of the council to provide a decent service. The climate work is predominantly focused on behavioural change, rather than shifting policy or lobbying. The wariness towards politics as a frame introduces space for the WCDT to claim they stand on neutral political ground.

Yet this was to some extent a strategic position. Illustrative of this was in a meeting with Oliver a year after the fieldwork formally ended. He was surprised at the strategic neutrality described in my research. He told me how he thought the garden *was* political and we discussed how this differed from his interview. His response was that in the interview, he had had his managerial hat on; whereas sitting with me discussing the research, he felt he could respond as an individual. What this is illustrative of, again, is the way that the organizational form taken by the WCDT constrains not only the concrete actions of the Woodlands Community Garden but how they publicly represent it. In this, they do not take strong positions on land ownership or use, because they have to remain amenable to funders and the local council (which is often a funder too). This is theoretically interesting in light of social movement studies which has tended to emphasize the importance of access to resources that becoming a non-profit entails for movements: a benefit too great to turn away from (McCarthy et al, 1991; Cress, 1997). In this case, this neutral framing is a result of that organizational form and its associated pressures, constraining directly the possibility of a grassroots organization staking a clearly political position in land use and local administrative politics.

An attempt to get beyond this exists in the search for 'unrestricted funds', through things such as the funding seminar mentioned earlier and the development of the Workspace project. As one of the biggest potential changes that the project faced between 2016 and 2020, the Workspace project built a small community meeting room in a neighbouring gap site to the garden. It drew in variety of groups engaged in crafts, community meet ups, health and wellbeing, or art. It held potential as a source of what they call 'unrestricted funds', that is, funding without a clearly mandated use for the organization, offering a degree of stability through renting out the space. As funding has been a point of precarity and a restraint on the organizational possibilities for WCDT, this was seen as an important opportunity and it has been important for supporting the more socially transformative work in recent years.

Oppositional organizing at the meadow

The meadow in turn provides an illustrative alternative of loud opposition, rather than quiet co-operative subversion. This reflects their emergence from contestation itself – from rejecting development and forging an alternative. It also reflects their different institutional formation and relation to funding, which is to say their general position in the community gardening field in Glasgow. Their squatting on the land had a significant impact in terms of how much of a political framing they are enabled to take. The North Kelvin Meadow and Children's Wood's engagement in direct contestation over the use of a piece of land in Glasgow has entailed a great deal of lobbying, campaigns, protesting and taking part in drawn-out bureaucratic processes of dissent through the planning system. That is, it has entailed a great deal of direct political action, in terms of engaging with the formal political system – especially in lobbying and contacting local elected representatives. In order to do this, they have mobilized support from local people and from those further afield. Indeed, in February 2016, the Children's Wood mounted a photograph campaign with submissions from around the world, from places as far afield as Arizona, Singapore and Belfast. Their antagonistic position, in contrast from the community garden, puts them outside of a number of the neutralizing facets of Woodlands' relationship with the council and funders. However, they become neutralized in other ways. Particularly notable perhaps is the need to position themselves as respectable community actors who want control of the space, thus they have to resemble something legible to the council and Scottish Government. Again, this recalls Scott's (1998) discussion of legibility.

The lack of official permission to be onsite, their challenge to the council as planners and landlords, and the fact the council themselves are a funding body – in essence their oppositionality – puts them outside of many pots of funding. This is a difficulty when it comes to resources, but a boon when it comes to avoiding the negative impact of funding's specificities. Being outside of those dynamics gives the meadow organizations the space to challenge power, and, as Toni puts it, get on with "doing things":

'I know with having been involved with community gardens, with Ivan having been involved in a lot, and I've been involved in a few a while ago, it's a bit different because they're very funding reliant and they have to then do things in order to appease the funders which might not have gone in line with the original principles. I think because this place wouldn't be eligible for any of that funding anyway, it's only private funders that would ever fund this place because of it being disputed land, then yeah we're just outside of that bracket. But maybe down the line that will change, but with the Scottish Climate Challenge things[2] and stuff like that, you've got quite strict criteria which almost stops it from being able to be quite radical in some ways, or just more direct. Just like directly doing things.' (Toni, interview, July 2016)

For those who are beholden to funders, "doing things" can be harder because of the need to adhere to "strict criteria". Toni's point holds to some extent for the Woodlands Community Garden, as discussed earlier, where funding shapes the activities on the ground.

While this position – largely outside of funding dynamics – functions to liberate the meadow, there remains too the immediacy of the threat to the meadow that connects collective endeavours there more easily to an idea of politics. The threat to the meadow has been imminent since 2008 when the plans were drawn up to develop the meadow. Campaigners argue this put them "on the back foot" as far as organizing goes – reacting rather than building a proactive campaign, but it has also meant that there was a tangible possibility of the site being bulldozed to make way for flats and townhouses. As Buechler (2004) argues, in early models of social movement mobilization, threat was highlighted as a key producer of solidarity. The threat to the space of the meadow itself was a large factor in what came to the fore in conversations, shaping them in certain ways, and determining the whole process as one of tension. It echoes Martinez's (2009) work that explores the mobilization of New York community gardens after they faced the threat of mass closure. At the meadow, as in New York's Lower East Side, collective mobilization was a means of pushing back against the potential loss of a growing site.

A pervasive sense of threat shaped conversations I had in the field, not only narrowing the scope of conversations to what might be lost (at the exclusion sometimes of what might perhaps be imagined) but it also led to a tendency to want to downplay difference for political reasons and to see a binaristic us–them between the council and the campaigners. I was often faced with evasion or participants who would avoid talking about tensions between the Children's Wood campaign and the North Kelvin Meadow, and this emerged from both sides. They almost all wanted to maintain a show of singular focus, of co-operation and common cause. To a large degree the sense of shared threat did lend itself to solidarity between often-divergent campaigns, though in the field it created unsayable things about frictions between people at the meadow (Walkerdine, 2016).

The daily frictions of two campaigns focused on differing aspects of the meadow could be understood to underpin comments from those like Ivan, who announced that community meant "really annoying [laughs]" (Ivan, interview, June 2015). These tensions are part and parcel of negotiating shared space, but it was notable that organizers often wanted to play them down. This chimes with social movement research that suggests that increased threat levels are likely to increase co-operation between movements (Morris and Staggenborg, 2004).

Threat also had a way of quickly turning people from bystanders into participants in protest, if only for a short while. It was notable how quickly people would become involved in the meadow. At a protest held on the land in January 2016, many people I spoke to had come along only recently, or were intermittent users. These individuals felt strongly enough, despite that minimal contact with the land and the campaigns, to attend a Tuesday morning protest in the pouring rain. It is notable that this kind of support for the meadow can be ephemeral, yet the immediacy of the threat and the foundation of the communal growing and other guerrilla practices there as a form of action mobilizes people to support the meadow and engage in such traditional political actions as protest. In doing so, this shifts participants' understandings of themselves in relation to politics, as the next chapter will turn to in more detail.

Keeping things private

By contrast, the position of Woodlands in the field, as a formalized and funded player, works against taking an antagonistic position against the council. Getting a lease for the Workspace project was a particularly difficult period for the WCDT, yet those difficulties were kept private. It was in the middle of those negotiations that Oliver expressed his general dismay at the council. His account of the process highlighted long delays on behalf of the council and inappropriate leases that the WCDT's solicitors suggested they reject outright. The cost of this on both sides and the drawn-out process by which an agreement was reached took its toll on Oliver and the staff at Woodlands. However, besides being occasionally notified of a delay with the Workspace project beginning, participants in Woodlands' other projects – whether the garden or the café – only came across details of this if they pressed Oliver for them. Otherwise, this was kept away from public knowledge as a negotiation between the landlord (the council) and the WCDT. Because of the position of the Trust as working alongside and within systems of land tenure, there is much to be gained from quiet subversion rather than outright contest. Indeed, it re-emphasizes the benefits of established players in the field working alongside rather than against local authorities (de Souza, 2006; Miraftab, 2009).

The position of Woodlands within the community gardening field can seem relatively stable, but it is still prone to existential threat (see St Clair et al, 2020). This precarity, however, despite its existential character, does not politicize the framing of the project in the same way as the threat to the meadow, or indeed the threat to the community gardens of New York in the 1990s (Schmelzkopf, 2002; Martinez, 2009). Unlike at the meadow, these are not flashpoints of mobilization. While the WCDT does have existential moments of crisis, they are usually around losing funding, rather than an external force trying to erase the space through development. Indeed, given the precarity and short-term timelines of funding, it is perhaps surprising these crisis moments do not come around more often.

This more nebulous kind of threat has no obvious opponent and did not seem to lend itself to mobilization in the same way, although Woodlands did try their hand at crowd funding (with limited success). While questions of food justice and food waste are often discussed in relation to the community café, for example, formal politics appears in the garden as a curiosity rather than a necessity – as a visit from a local MP or MSP to talk about the café or have their picture taken with local children, a local councillor on the board. This lends a very different environment at a local level and a different organizational relationship to the idea of politics.

The lack of public struggle against the council at Woodlands meant political imaginations of the project were not focused on the uselessness of the council, or their distance from reality, as they often are at the meadow. Instead, participants tend to reflect on what is gained locally, and their personal feelings and reasons. The difference between the projects partly derives from the publicness of contestation – and also its existential implications. The meadow organizations cannot afford to keep quiet about their difficulties with the council because they needed mass support to help them succeed in rejecting the developers' plans. The garden's internal position as a potential leaseholder with the council, not to mention its position as a funded organization, restricts the benefits of publicizing its difficulties with the council. The different pathways taken by the organization relate in many ways to their position within their institutional context: their relationship with the local authority and to funders.

Organizational responses to field pressures

The WCDT and meadow organizations are reflexive about their relationship with the council and their funders. By reflexive, in this context, I mean that not only are they aware of the dangers of taking on a funder's aims, and its potential to disrupt their own aims, but that they actively take steps to try to optimize their relationships with funders, shifting their actions over time. In this, they are engaged in critical assessment of their own position, in the WCDT's case through a history of having been pushed away from their aims to some extent in the past – particularly obviously in providing eco-driving lessons to get funding, but latterly feeling this sat very much outwith their remit. Seeing the WCDT as a reflexive agent brings in the organization's agency in relation to the field, in order to recognize their role in trying to change it. In this, the WCDT introduce an idea about independence and the ability to be critical: they argue that they have not been co-opted. In this, they show an understanding of the potential for co-option, as shown too by Miraftab's (2009) respondents in anti-eviction campaigns in Cape Town (see also Osterman, 2006). They argue that they are independent and able to mount sincere and vocal criticism, rather than be cowed by the institutional bargains made by accepting funding. Oliver, manager of the WCDT, posits this as the potential to work locally.

Oliver: The remit of the trust is really working in the locality and I think that has real advantages.

Helen: What do you think that helps? What kind of advantages do you see?
Oliver: I think it gives us more independence ...
Helen: I just wondered what you were independent from?
Oliver: It's something I've noticed if we go to, we're not part of like, we're not part of a council, we're not part of the NHS, um, we're not part of what you might call the vol- well, we'll call the third sector, voluntary sector, I've kind of noticed if I go to networking meetings of development trust associations, we are one of a body of development trust associations, the DTAS [Development Trust Association Scotland] are a lot more *outspoken*, a lot more independent than uhhhh a council, NHS, a lot of the bigger voluntary sector organizations. (Oliver, interview, July 2015, emphasis added)

As Oliver notes, that the WCDT does not have allegiance to a political party nor an established governmental body allows them room for manoeuvre. He attributes this to the specific status and resources of a development trust. The WCDT is a member of the Development Trust Association Scotland, who have been instrumental as a lobbying body, pushing for development trusts to be recognized as representative of communities in their local areas, something the Oliver highlighted as important during a funding workshop he ran in September 2016. This urge to be noticed is a play for legitimacy, a quest for status within the system: to be recognized as representative of the community by decision-makers and therefore targeted for inclusion in consultation exercises. This again bears resemblance to quests for legibility in Chapter 5.

Recognition gives the Trust a legitimate place in the bureaucratic landscape and a say in local matters. They become in this sense the community to be consulted. This has relevance to the rising importance of participation, described more than 20 years ago by Cooke and Kothari (2001) as a 'tyranny' due to its pervasive appearance in local governance strategies as a form of tokenism and still relevant in many contexts from climate change adaptation (for example, Masud-All-Kamal and Nursey-Bray, 2021) to methodological innovations (Pánek et al, 2020). In this context, however, there is a voice, however limited or partial, in being the recognized 'community' to be consulted. But it is precisely the limitations of this position, precisely the way working within the system can curtail the ability to be critical, that lead to analyses suggesting the co-optation of communal growing projects or alternative urbanisms, a process de Souza (2006, p 334) discusses as 'adjustment of agendas or dynamics' to the system. Unsurprisingly, this is not how the WCDT see things, preferring the limited power of minor bureaucracy to the ambivalent and at times nebulous gains of contestation and antagonism.

In this context, however, the WCDT still argue they are independent. Independence here is about being separate from political parties and governmental interference, about the ability to be critical. This is exemplified best by the engagement with alternative food insecurity support. Besides the community garden, the WCDT are also known for their community café, which provides a free weekly vegetarian meal. All are welcome to attend and, having grown this model from a handful of attendees to regularly feeding over 30 attendees a week by 2016 and reaching between 70 and 80 by 2019, the Trust are often invited to talk at conferences and events. At such events they are critical of food banks' methods of support, and increasingly emphasize the need to engage with both food poverty and food ethics at the same time. Reflecting on this, Oliver proudly described how the Trust provided a number of speakers at a conference on food insecurity: "We went to the, there was a Beyond Foodbanks conference in February which was looking at alternative ways of tackling food poverty and the first four people that spoke in February were me, were all WCG café volunteers or me" (Oliver, interview, July 2015). This signifies, for Oliver, the real critical voice that the Trust is able to have. It demonstrates their role in the wider conversation about food provision and scarcity. This is how the WCDT demonstrate their putative independence from funders to themselves and to others, and how they envision their capacity to enact change.

Naturally, this sits in tension with the influence that funding and the structure of community gardening as a field has upon the Trust and the Woodlands Community Garden, especially in terms of agenda setting. What emerges in this tension is a critical reflection on the co-optation versus radicalism debate that lends sympathy to accounts that try to synthesize these (McClintock, 2014; Williams et al, 2014). What is interesting in the case of the Trust is that they note the issues associated with funding, are reflexive about those issues, and try explicitly to manipulate that situation to suit their desired aims. Further, they have wrested a position as a recognized community – and thus being consulted on projects such as cycling infrastructure – which gives them a limited amount of power within the system, at least to voice the criticism they claim as theirs. Within this messy picture, it remains that this is municipal level struggle, and the influence that a community organization can have, is primarily through voice and through disruptive practice. The ambiguity and flexibility of the position of the Trust regarding funders leave them free to negotiate, and to be creative in the gaps left to them. This is contrary perhaps to the interstitial urbanisms discussed in the scholarly literature which emphasize, as Tonkiss (2013) has done, that these projects are anti-utopian because of their willingness to work within the gaps. Instead, Woodlands explicitly use their marginal position to pose criticisms and pride themselves on their independence within this. They have made a difference to community food provision, the green space around the garden, worked with schools to educate young people, and made a small but significant difference to levels of litter around West Princes Street.

Implicated in this is the organizational form of the WCDT which positions the Trust as a professionalized figure within the field as much as it constrains them. Charitable or non-profit status – which the WCDT have as a registered Scottish charity – can be situated as a resource that offers too much to be turned down (McCarthy et al, 1991), certainly it allows access to grant funding for communal growing projects. However, non-profit status can also be a hindrance to social movement aims, and the path taken to non-profit status is of great importance to understanding whether that charitable status is effective for the movement or not (Cress, 1997). What is at stake here is the question of whether becoming bureaucratized and professionalized is a key resource or not: something Woodlands claim. But since the garden began as a collaboration between a development trust and guerrilla gardeners, rather than as a community movement, they have always worked within a non-profit framework. While a non-profit status might be a necessity for accessing funding, it was not a condition adopted by the WCDT in order to do so: it was the organizational structure of the group prior to taking up communal growing. Indeed the involvement of the Trust was predicated on their position as landowner. The impetus that began with Garden Revolutions of the West End was subsumed into the Trust when it became a community garden. In this way, a similar narrative emerges around reduced radicalism (from guerrilla gardening to development trust), although it is not a straightforward pathway of professionalizing in order to access positional goods.

Thus, organizational dynamics are important in terms of how the field of communal growing works, and they are part of a larger question of the limited range of non-corporate entities and their organization. The pressures against an overtly political framing within the field of communal growing is broader than funding or organizational pressures, and this is well illustrated by turning back to North Kelvin Meadow. Although not formally tied to landlord relations or some of the starker vagaries of funding, they remain subject to the pressures of the broader systemic structure of growing and charitable work in Glasgow. In this, communal growing projects adopt neutrality as a strategy to navigate the field.

The importance of non-alignment

Within the approach of the campaigns to the defence of the meadow and wood, there is strategic partisan neutrality when it comes to political parties. Again, this is about navigating the political landscape within which they work. At the meadow, this returns to the idea that the meadow and wood, children's education, green space and open space in the urban environment are above the pettiness of party politics and are social goods or indeed rights. It is also about a willingness to work within rather than against systems. In short, for campaigners this is about *strategy*. Michael put it with clarity, when asked if the campaign was political: "It is quasi-political, yes. OK. But don't let that interfere with a strategic thing. There's no point coming out and starting to make threats and impaling people. That's not going to work" (Michael, interview, July 2016).

The idea that it is important to be "strategic" in order to get things to "work" was key to the way that both the North Kelvin Meadow campaign and latterly the Children's Wood have operated. This has practical applications. Claiming neutrality in partisan terms allows them to move fluidly between politicians of different hues without conflicting memberships or loyalties. That said, both the Woodlands Community Garden and the meadow and wood campaigns have a natural affiliation with the Green Party. The co-convener of the Scottish Green Party, Patrick Harvie, has shown support for both case study sites at various points over the years. Indeed, he attended the meadow to put up bat boxes in protest at the indictment of two members of the meadow campaign in 2009. This affiliation stretches as far as the local Green Party chapter visiting the meadow (poor turnout notwithstanding) in July 2015, and Terry showing them around. As he did so, he emphasized the ways they could use the party apparatus to help put pressure on the council to save the meadow.

However, the obvious ideological overlap between the green spaces studied here and the Green Party was strategically of lesser importance to saving the meadow than the Labour–Scottish National Party (SNP) tension between Glasgow City Council (which was Labour-dominated between 1980 and 2017 [*Daily Record*, 2017]) and the SNP-dominated devolved Scottish Parliament. The SNP have offered what activists have called 'cagey' backing for the North Kelvin Meadow, offering noncommittal support for their case. Many however saw the Scottish Government's SNP dominance as an opportunity, as the SNP's putative wish to point-score against the Labour-dominated council was considered a factor in their favour. This does not necessarily demonstrate how Scottish regional politics works, but it does offer a viewpoint on how they are understood – as competitive, party-dominated, and led by partisan (rather than social) concern. This is, I argue, a key facet of what I discuss as the subjective disaffiliation with politics, that I will discuss in greater depth in the next chapter.

This understanding of politics as sullied lends itself to the demarcation of the meadow as above municipal politics. Terry, the backbone of the North Kelvin Meadow campaign, has put it similarly, discussing how he wants to sit down with the council at the end of the day, so you don't go about saying bad things about them, although he usually caveated this with an "at least not to their faces". This reiterates a tendency to narrate the struggle as a strategic campaign fought rationally with one sole objective – to save the space. A member of the Children's Wood committee, Phil, discussed in an interview how he felt that the space was not aligned with any political school and was somehow more "pure-hearted":

> 'It's not really aligned with any political ideology I think. There probably is, are ideologies that are more associated with the people in the Children's Wood but yeah it isn't really associated with conservatism or liberalism or even anarchism, but there are people who view it in that way, maybe. But yeah in general it really is more *pure-hearted* than that. It's just about wanting the space to work as it does and I think that's *independent* really of political ideology.' (Phil, interview, July 2016, emphasis added)

Again this idea recurs that the Children's Wood campaign sits on a more moral plane than politics more generally and that ideologically there is little alignment of the campaign with any one set of ideals. It is possible to argue to the contrary that there is a great sympathy between projects and the Green Party, but that is not the point here. There is a deliberate concern here to position the meadow as a broader concern, superseding ideological concerns – to present it as neutral.

While disavowing a connection to ideology, there is nonetheless tactical struggle and strategy within the organizational side of the Children's Wood, and to a lesser extent the North Kelvin Meadow campaign. The latter concern themselves with their discourse not alienating those in power, and trying to make strong arguments in favour of saving the space ecologically. The Children's Wood go beyond this. At committee meetings in early 2015, there was the sense that the campaign should reach out to more politicians, leverage public opinion and the media as far as possible, to apply pressure on the council to concede the land. To this end, their partisan neutrality helped them claim ground as a wide social good, rather than an ideological outgrowth of one specific party or movement. The ramification of this is an elevation of community as above politics, framed often as a social good in and of itself. In determining the direction to take when countering the development, the Children's Wood had support from the Development Trust Association Scotland, who advised them that they should absolutely consider the decision as a political one – and that in recognizing this, they might want to go up a political level and lobby the Scottish Government, which they eventually did do. Nevertheless, the campaigns saw their involvement in lobbying, utilizing politicians and trying to apply media pressure as extraordinary activities.

Politics is thus a means of saving the land, rather than a framing through which to see everyday activities on the meadow. Neutrality is implicated in this – in a manner of speaking, their neutrality was a tool, it became a way of engaging in strategic action (for change). It is also a means of not identifying with the imagination of a divisive, competitive, party-dominated local politics. It is in this latter sense of politics as divisive that the moral framing of these projects come to have salience: as a non-conflictual way of framing activities.

To consider politics analytically in this context then requires an appreciation of how organizational context and the broader field of action constrain communal growing projects, pushing them towards a strategic neutrality. Taking politics not only as an analytical category but as a contested terrain makes obvious the necessity of getting beyond a conversation in which arguments are made for the political, co-opted or always both nature of community growing projects, to appreciate politics as a category that is fought over and understood in a myriad of ways. While communal growing projects may not live up to Rancière's (1999) insistence that only that which engages with the foundation of equality upon which democratic society rests (and the question of who can be counted as an equal) can be counted as political, there is clearly something critical and transformative at play in communal growing projects which attempts to situate something autonomous and new; and yet which meets resistance and pressure to be legible and neutral from more powerful actors within the field of action. Even on a terrain of politics that considers the everyday as source, site and stake of struggle (Beveridge and Koch, 2019), with perhaps less stringent and totalizing criteria for being political, needs to attend this interplay of autonomy and curtailment. In outlining both the ways growing projects open up new space for alterity and autonomy and the ways this is curtailed and neutralized, this echoes McClintock's (2014) insistence, building on the work of Polanyi, that community gardens are necessarily both radical and regressive. Yet the argument around the political (or otherwise) characteristics of growing projects is not simply an academic one, finding its shadow in an empirical tension within these projects that can highlight the subjective terrain on which this can play out, and point to a functional fluidity within communal growing projects that reasserts the fundamentally ambivalent character of escapist places, as the next chapter unfolds.

8

The Political Imagination of Common Justice

Ambiguity, interpretations and imaginations

One of the myriad reasons to take the politics of communal growing projects as an empirical puzzle relates to the breadth of interpretation of the case studies. This vexes any easy conceptualization of the projects as political or not, without asserting that participants are wrong in their understanding of their action. This is to say that irreconcilable attitudes exist between participants' views of the projects as completely political, as totally apolitical or somewhere fuzzy in between. I discuss this as the political imagination of the sites, in order to capture the interrelation of participants' understanding of the sites and their broader concept of what politics means. That a space exists between an understanding of communal growing as commoning and productive of an autonomous space in the city; the strategic neutrality at an organizational level; and a multitude of subjective understandings of politics illuminates some of the challenge, and often operatively fuzzy nature, of collective escape. Some of the productive ambiguity within escape as a concept sits precisely in this muddle of political interpretations, in opening up a space that is fluidly understood and governed to a degree by autonomously negotiated cultures and dynamics.

That communal growing can be both deeply political for some and apolitical for others was indeed partly a question of different conceptions of politics itself in the field. Some were drawing on a broader, feminist-inflected sense of everyday life as political, while others purely identified politics with different levels of the state (local council, Scottish Government, UK Government) and the political party structure. The difference in interpretation was spread across both sites and also related to personal trajectories, project involvement and experiences of protest and politics. This recalls Nettle's argument that: 'As in many social movements, community gardeners' collectivity is plural, ambivalent and often contradictory (Melucci, 1996) and does not necessarily coalesce around a clearly articulated political philosophy or model of change' (Nettle, 2014, p 170). The empirical variation in the political interpretation of communal growing confirmed this plurality, but one commonality emerged: the importance of the spaces themselves and their transformative potential. That transformation is at times imagined *apolitically* is a notable empirical artifact that requires some exploration; though it recalls the sense from the previous chapter that a commons is often more an analytical label than a lay category (de Angelis, 2017).

In exploring this variation, there are two things of note. First, this ought to lend a caution to totalizing statements about the political or otherwise nature of communal growing as a practice: these function at an analytical level only, and a great degree of subjective variation exists in terms of how the projects are imagined. This chimes with Nettle's (2014) arguments around not seeing all community gardening as social action, since much of it occurs with no political or autonomous intention, and not expecting political gardening to exhibit a clear, coherent and unitary ideology. Second, the case studies' ability to contain the variability of interpretation, not just of their political nature but also of community itself, can be seen as a strength characteristic of some urban communal activities, lending itself to a greater inclusion and therefore greater capacities for exposure to difference and discussion. Again, Nettle's (2014) work demonstrates similar propensities to avoid dogmatic adherence to principles and attempts to embrace different viewpoints within growing practices. Although this must always be tempered with the awareness of the bounded limitation of community as a vessel for social change, we can see this as being potentially beneficial for democratic polities through 'everyday exposure to difference' (Atkinson and Flint, 2004, p 876).

The broad variation in political imaginings was personal, in that it unsurprisingly reflected the person's worldview and experiences. The breadth of perspectives in many ways reflected the breadth of participants in the projects, although in general there was a consensus on the social justice orientation of the projects themselves. This soft-ideological orientation is common to communal projects in Glasgow, and probably much of Scotland and beyond. A general left-inclination seems to be common to many growing projects (see Nettle, 2014). In Glasgow, this has suggestive links to notions of the city as a 'friendly' and welcoming place; an idea that Glaswegians often take pride in. The city was voted the friendliest city in the world in 2014 (Rough Guides, 2014), but a general tide of left politics also links back to Glasgow's broader partisan history. Glasgow socialism and Red Clydeside are historical precedents in industrial politics, but with industry largely now gone from Glasgow there are more recent touchstones for local partisan leanings. Particularly the Thatcher years and Tory rule in Britain instigated a widespread rejection of the Conservative Party in Scotland, with Scotland's political consensus moving to the centre-left (McCrone, 2001; Soule et al,

2012). Within the imagination of Scottish political identity, there is also an extrapolation from the autonomy of Scottish civil society over the years to an 'inclusive, civic Scottish nationalism' (Soule et al, 2012, p 5) based in residence and culture, rather than birthright or tribe. This lends itself to an openness to the other, within an understanding of Scottishness that is not ethnic in its basis but rather residential (Leith, 2012).

This is the context in which organizations such as Refuweegie resonate. Refuweegie is a neologism composed of refugee and 'weegie', the latter of which is shorthand for a Glaswegian. Refuweegie is also an organization that sends welcome packs to new refugees arriving in Glasgow, including warm clothes and a 'letter fae a local'.[1] Anti-racist activism in recent years is also worth mentioning here. On 13 May 2021, during the Islamic festival of Eid al-Fitr, an immigration detention van on Kenmure Street was forced to release two men after a spontaneous sit-in protest and the emergence of local Glaswegians in their hundreds to block the van's exit from the street. This remarkable event emerged at a time when COVID-19 restrictions meant people in Glasgow were not allowed to meet in groups larger than six and were not allowed in each other's houses. The pubs were closing at 8pm. This was celebrated in 2022 with a two-day 'Festival of Resistance' organized by community organizations in the south of the city to mark the event.

Yet orientations to social justice, particularly among the community organizers in this research, are often similar enough to present a tacit vaguely left-wing consensus. This means this orientation becomes a kind of self-evident backdrop against which to do community growing, rather than an explicitly political or antagonistic terrain.

Garden variety politics

An illustration of this interpretive variation is found in the personal narratives of participants, which offered a wide array of reasons and values embedded in the way they discussed their involvement in projects. For some, this was about prior political engagements and seeking opportunities to express their politics; for others, it was more nebulous, a question of connection and moral engagement. For most, it was along this blurry boundary between politics and ethics that involvement in the meadow, the garden, or both, lay.

Some participants viewed involvement in communal growing as political activity. Ivan has lived with his family in Transition Towns[2] and worked in community gardens across Glasgow. He, his partner Toni, and their family live an alternative lifestyle, engaging with alternative health, trying to grow much of their own food and home-educating their children. When asked whether community growing itself is political, he tells me that he gardens for himself, but that he can see how gardening in this communal place can be political. In echoes of Hodgkinson's (2005) argument that digging is anarchy, he tells me that all growing is anarchic, is political, in contemporary society. He illustrates this by describing interactions with those who ask 'Why bother putting the effort into growing potatoes on the meadow when you can buy them for 20p a kilo in a supermarket?' But he tells me that he came across some figures recently that suggested 90 per cent of the chemicals put into the ground are absorbed by potatoes, and potatoes have large amounts of pesticides used in their production. He tells me, "Mate [he calls everyone mate], you're literally poisoning yourself eating those potatoes. You couldn't pay me to eat one of those potatoes." And then he blames capitalism. That, for him, is why it is political – because growing potatoes is going against that system of poisoning people via potatoes for profit.

Ivan is not alone in seeing using the land like this as political – a similar idea that growing goes against the food system and that globalized food systems are potentially dangerous and immoral was occasionally found at the Woodlands Community Garden too. This was most prevalent in conversations about and at the Woodlands Community Café, which directly engages in food provision within the city and offers an alternative to food bank provision, its practitioners argue. I would find myself, at the café, moving from conversations about how best to grow cucumbers or make salads, to the suspicious ways cucumbers are packaged and the purported evils of sterile F1 hybrids. The slippage between cooking and eating food to the broader systems in which they are enmeshed is easy enough. But a wholly political view of growing or even the café was not a common notion.

One such participant was Mark, a raised bed gardener at Woodlands, a long-time volunteer and latterly also a staff member. Mark's history of unemployment through ill-health, and poor mental health as a result, meant that his connection with the Woodlands Community Garden was one of salvation. His life has been, by his own account, vastly improved by the social connection and meaningful interactions found there. When talking with him about his particular trajectory from volunteer to employee, I asked him about the wider role that the Trust was taking – organizing clean-ups, trying to 'green' West Princes Street where the garden is sited. His response was one of closing down:

Helen: Is there anything political about the WCDT [Woodlands Community Development Trust] taking a more hands-on approach?

Mark: Oh no, I don't think so. I like to stay away from politics, I don't bother with that stuff. I don't think it's worth it. But that's my personal opinion. (Mark, interview, July 2016)

His response was typical of those who want to avoid politics altogether, but it is notably different to that of Ivan. Although they are involved at different projects (mostly, Ivan has had some contact with the Woodlands project through his partner, Toni, and worked in community gardens elsewhere in Glasgow at the time), this is less a contrast of projects and more of political imagination. Mark completely disavows politics, as it is not something he thinks is "worth it". This dismissal of politics in its entirety starkly contrasts with Ivan's profession of the innate politics of growing and anarchy within the system of globalized food production and chemical poisoning (by food production giants, with Monsanto getting particular attention as the embodiment of this social ill). They offer opposite ends of the political imagination of the spaces, and if we see the projects as part of the semi-continuous food growing community project scene that overlays Glasgow's informal green spaces, this offers an array of interpretations. If a continuous, or singular, statement about the absence or presence of politics in communal growing was sought, this would clearly be challenged by one or other of these participants. Critically, this wide variation raises questions about how action is understood, and whether it matters for analytical perspectives on social action.

They are engaged in very similar activities, but one's point-blank refusal of politics seems to problematize the notion of the other that digging is *innately* political. As Oliver, WCDT manager put it, "it kind of is driven partly by the people and personalities that are involved". Thus, since Mark has always avoided politics as "not for him", whereas Ivan has sought alternative ways of living such as Transition Towns and is largely anti-capitalist, they have very different interpretations of growing. These are the results of different life experiences and predilections. But what is interesting here – more so than the affirmation of difference of subjective interpretation – is that this suggests an innate flexibility to communal growing as a practice. That is becomes a little like community-as-idea itself in its mutability to individual meaning and practice. Communal growing can be Mark's salve from unemployment, a chance for others to engage in greenness and a site for engaging in conversations on agro-capitalism. Yet, it is not a totally free-floating signifier. There are some things that would not fit. Communal growing obviously needs some orientation to growing and a collective aspect. Further, the ideological commitment to social justice seems entrenched, however restricted it might be in practice. Particularly in the context of these case studies, a more closed approach to community boundaries is difficult to imagine given the ideological norms of Glaswegian growing projects.

Both sites thus share an orientation to inclusivity that provides an important ideological commonality to their activities, and underpins their work to enact a more just city. Both sites reflect this in their work to be open and inclusive, as discussed in Chapter 4. At the meadow, social justice becomes a way of positioning the space as moral. The meadow becomes framed as a moral value in itself. This has value for participants in that it moves away from an idea of divisive politics, towards a more conciliatory, communal ideal. Arguably, this returns us to the ideological work of community as an idea too, in that it reinforces these ideas about collectivity over division. If this is a politics, it is one that differs radically from a common understanding of politics as related to political parties and systems of government detached from everyday life. The political and the economic become entwined in this, in that they are both dismissed as ways of valuing the space; seeking instead a common space and time to forge connection.

In this context, it is interesting to place the conversation that Yolanda and I had at the café one week. Yolanda is an explicitly left-wing economist, by profession, and we had been discussing redistribution of wealth in society. I asked if she saw a connection between the community café (where we were at the time) and the garden in working to expose people to difference and to more perhaps political ways of thinking about redistribution. What she said to me was that, while it was definitely important for creating space for those conversations, "you can't start from politics". The implication in this, however, is that you can reach that point, and that the potential to become political (or beginning to frame and think of social problems as politics) is inherent in the projects.

Similarly, Ivan has suggested that consciousness-raising is inherent to community gardening. He is not alone in this – other community growers I met during the process of the research project said similar things about the need to begin with the question of "why grow?" This had a class inflection, in that Ivan noted this was a more difficult conversation in places without cultural preferences for organic, or indeed with people who had never gardened before. The class implications of this, given the higher price of organic food, are obvious, but implicit in the way Ivan talks. In this, the notion that communal growing can be an awareness-raising exercise emerges, echoing Nettle's (2014, p 191) argument that community gardens represent a 'politics of example'. This notion of demonstrating another way of living the city is again analytical but connects the disruptive pathways of communal growing to a social change dynamic – through demonstration and didacticism. What is suppressed to some extent through field pressure towards a strategically neutral framing is the potential to connect the example of communal growing to an explicit agenda for social change or a systematic critique.

Subjective politicization

Yet the potential proselytizing force of these spaces is suggested in the narratives of those who become activists through their involvement in the meadow. Because of the threat to the space, the constant battles with the council that provide the backdrop for the meadow, participation in mundane activities can lead to a greater degree of political activity, despite the formal distinctions in sub-committees and everyday management.

At a Children's Wood committee meeting held in a pub close to the meadow, tactics were discussed. Particularly, lobbying came up as an important way of gaining political support for the campaign. Initially this was focused on the council planning committee but latterly widened to include local MSPs in the Scottish Government who were petitioned to 'call in' the decision (that is, to utilize their powers of oversight over planning decisions to scrutinize the decision), with a focus latterly on Angela Constance as the Scottish National Party MSP who was then Cabinet Secretary for Communities, Social Security and Equalities, and therefore the person whose decision this might ultimately become.

However, at the meeting I attended, for two of the committee there the idea of lobbying was uncomfortable. Both Joan and Margot said they were uncomfortable with the idea and felt that challenging politicians at their surgeries and having to defend the campaign on the spot was daunting. The fear of exposure for not knowing enough was prominent in these accounts. Polly, as meeting chair and Children's Wood keystone, allayed those fears with reassurances that they wouldn't be alone, that more experienced campaigners would be with them to support them.

What was notable in this was the anxiety and unease that the idea of lobbying drew from Joan and Margot. This emotional insecurity stemmed, it seemed, from inexperience and the way that the campaign has opened up new experiences such as this for participants. That the meadow put them in a position to engage in this political process suggests a way in which the meadow has drawn campaigners into more active engagement with formal politics, transforming their relationships and offering new political experiences. As she narrates it, Joan has been politically involved online, but spoke in an interview about how the campaign moved her beyond online activism to making a difference in her local area. For her, it was a natural extension of her ideological beliefs, yet it was the first time she had lobbied anyone. Margot, on the other hand, explicitly talked about not being involved in politics before.

Nevertheless, Margot had been involved in the meadow since her husband took part in the first litter picks in 2008. She was not physically active at that point due to being heavily pregnant, but latterly has taken on a central role in the administration of the Children's Wood committees. Reflecting on how she got involved, she laughed and noted that she had 'never been an activist' before:

Helen: Have you ever been involved in any more activism, or anything similar?

Margot: No, I've never been political til this project. No, I never have been [laughs]. I've just always been, I've always supported Green issues but I've never been involved in any, it's probably

	just my family background. It wasn't what we did. I've been to a couple of demonstrations but I've never been an activist.
Helen:	So what's different about the Children's Wood that's made you an activist?
Margot:	Well, obviously, because it's right there and obviously because I can see it every day that probably has lots to do with it. But it has a lot to do with my son as well. I think when you have a family you sort of start to appreciate things that are really important, how important it is to have wild spaces and this country really lacks them? (Margot, interview, July 2017)

She thus put her activism down to proximity and to motherhood, but she has also been socially close to the meadow for many years now. A similar sense of prior social ties facilitating activism has been found in social movement work, such as Hensby's (2017) work on student protests in 2010–11. The meadow became central to Margot as an issue and she has lobbied councillors for the meadow and is part of the committee. Given the Children's Wood's focus on children as a means to reach people, it is interesting that Margot also relates her activism to a perspectival shift associated with becoming a mother. In a sense, this becomes about an idea of the common good via an understanding of what is best for her child.

This was repeated by a few other activists too – that having children was an important wake-up call to engaging more with political questions and ideas, particularly environmental politics, as it extended the temporal imagination far into the future, creating questions of what world will be bequeathed to offspring. This rationale, echoing the discussion in Chapter 4 of the meadow as a 'mothers' campaign', reconnects the political imagination of the campaign with its everyday users, which is to say, families. In the face of organizational pressures towards neutrality, this transformational capacity, its consciousness-raising character, presents a counterpressure. Yet in order to be understood as political in the everyday, the meadow has to overcome negative associations with the idea of politics. This relates back to experiences of party politics and the political machinery that those involved in projects have. Part of the unpolitical imaginary of communal growing for Mark, the Woodlands raised bedder and avowedly apolitical gardener, is a sense that politics is itself not "worth it". In a sense this is the idea that *politics itself* is sullied.

A common justice thing

The lay political imagination of the sites is complicated by a moral ambivalence towards politics itself, shaped in part by the recent political history of Scotland and the UK more generally. There are those, such as Ivan at the meadow, who see growing and social connection as potentially emancipatory and political acts. However, there are those at the meadow who deliberately separate out the murky political and strategic campaigns from the everyday mundanities of playgroups and allotmenteering. Despite Polly's framing of much of the activity on the meadow as "guerrilla events", in recognition of the unsanctioned character of the social gatherings that take place there, there is a tendency among participants to depoliticize the space, to see activity there as *above* politics. In this they propose a kind of mundane ethics – a social right to wild space and to children's play especially.

In interviewing Alasdair, a long-time activist with anarchist leanings, his disavowal of any political nature of the activities on the North Kelvin Meadow emerged. Alasdair was a Yes-voter who was wearing a badge saying '45', displaying his dissatisfaction with the Scottish vote to remain part of the UK.[3] He has nothing but disdain for the "corpie" as he calls it – Glasgow City Council (a similar function was fulfilled by the Glasgow Corporation until 1975). He nevertheless disavows a political framing of the meadow. He frames it rather differently. A journalist before he retired, Alasdair noted: "You know. If I was writing a new story it'd probably start: fat Tory bastards fuck up the community yet again" (interview, December 2014). But he went on to say that the meadow was not a political thing in the same way: "I don't really see the taking over [the meadow] as a political act. It's – it's more like a, it's more like a common justice thing. You know, we use the land, for leisure, to educate our children" (Alasdair, interview, December 2014). The vehemence of Alasdair notwithstanding, framing the issue as "common justice" rather than "a political act" importantly separates out the morality of the space from Alasdair's far-left politics in his narrative. His anti-Tory and anti-council positions are separated from the meadow, in a sense purifying the space from the murk he associates with politics. In this sense, disillusionment with certain aspects of the political system (for example, austerity; Conservative government) is associated with sanctifying the space. Yet this vision of justice as itself apolitical – as principally a moral contention – belies the pursuit of such justice through political means, especially in protest and lobbying.

It is perhaps little wonder that within the Glaswegian context there is a deep ambiguity towards politics as an idea, since politics for many is primarily associated with Westminster, Holyrood and political parties. Although for some politics means the promise of something better (Ivan's anarchic growing), for others it signifies the council's petty manoeuvring, the rise of the Scottish National Party and deep divisions within Scotland and the UK more widely, not to mention the recent divorce from the European Union. When Alasdair proposes that the meadow is about "common justice" rather than politics, he signifies a wish to distance it from a sense of pettiness and division. This is importantly connected (albeit in a fragmented way) to the enduring sense of political cynicism at the case study sites regarding the local authority. Glasgow City Council evoked responses from disdain through to apathy at both the meadow and the garden. The council are deeply unpopular and participants often found them to be frustrating to work with. Within this is a strong sense of the council as self-serving, functioning only to perpetuate their own desires. This was reflected at the planning protests on the meadow in a deep fatalism.

In January 2016, the planning committee sat to decide on permission for the development of the site, and also to consider a community concept plan put in by the Children's Wood. As part of their decision-making process, the councillors of the planning committee visited the site in high-visibility vests. Knowing in advance of this arrangement, the campaigns organized a protest of sorts on the site, gathering a demonstration of local support during the tail end of a winter storm known as Storm Jonas. In the pouring rain and fairly dismal conditions, hundreds of people – including at least one class of nursery children – turned up to support the meadow. Despite this support, the prevailing attitude among key campaigners and members of the Children's Wood committee that I spoke with was that there was little that the protest could do to change minds, that it was in fact a "done deal". This fatalistic attitude regarding the council's deliberations ran through those like Michael, who has been involved in trade union negotiations, to mothers who had come along to the meadow for the first time. This scepticism regarding the council's actions led to interpretations of the site visit as "window dressing". It was compounded by the lack of engagement of the protesters by the councillors, despite megaphone heckling from Bob, a prominent campaigner and minor local celebrity, to "engage with us, engage with the community". It later surfaced that due to the 'quasi-judicial' nature of the planning process, there are rules about site visits that include not talking with people outside of the official party. Not having this explicated, many of those gathered found the councillors' non-engagement rude but expected. It reflected expectations regarding the council as distant and unwilling to engage outwith their narrow interest.

Despite this, as they leave, the protesters applaud the councillors, encouraged by Bob with a megaphone, to thank them for coming to see the site. Despite a deep-seated pessimism regarding the actions of the local council, this reflected a certain attitudinal approach of the Children's Wood, and to some extent the North Kelvin Meadow, that not only refused to be adversarial with the council but also refused negativity and fatalism, discussed earlier in their determination to take a 'can-do' approach. Within this, it is possible to see the Children's Wood's efforts to reframe debate in Scotland around land use in terms of possibility, rather than the inevitable pettiness of politics. They do so in a partisan neutral way in order to distance their efforts precisely from this perceived pettiness and in doing so create a discursively complicated field of interpretation around the politics of the space.

A temporalized politics, or politics over time

Threat is innately a temporal condition, and thus the politics of a space framed by threat shift over time. In 2016 when the major ethnographic work underpinning this book finished, the meadow had reached a relatively stable condition – development had been halted, and the question that remained was how best to protect the meadow as an asset for the longer term. Revisiting the site between 2016 and 2022 would suggest that although the space continues to provide space for communal activities and daily leisure, its formalization and the movement of disagreements with the council behind closed doors, has reduced politicization around the site. In 2022, a lease was finally signed with Glasgow City Council for a 25-year use of the space; but it was a long-drawn-out process involving extensive back and forth between lawyers and a degree of manoeuvring on both sides, particularly as Polly narrated to me in 2021 with much frustration, over the right of the council to take back the land or reserve some for the use of one state nursery. As a contract negotiation, this was largely not done in public, though it did at one point require a public hearing. Campaigners mobilized the usual networks of outraged parents, dog walkers and educational specialists into attendance. Outwith this phase, the meadow, once saved from development, is now a leisure space, with vegetable and fruit growing, toddler groups, dog walking and educational activities on site. Continued everyday challenges around who can use the space are not principally seen in political terms, despite the tensions it raises for inclusivity narratives.

Thus, success and stability at the meadow may incline them away from a political framing of the meadow. Maintaining a politically neutral face in partisan terms worked well for them in the campaign due to the capacity it holds to mobilize those who would otherwise be put off, allowing them to leverage support from schools and other charitable organizations. It also meant that when the time came to sit round a table and negotiate with the council, as Terry always held was the endpoint of any campaigning, they were not seen as political actors per se. In a sense, the meadow came to hold a similar position as the WCDT of productive ambiguity and strategic neutrality. The WCDT also had extended negotiations with Glasgow City Council over a long-term lease of a site (and found it equally vexatious). In this, they take up similar positions as acceptable actors, fundable community organizations and indeed organizations whose capacity to be critical only extends to the available space of the field.

This would appear to echo concerns around the impacts of working with institutions and systems, but taking a wider temporal lens complicates this picture suggesting possible waves of transformative action within the projects. In the social movement literature, such concerns emerge in discussions on the difficulties of working with funders and formalization, both of which are purported to lead to deradicalization (for example, Miraftab, 2009). Equally, the community gardening literature is highly attuned to the challenges of becoming shaped by the environment, whether it is through increased competition in the sector (St Clair et al, 2020) or through producing docile organic consumers (Pudup, 2008). Neither literature takes for granted the complex interplay of intention, daily practice and interaction with a system that is often assumed to be coherent (erroneously, Gibson-Graham [1996] and others would argue).

Both case studies here would appear to have taken up field positions that require a degree of docility while introducing local populations to organic growing and outdoor education, and thus raising questions about their own purported critical and independent role. Yet they have done so in different temporal arcs. Until fairly recently, the meadow site was in open contention with the local council, and drawing into the dispute a wide array of characters, including civil servants and politicians at a national level and international support. Thus their period of quiescence has only emerged in the last few years, with ongoing disputes behind closed doors. The WCDT have a different rhythmic arc, fighting to stay afloat since 2010 through a cocktail of funding and learning from wrong-turns. It is notable, then, that in more recent years, the WCDT have engaged in a series of more socially transformative projects, facilitated by providing more meeting space and reacting to a social politics demanding a way to reckon with racism and sexism in everyday life.

In this, Woodlands – despite tensions in their relationship with funders and a need to remain to some extent apolitical – have shifted towards a broader claim-staking and action-oriented role, though they do so with the same "community-led" or "grassroots-ish" ethic that Oliver highlighted as core to the functioning of the Trust. They founded in 2021 an anti-racist library, an idea that emerged from their anti-racist discussion group that ran weekly, first online and latterly in person, where they read Black-authored texts and discuss racist discrimination. The library itself sits in Millennium Park when the weather is clement and catches passers-by, offering an array of fiction and non-fiction books across age ranges. Their children's books, for example, offer an array of stories, some encompassing racist themes and others simply with a more diverse range of lead characters.

Another discussion and action group that has emerged is the Women of Woodlands. Initially a small group, it was galvanized by the deaths of Sarah Everard and local woman Esther Brown, the latter a devastating local event that I deal with in greater detail in the next chapter. It has led to an array of activities that span beyond the weekly meetings to encompass a local survey on gendered experiences of the neighbourhood, self-defence classes and building relationships with the local community police.

The food offering at Woodlands has also become more explicitly plant-based, shifting from a principally vegetarian to a fully vegan menu, as a result of involving staff who were interested in taking this extra step. This aspect of the café emerged in 2021 as a minor but important theme for some café attendees – providing both food access *and* vegan food, and thus not separating out food ethics and sustainability concerns from the practice of equality inherent in people from diverse backgrounds eating together (see Traill, 2022). Further, a degree of support for those experimenting with dietary shifts, a weekly online drop-in for a while known as 'Chickpea Chats', also offers space for more explicitly transformational work.

As such, a trajectory emerges for Woodlands that takes on a range of broad transformational issues from anti-racist campaigning to dietary shifts; asking critical questions around how society may need to change. The ethic of being community-led opens the door to providing space for a range of more challenging activities aiming at social change, including inviting people to protests, although it does so with a specific tenor. The more lifestyle-oriented elements of this more radical programme cannot be ignored and the critiques of behaviour shifts in community garden do resonate here (Pudup, 2008; Ghose and Pettygrove, 2014). Nevertheless, the advocacy within Woodlands in the everyday for ethical social behaviour change and the space for reflection around the role of race and gender in society does create capacity for broader shifts, raising awareness of issues such as intersectionality, and creating new infrastructures for social transformation, like the library and space to talk about dietary shifts.

As far as this remains grant-funded, this will remain constrained by directions, preferred methods, and fashions among funders, including the Scottish Government and Glasgow City Council. But it does offer a degree of wiggle room, room to reimagine and work towards a more just future. In turning towards gender and anti-racist action, Woodlands began to actively reach out, rather than simply welcome in. Thus, this new pathway intervenes on the terrain of previous critiques, and demonstrates iterative work towards justice in action (Fraser, 2008). Behind the scenes, the WCDT also engage in a dialogue with contacts in the Scottish Government, one of their funders, pressing for more funding and asking why no connection is made between food ethics and food access. This backroom activism serves the WCDT in terms of pressing for their future funding, though it remains largely invisible to the public eye.

In offering a rising wave of more transformative actions, Woodlands suggests the possibility of fluctuating periods of greater political framing and more socially transformative work. Attuned to a "grassroots-ish" approach, but also steered by the politics of staff members themselves, this means that things move in relation to wider social shifts and personnel changes – particularly in paying greater attention to race in response to the Black Lives Matter protests and the prominent conversations after the death of Sarah Everard around policing and gendered violence.

Does this leave room for a future wave of more transformative action at the meadow? These are different spaces, and the lack of public support from the North Kelvin Meadow campaign or the Children's Wood for local struggles to save nearby flats at the Wyndford that have been scheduled for demolition in 2022 would suggest limits to local solidarity. But the trajectory at Woodlands does highlight the way a longer temporal lens can attend to community projects reacting to social shifts, and as such highlights waves of action in community politics.

9

Escape, Crisis and Social Change

Communal growing projects over time

Time emerges as a critical element in understanding the evolution and implications of communal growing practices. Projects react to opportunities within funding structures and the broader social landscape, adapting and filling spaces that emerge. This is most clearly demonstrated by attending to continuities and crises that have emerged since the initial in-depth fieldwork of 2015–16. Reflecting on the enduring problems of communal growing projects, I argue that a longer temporal lens is required to understand communal growing projects as emerging in context over time. This allows for a deeper engagement with the question of how communal growing projects might become more transformative, more political, over time and what conditions facilitate this.

Naturally, attending to the period between 2016 and 2022 requires some reflections on the COVID-19 pandemic. Both case studies had social value during the height of the COVID-19 crisis because of what they already were – spaces of release, of decompression, of time sovereignty and of collective meaning. That is, because they were spaces of escape. This longer-term basis is important to recognize, against a prevailing narrative around interconnection and mutual aid as suddenly emerging. The quick praise for mutual aid and solidarity that emerged during the pandemic overlooks perhaps the slow burn of social connection that we are always already enmeshed in (Studdert and Walkerdine, 2016b, 2016a; Blokland, 2017; Care Collective, 2020) and which is a crucial element of what makes the social infrastructure of cities function. Underplayed too within narratives of mutual aid's explosion is the important collective imaginary underpinning such work – and underpinning the work of the community gardens here. The *idea* of community, of collective life, of mutual support is critical (see Chapter 6 and Traill, 2021). Moving from the extremely local to the global, the lenses of tragedy and crisis demonstrate how the key analytical themes of the ethnographic fieldwork echo, morph and survive through tragedy and crisis, reflecting the broader significance of spaces of everyday escape.

Many of the most acute critiques around justice and politics in the growing projects studied here take on a different hue when viewed with a little extra hindsight. In returning to the projects again across the years between 2016 and 2022, changes emerged which shed new light on growing as a situated phenomenon. The key question around politics and inclusion, particularly as it pertains to justice, is: who does it encompass, and what does it redistribute to them? This is in a sense also to ask, how is justice actualized and to whom does it apply? The creation of a communality that excludes, in effect creating an internal 'community within a community', creates challenges at the two case study sites around claims to inclusion, even as they prove somewhat porous to newcomers. What barriers exist to entry, even in the face of a nominal claim to inclusion? What incremental progress had been made to face up to the existence of exclusions, between the period of intensive data collection and my putative return? Some of these mundane developments have been covered in previous chapters, but I want to pull out three main themes that deepen the ethnographic findings from this re-tuning work, around actively reimagining Woodlands; the recurrence of anti-social behaviour at the meadow; and ongoing project fragility and tenure stability that runs as a backing track to community organizing.

Evolving challenges

First, then, as the previous chapter began to unfold, the direction taken by Woodlands since 2016 is worth some consideration. As the Woodlands Community Development Trust (WCDT) reach out from gardening and a community café to include a more active reimagination of Woodlands, through street clean-ups, the Workspace project and an increase in activity around organizing and behavioural shifts, the organization takes on a more transformative remit claiming more space and more explicitly working towards social change. As previously noted, this is framed in a specific way – community-led and culturally focused. Cultural touchpaper moments like the death of Sarah Everard, the Black Lives Matter movement, and the increasingly mainstream environmental movement, encapsulated perhaps in the Fridays for Future school strikes, have opened up for the organization a role in facilitating conversations. This work, which mostly provides the social infrastructure for bringing people together, stems almost directly from the community meeting room and the growth in the sense of the WCDT as a place to meet, and not just garden or eat. This has led to more radical interventions such as the anti-racist library, a project imagined from the anti-racist meetings that brought together locals interested in reading anti-racist texts and discussing race and its impacts. The anti-racist community library opens once a fortnight, outdoors where possible, staffed by volunteers and sourcing books from the avowedly political, independent bookshop Aye-Aye books. In this, what the WCDT are facilitating goes beyond an infrastructure for resilience or cohesion (for example, Klinenberg, 2019). It allows for a transformative dynamic – an exposure to ideas, a place to challenge and build new ways of thinking about social issues, to think about food justice and be invited to demonstrations against climate breakdown or racist immigration legislation. In this, creating spaces of coming together to escape can also create a terrain of reimagining other (potentially more just) futures (see Valle, 2021).

This emerges in novel ways around the community café, which, as noted earlier, demonstrates a rich practice of justice where people can come together to eat as equals (Blake, 2019). The café was a site of eating together but it also presents a novel intervention in food insecurity that refuses to use waste from the food supply chain through the FareShare scheme.[1] Instead, it uses local suppliers to buy high quality food with which to make community meals; staking a claim to the need for emergency food to be ethical food, rather than perpetuate a sense of waste food for waste people. Yet the café, as a multifunctional space, also begins to subtly change foodways for those who attend over time. As was noted in an evaluation exercise I carried out with the charity in 2021–2, the community café's quiet veganism can bring about soft change in people's lives, introducing new foods and ways of thinking about food justice. In this, the practice of collective escape, of curating spaces to enact community differently, lives up to some of the more radical potential within communal growing, though it does so through side projects only tangentially connected to the garden itself.

A second point of note from taking a longer timeframe into consideration is the intervention from Polly at the Children's Wood in creating a specific space for teenagers coming to the site and causing trouble. A long-standing issue often discussed in relation to an idea of 'anti-social behaviour', the fire-setting, noisy and often destructive behaviour of local teens, had previously led to working with the police to move on teens, and a distinct boundary between a sense of the local home owners of the West End and young people who are seen as destructive "bams", as Howard's account from Chapter 4 frames it. Yet sociality is about what is built between and around people (Studdert, 2016). The 'anti-social' of this anti-social behaviour speaks as much to the incapacity of those at the meadow to engage productively or inclusively with those coming down from north Glasgow's estates, instead seeing them as a threat. Which is to say: it is a relational failure in a context that claims to value inclusion and making space for 'everyone'. It connects back to comments made in 2014, at the very start of the fieldwork at the meadow, that the committees and organizers who were so keen to save the space were not always capable of talking across difference. To repeat Craig, a well-known local critic of the Children's Wood, "some of them don't really know how to talk to people outwith their own social demographic".

Polly's work emerged from explicitly trying to bridge this kind of "demographic" difference. Continuing issues with fires and noise, with racist, homophobic and sexist comments in this particular phase, seemed to the committee to require a response from the Children's Wood, and as Polly tells me, over a cup of coffee in an empty youth club one morning in June 2021, she pushed to engage the kids, rather than get the police in. Polly got youth workers involved and staked out the meadow, there every night in every weather, to try to build a relationship with these young teens. Demonstrating the attitude she discusses as 'can-do', she built relationships, but she realized that with dark nights and often-inclement weather, they needed somewhere to be that was not only the meadow, and that part of the issue these kids were facing – one of a great many – was a lack of space that was *theirs*. Gesturing round her as she spoke, she told a story of looking for places to rent, finding funding, drawing in boxing tutors and graffiti artists, and trying to support the children to develop skills and programmes they want. It hasn't been straightforward. These are children, Polly tells me, laughing, banned from all the other youth clubs, banned from the local Tesco and McDonald's. Polly's refusal to see anything but possibility means she and the youth workers at the club work hard to find ways to introduce a different way of engaging with the world. There's a small library of books, a chill out space with games console, a kitchen, a pool table, and the walls are heavily tagged. Upstairs in an old industrial unit, they can be noisy and paint the walls. The continuity in terms of autonomy and empowerment is striking, but it also constitutes an enclave away from the meadow – though Polly insists they still get out as often as they can, including to allotment beds they've taken on.

Polly's extraordinary work in finding space for local youths and building, as productively as possible, with them, a space of their own laid the foundations for local youths to engage in meal delivery during the pandemic, for fundraising and youth festivals, and for making space for exploring creativity and options beyond criminalization. This could easily be romanticized, and it is hard work, but it returns again to an ethic of care and responsibility that is arguably at the heart of communal growing and related activities (Crossan et al, 2015), but stretching out, moving, in interesting ways. Extending the ethic of ownership as a practice of justice, and moving it into different spaces attuned to a set of specific needs, suggests the possibilities that might emerge, the contagion which could spread from the meadow – though it does so through the evidently charismatic and driven character of Polly herself.

This ethic of care was strained by the pandemic at the meadow site itself with tensions around whose space it was becoming heightened by patterns of high use. Signs were put up reminding people not to stay too long to allow more people to use it safely. Polly noted that this played into a longer-term issue with the meadow being a victim of its own success: "[W]ith the wood, we're trying to get people to use it less and spreading people out a bit more, so we'll [with the G20 youth club] probably go up a bit more to Ruchill Park" (interview, 2021). Polly's concern to use other green spaces, including Ruchill Park and Maryhill Park, which are both further north away from the West End in more working-class areas, speaks to a concern about sharing the meadow evenly, with the organizations at the meadow increasingly concerned about overuse from an ecological perspective, wearing out the grass and reducing its ability to function as a meadow. Although the youth club has its roots at the meadow, the need to spread out and get beyond the site pushes them into other green spaces around the city. That said, it still retains a strong connection to the wood, using it as a base, learning from and with it, and with some of the older kids regularly returning to sit in the treehouse and talk. In this way, a longer time perspective allows for a sense of the ebb and flow of inclusion at the meadow, as it shifts priorities towards an ecological inclusion and offshoot projects emerge to encompass, however uncomfortably, younger people more usually positioned as problematic.

The final point of note here speaks to the trajectory of these community organizations over their history. The fragility, around funding and tenure, continues to threaten the existence of both sites. The ten-year anniversary of the Woodlands Community Garden suggests that despite season to season living, the garden is not going anywhere and neither is the overarching Trust. Explorations of alternative funding sources, from the new Friends of Woodlands scheme to invitations to community fundraising, suggest the continued awareness and work to address the ways in which funding instability plays into organizational fragility. The Children's Wood's new tenure stability invites a greater possibility of funding, but its ongoing struggles with the council to agree the terms of a long lease speak to the real issues that community organizations face in taking collective responsibility. In March 2022, the Children's Wood and supporters celebrated signing a 25-year lease on the land with a community event on the meadow with storytelling, planting session, a bee workshop and live music. This heralds a degree of stability for the meadow at least in tenure but it also changes their position in the field of communal growing spaces in Glasgow, taking them closer to the position held by Woodlands and the associated pressures towards politicization discussed previously, reliant as ever on project-based grant funding to continue to survive and build social connections. The instability in this makes building for the long-term difficult. Thus, there is still a deep-rooted instability to the projects.

As such, taking a longer temporal view confirms and discomforts some of the initial findings of the project, reiterating the sense of research findings as a snapshot of a process with longer-term dynamics. New directions have emerged for both projects, as the meadow settles into what should be a greater period of stability, and Woodlands embarks upon a more obviously transformative trajectory through having space to unite people for their interests. These longer-term rhythms are notable in that they confirm a fluidity to imaginations of politics, justice and community across the sites.

Emerging crises

In contrast to these relatively continuous themes and movements, the period 2020–1 proved to be particularly intense for both sites, due to the global COVID-19 pandemic and the death of a community gardener. While the former has been a global event of historical intensity, the latter – a few months after the public outcry over the death of Sarah Everard in London – was a more local crisis, but one not less deeply felt. Both illustrate the enduring relevance of spaces and practices of communal escape in exceptional times, as well as in the everyday.

The rape and murder of Esther Brown[2] in May 2021 rocked the WCDT. As a former board member, active gardener and café volunteer, Esther was well known and liked locally. She was heavily involved in working with refugees and an active member of the congregation of the nearby St Silas church. Esther was first noticed missing by people in the community garden, and in the days that followed her death, flowers appeared (despite Esther's pronounced dislike for cut flowers) tied to the fence on the corner of the private park across the street from the garden. The cards that festooned it expressed grief, shock and love. Esther's raised bed became a site of pilgrimage, where people left living plants with messages on the pots.

A week after her body was found, a candlelit vigil was held in the community garden to remember her. Stories were told of what Esther taught us, what good she brought to the world. Despite the COVID-19 pandemic that at that point still kept people mostly apart, despite the masks everyone there wore, despite the grief and the pain of losing someone who had been such a keystone to building community around the garden and café, as well as elsewhere, it was a spontaneous celebration of the things that we all appreciated in Esther – her care for others, her compassion, her Christian spirit of forgiveness, her strong sense of social justice, and her unwavering willingness to get involved in local activities. The garden and its networks of knowing and caring became not only the way Esther's death was first noticed, but also a means through which it could be collectively processed. The garden was a place to talk about Esther, and to process grief both materially in leaving plants and messages, and through everyday conversations around shared loss.

The emergence in 2019 of a novel Coronavirus first identified in Wuhan, China, reshaped the world in more global ways. In the UK, this was experienced in successive lockdowns as rising waves of the virus caused extreme strain on the NHS and mass casualties. It reshaped everyday life: shifting jobs that could be done remotely to online and furloughing many jobs that could not; requiring masking, social distancing and intensive cleaning; causing panic buying and food shortages, moving shopping online and generally restricting movement; intensifying policing and generating widescale anxiety, stress, isolation and depression; and throwing light on the work which is essential for our lives to function – including nurses, shop assistants, refuse collection workers, delivery drivers and the postal service. For many, in Glasgow and worldwide, this caused financial strain and increased reliance on food aid. Financial insecurity, most often at the heart of food insecurity, is likely to have increased during the pandemic (Weakley, 2021), with the Trussell Trust, the largest chain of food banks in the UK, reporting big increases in food bank uptake due to 'the erosion of households' financial resilience' by the pandemic's effects (Trussell Trust, 2022, p 1).

The pandemic also fundamentally changed how Glasgow felt. People suddenly stuck in place explored new nooks and crannies within the city, and in some cases discovering in their backyard outdoor places where it was safe to meet others and experience some joy in nature. Space for exercise – for cycling, walking, running, wheeling, scooting, dawdling – emerged, including the closure of roads, some of which remain closed to this day. But the eerie stillness of the motorways in Glasgow, with only a handful of cars passing, was a reminder of the deeply unsettling nature of everyday pandemic life.

In such a time, places of urban nature faced higher demand, for their dual capacity of providing soothing natural spaces and for creating space to encounter others at a distance – deliberately or otherwise. Speaking in a personal capacity, I know that the Woodlands Community Garden became a space we would seek out time and again during the weeks of lockdown, as a safe, relatively uncrowded space to linger during our allotted outdoor hours, where my son could run around in relative freedom. Others felt the same, and we would stop for illicit conversations – unsure of the exact restrictions on conversations with acquaintances in outdoor settings. The Children's Wood experienced an uptick in use too, though organizationally they struggled with it more, as noted earlier. While the WCDT moved community events online, providing support groups and therapy sessions remotely at first, and then outdoors when they could, the Children's Wood proved a victim of its own success.

When I interviewed Polly again in 2021, she noted that the "ethos has changed a bit", with a greater emphasis now on protecting the land ecologically, rather than simply bringing people in. Again, this is reactive in the same way that the earlier campaigns were, but it has in the longer term meant that with the G20 Youth Club and future planned Forest School training sessions, there is an emphasis on using a range of outdoor locations nearby, including Maryhill and Ruchill Parks, the canal and some allotments the Youth Club have taken on. The greater use of the meadow led to signs around the park saying 'no fires' after branches were regularly being pulled off trees to feed barbeques, and asking people to use the meadow considerately. Signs later on in 2020 also appeared asking people to stay a 'red deer' away from each other, and pointing out that the virus had 'not gone away'. The space of the meadow in this way took on characteristics of the broader pandemic city; reminding people of the need to remain apart while creating in a small way a space to relieve some of the pressures of pandemic life. Similar signs appeared at Woodlands Community Garden, along with hand sanitizer stations next to the gate, but perhaps in part because it is smaller and more dissimilar to a park, the garden struggled less with the need to keep numbers down.

In this, both case studies during the pandemic became important because of what they already were – spaces of release, of decompression, of time sovereignty; spaces of escape. It has been suggested that community gardens can play a role in disaster mitigation in a pandemic, providing flows of reliable information, access to resources and, from a governance perspective, an understanding of how local power dynamics will be effected by interventions, based on work in Freetown, Sierra Leone (Osuteye et al, 2021). From a more mundane experiential level, they also provide a reassuring point of contact and a sense of constancy, of slow seasonal change. The rhythms of these spaces, outlined in Chapter 3, speak to the importance of the time-space of the meadow and the garden as multifunctional in addressing different needs. Escape is not a surprising thing to seek at such a time of international crisis, and neither is it surprising that reconnecting with nature as a salve for the psyche was a common coping strategy. Indeed, as Ginn (2016) argues, gardening is a means to reconnect with nature and ourselves; building identity narratives that complicate the commercialization of growing and emphasize sharing and long histories. In this way, growing as activity and gardens as spaces hold specific capacities to soothe and situate – a critical feature in a time of deep uncertainty. Everyday conversations and visits across both case studies highlight the relief these spaces offered in a time of stress and uncertainty, of disrupted life rhythms and new distances and proximities. In this, communal growing spaces work as a resource for hope and connection in divided cities and difficult times.

Emergency food in unprecedented times

Where the WCDT and the Children's Wood most obviously shifted gear to address the pandemic (rather than simply moving online) was principally in relation to food aid. At the Children's Wood, this predominantly involved the offshoot youth club, the G20 Youth Festival, founded by Polly out of the increase in anti-social behaviour around the meadow. The idea to support the local area through food came, according to Polly, from the kids themselves, who wanted to help, offering so-called 'food from the wood' (though no food was actually produced there) throughout lockdown, with young people coming along "religiously" to deliver food around Maryhill, developing networks and setting up a pantry in the Wyndford on the street.

At Woodlands, this took the form of a highly structured programme of food production and delivery known as the Neighbourhood Food Service (NFS) in collaboration with three other organizations across north Glasgow. During lockdown periods, Woodlands could not run the community café, which at its height pre-pandemic fed 70–80 people a week at the Fred Paton Centre, home to an organization which supports older people in the city. The NFS acted to some extent as a stop-gap, but it also reached far beyond the bounds of the café in part because of the collaboration with other partner organizations. Over a 13-month period, the NFS delivered more than 22,000 meals and 3,800 grocery bags to over 350 different households. In 2021, I was asked by the WCDT to help them evaluate the NFS and their food work more generally. As part of that, I interviewed collaborative partners from the different organizations involved, staff at WCDT, and we collected a small amount of user data. The report from that work highlighted both how valuable the NFS was in providing food aid at a time of great uncertainty and insecurity, but also how much the community café was valued when it returned in a stripped-back outdoor setting between July and November 2021. This echoes work by Oncini (2021) on Manchester, which highlighted how community food provision goes beyond simply eating a free or cheap meal, but encompasses various forms of advice and social connection. The evaluation work also reiterated quite how important the act of eating together is, how much dignity and value people find in coming together in a non-judgemental setting (Blake, 2019).

The proliferation of food aid, across Glasgow, the UK and elsewhere, during the COVID-19 pandemic spoke to widespread increases in food insecurity. Jafri et al (2021) surveyed people in 82 countries, with a majority on the African continent, the largest contingent in Western Africa (24 per cent), and a minority in Northern America and Western Europe. They found common difficulties around accessing food, and heightened food insecurity across a wide range of settings. In the UK and elsewhere, mutual aid emerged as a solution (Mould et al, 2022), filling gaps that oversubscribed food banks struggled to fill. In 2020, an early report by Rachel Loopstra (2020) noted a fourfold increase in demand for food banks in Great Britain. While this major headline is important, it also hit specific areas of the population harder than others: there is an underlying equalities issue here. The report explicitly draws attention to the ways people from Black, Asian and minority ethnic groups, unemployed adults, households with children and people with health conditions and disability were most at risk (Loopstra, 2020; see also Power et al, 2020). This level of need has lasted through the pandemic. The Trussell Trust, the largest UK food bank chain, noted an 'acceleration' in food bank usage in their end of year report in 2022, suggesting this problem was not isolated to the highly uncertain conditions in the early pandemic (Trussell Trust, 2022). Yet financial support for food aid from governments has largely ended in Glasgow. The NFS wound up after 13 months in May 2021. The G20 Youth Club still do food deliveries, but it is principally now a fundraising tool. What does remain is the community café: struggling to find funding, still reliant on the next piece of grant funding to come through, still frustrated at the endless cycles of justifying the need for their work.

Praise for emerging pandemic responses does so often with an emphasis on mutual aid and spontaneous emergence (Springer, 2020; Mould et al, 2022), but at the meadow and the community garden, they grow as much out of pre-existing social networks, particularly at Woodlands where relationships with collaborators, a network of volunteers and potential recipients, staff and a strong reputation facilitated success.[3] This is not to downplay what was achieved elsewhere but to situate this particular action in an existing trajectory. Similar remarks could be made about another community project that I spent 2019 researching the ethics of sustainability alongside, the Baltic Street Adventure Playground. The Baltic Street Adventure Playground is an adventure playground whose work focuses principally on providing space for children to be empowered and to play, but whose broader neighbourhood context in an area of high urban deprivation means their care extends outwards to include community meals, feeding children in ad hoc, daily ways, running large school holiday programmes and proving a free food pantry. Their pandemic response escalated their food aid from this varied but small-scale scope to delivering food parcels and groceries to approximately 300 families a week. This built to a large degree on already existing capacities and local trust.

Equally, the work by the Glasgow Community Food Network during the pandemic to connect up producers and food aid projects also grew out of existing partnerships and capacities (GCFN, 2021). This is not to downplay the emergence of spontaneous mutual aid, but to note the longer history and relationships that underpinned some of the aid response; and particularly to point to ongoing work at Woodlands and Baltic Street that continue to provide food aid in the face of a wider range of crises including the current so-called 'cost of living' inflationary crisis, ongoing and widening socioeconomic inequality, and the looming climate crisis.

Thus, a longer temporal lens illuminates continuities and shifts within communal growing projects as they respond to the shifting environment, or field. Precarity and boundary work remain important, but as the broader environment shifts, the space open to communal growing projects to act moves with it. The WCDT demonstrate a shift towards more outwardly transformative work; the Children's Wood opens up space for often disregarded youth, though it does so often away from the meadow itself. In this, the possibility of transformative work within projects moves in relation to the space afforded by external social shifts, such as an increased focus on anti-racist work and environmental crises, and responds to other actions, such as periods of increasing anti-social behaviour.

In the major crises of both COVID-19 and local murder, the strength and potential of escapist space becomes clear as a social infrastructure not simply for transformation and escape, but also for resilience (Klinenberg, 2019). The effective response during the pandemic's peak that emerged from the WCDT and that lives on in vegetable boxes and the community café raises questions for the narrative around the spontaneous efflorescence of mutual aid during the pandemic. Growing out of the embedded social infrastructure of the space and persisting long after funding and enthusiasm for mutual aid died back, the community café presents a much longer duration of support built on strong local relationships of trust. Given the emerging crises around food, energy and inflationary pressures in the early 2020s, understanding and supporting such social infrastructure is critical to address both immediate relief and building new, more sustainable futures. Important in this will be taking an approach that allows for an understanding of how such interventions move and grow over time, including work that is more longitudinal in scope.

10

Conclusion

Community, politics, justice

The field sites of this book demonstrate the possibilities and tensions inherent to carving out places of collective escape in the city. Community underpins these escapist spaces, both as an idea and a set of practices, and intersects sometimes uncomfortably with urban justice, the right to the city, and the commons. This intersection complicates easy conclusions around the politics of communal growing projects. Attending to urban land politics, organizational pressures and the cultural implications of political interpretations demonstrates the breadth of action and beliefs, all of which might contribute to an understanding of the politics of such spaces. Questions of who belongs in a community garden in the West End of Glasgow thus have broader significance, giving us space to think through what it means to make a city and what stymies the remaking of the city in different ways. The organizations and movements in this book are attentive to justice through the idea of inclusion and opening up green spaces for broad usage. Yet there are tensions between doing the work to build green, social spaces and the exclusions and incursions of others, and such tensions are illustrative of the broader tapestry of social justice in the city as they are enacted through the seemingly mundane terrain of growing plants together.

That community, justice and politics are entangled in such a way is most evident through the analytically political work of building a commons as it sits against a sometimes limited political imaginary. While the political (or otherwise) status of communal growing projects is a well-worn terrain for debate, this needs to be understood on the one hand as emerging from both internally transformative capacities and a claiming of space in the city that we might understand as staking a claim to the city (Lefebvre, 1996); but also as restrained in its imagination in everyday life by organizational conditions and popular ideas around what politics means (often seen as divisive, especially around constitutional matters that were very much present in the field between Scottish independence referendum in 2014 and the Brexit vote in

2016). Politics is thus as amorphous a category as community at times; yet people at both sites often felt the moral content of their action, the *common good*, was fundamental to understanding the significance of what they were building in communal growing projects. In this, community, politics and justice emerge as categories that blend into one another, empirically rich and sometimes contradictory in their emergence.

The afterlives of growing

One benefit of the longer timeframe that this research can reflect on is that it allows for a consideration of how some of the tensions and politics around communal growing shift and change in sometimes subtle ways over the years. Some of the most difficult or awkward conversations in the field circled around the tacit exclusions made both at the North Kelvin Meadow and Children's Wood and at Woodlands Community Garden; and around how political or not such spaces can be. This mirrors to some extent some of the controversies in the extremely broad literature on community gardening – where whether growing or urban agriculture can or does embody certain values are debated at length. Such debates are deepened when a longer timeframe can be taken into account. Thinking with longer cycles of rhythm and change, taking longer trajectories into account, means attending to cycles of funding that have increasingly allowed Woodlands to support women's groups, support groups for people of colour, and develop an anti-racist library; sensitive to rising tides of public awareness around gendered violence and racial discrimination, and to advocate, however softly, for climate-friendly behaviours such as cycling and veganism. The developments over in the meadow and wood seem to have shifted action away from public campaigns or overt attempts to modify behaviour. This seems to relate directly to a degree of stability of tenure, though a recurrence of anti-social behaviour raises continuing challenges for the organizations based there. Yet the offshoot project in Polly's new youth group speaks to a similar ethic and values, suggesting more complex afterlives to the activism that to some extent is no longer necessary in North Kelvinside. At each site, then, a glimpse of the longer-term temporalities of communal growing can be seen as cyclical – responsive to broader social dynamics, actions of landowners and developers, city councils and pandemics.

The question of legacy, raised in John Urry's critical question (in Bialski and Otto, 2015) 'how does it move', is an important and often understudied element of social action. It poses something of a methodological question too. Taking an ethnographic snapshot in 2015–16, and returning and re-tuning in later years allows some attentiveness to longer-term effects, to the afterlives of action, but a more systematic ritornello might be designed to think with shifts in practices over time. Certainly, the COVID-19 pandemic seems to require an attention to afterlives, especially in relation to the surge of mutual aid and local support structures that flourished during lockdowns. With restrictions easing across the UK to something approximating normal as the 2020s unfold, this question is one that we must now turn to face – how to not only live with the dragging tail of COVID-19 but to reckon with what we have lived through. Does the surge of enthusiasm for being outdoors, for gardening and being in nature stick? Does a greater recognition of the value of human connection change things, and provide some political room for manoeuvre for communal gardens in Glasgow, and what does this mean for the necessary transition to a more sustainable future? These are not questions this book can answer, though they emerge as lines of future enquiry as the afterlives of the pandemic become clearer.

For communal growing, some shifts may be occurring at the Scottish national level in particular, that appear to support an increased sense of value attributed to projects. The development by the city council of a Glasgow Food Growing Strategy, an outshoot from the Community Empowerment Act (Scotland) 2015, was legally mandated, which not only mapped existing but had locally sourced suggestions of available land for potential allotments or community gardens. In 2021, the Glasgow City Food Plan was launched, which spans food injustice, food systems, local sourcing, waste and community growing, and emphasizes that '[c]ommunity food projects impact positively on our communities wellbeing and do much to help the local environment' (Glasgow City Food Plan, 2021, p 6). The city council was one of the partners involved in developing the plan, tying them into supporting the development of a system designed to provide 'fair food for all', although the plan holds an ambiguous territory as it is imagined to be held by a putative 'everyone'.

Thus, the potential to apply pressure to support communal growing in Glasgow would seem to be there, though the question of course exists as to whether the movement to do so does. Despite the existence of a Glasgow-wide organization that represents community growing across a number of different sites and scales in the Glasgow Community Food Network, neither field site was greatly engaged with the network. The Glasgow Community Food Network are visibly involved in a variety of endeavours from pandemic food support, small research projects and climate activism. They are, however, not universally seen as a representative organization by community organizations. Nonetheless, the broader political opportunity structure which in 2015–16 in particular appeared predominantly to close off transformative action and circumscribe the activities of growing organizations may be shifting. In the years to come there may be a more politicized role emerging for community growing organizations and movements, though it may hinge on the capacity of the Glasgow Community Food Network to legitimize their efforts to speak for the sector. Their marginality to this book speaks to a certain lack of recognition for them as helpful partners by some in the field.

Open terrain

There are also other broad questions and justice horizons that emerge with which communal growing naturally intersect, and that this book has not directly engaged with. The most crucial perhaps, especially given Glasgow was the host city for COP26 in 2021, is that community gardens are often sites for imagining a more sustainable city. While this book has focused perhaps stubbornly on the social aspects of community gardening and their escapist capacity, both sites lay claim to what a sustainable future might look like and what kinds of action might take us there, from the soft promotion of veganism to preserving wild spaces in the city. Although I have not taken a strong focus on sustainability here, a broad definition of sustainability would include not only environmental but social elements. Wheeler and Rosan (2021, p 4) define sustainability as 'a process of continually and actively moving in directions that promote ecological health, social equity, quality of life, cooperation, and compassion'. Within such a frame, community gardens as imperfect attempts to reimagine a just, collective city give us somewhere to start when considering what a sustainable way of life might look like. Indeed, visions of the sustainable city often do include an element of home-grown or collectively managed orchards, gardens or meadows within the city and without (see, for example, Worldwatch Institute, 2016; Wheeler and Rosan, 2021).

It seems abundantly clear that, for all the lifestyle sustainability work that explores an individualized, classed set of consumers (S.M. Hall, 2011) and classed politics within that (there is a a good summary in Littler, 2011), there is a need to think about how we engage in a collective project of sustainable life, and what that might look like. Bonow and Normark (2018) suggest that the power of community gardening is creating leverage, for demonstrating and pushing for greater sustainable development, rather than necessarily contributing itself to sustainable development directly. This conclusion, itself aimed not at everyday life but at transformation at scale, seems to overlook the potential for reimagining life that occurs in the spaces of communal growing projects. Against this, I would echo Ginn (2016, p 4) when he makes the case for any 'ecologically sane future' requiring more 'unproductive' and more ecologically rich human and non-human elements. Hanmer (2021) describes this well when he discusses growing's capacity to provide space for self-determination and autonomy for retired gardeners.

Reimagining sustainable cities is a huge project, and one that the remaining pages of this book cannot begin to unfold in any depth. But such work might take as a starting point key themes that emerge in communal growing. If sustainable life must involve consuming less, being more rooted in place, and working together to find collective ways of doing things, then there may be things to learn from communal growing projects – from their slow advocacy, their meeting people where they are, from reflexive practices of equality in food aid, and from the difficulties of balancing a myriad of different opinions, perspectives and people in pursuit of a common goal. Nevertheless, this of course needs to take into account the intersection of inequalities with urban greening (Wolch et al, 2014; Mabon and Shih, 2018; Rigolon and Németh, 2020; Garcia-Lamarca et al, 2021) in order not to take the internal political dynamics of alternative spaces as a sufficient terrain for their promotion as 'solutions' to problems of sustainability.

For the gardens to come

This is not to reify community growing projects, but to address them as a terrain offering ways of imperfectly pursuing practices of justice and community. It is to argue for growing projects as a means to understand how local projects are situated phenomenon that might contribute in complex ways to wider social change. As Barron (2017) puts it:

> One explanation for the strong and sustained interest in community gardens is that they bring to the fore some of the tensions that characterise our era, particularly in terms of how land and property are valued; how nature and public space are understood in cities; whose needs are served by urban agriculture and public space; how such spaces are produced, and who can participate in these processes. (Barron, 2017, p 1142)

If this book has succeeded, it has built on these tensions, demonstrated the interplay between attempts to escape and create something collective and autonomous in the city; and the broader structures of opportunities that constrain and facilitate action. It has also illustrated the way practices attempting to actualize community are importantly shaped by an idea of what community is; expanding our understanding of community as not just a practice, but also a core social idea.

The case studies of this book are situated in a specific milieu in which community is made responsible for taking on welfare functions (Amin, 2005), and is slid easily into political discourse (Wallace, 2010). In this context, community-as-idea can itself be seen as a site of contestation. Practices of care, solidarity and support lay valid claim to being an actualization of community-as-idea; and yet the positive symbolism of community-as-idea is evoked as a means to co-opt local caring and reduce local authority funding for care services. This is the difficult context in which communal growing negotiates existential questions of funding and organizational form, while crafting connection. This is no mean feat. Yet in the morally situated idea of community that frames growing projects is a deeper problem about what is and is not contestable.

The tensions between the way the space of action for community growing projects is constrained and the transformative capacity of the projects illustrates a broader struggle over what community is allowed to be and how much autonomy they are allowed. Whether a project is political or not is in many ways a vexed question, and a red herring, because the sense in which it is political relies principally on whose definition of political one uses and whether analytical or practical concepts are being utilized. Yet what is at stake in these cases is not just the sites themselves, but questions of who gets to determine the city and what the proper place of communality is. Community-as-idea is imagined by research participants largely apolitically and the prevailing norm in these case studies is for communal practices to conform to a moral rather than political framing, that sense of 'common justice'. The context of increased urban participation – particularly consultation, but also the increasing involvement of non-governmental actors in the production and maintenance of the city (Cooke and Kothari, 2001; Tonkiss, 2013; Arapoglou and Gounis, 2015) – lends a greater importance to the idea of community than might otherwise exist. This extension of governance has provoked a great deal of debate as to its democratic or neoliberal character in community gardens (Pudup, 2008; Rosol, 2010; Ghose and Pettygrove, 2014; McClintock, 2014; Crossan et al, 2016; Ginn and Ascensão, 2018; St Clair et al, 2018), but it also shifts the way that community projects emerge, as suggested by the pressures on communal growing projects here to remain strategically neutral.

One challenge of community organizing becomes in this sense a struggle for recognition and, in pushing the boundaries of participation, a struggle for the role of communal organizations in urban life. Indeed, the North Kelvin Meadow's starting point in 2008 was the rejection of the veneer of participation established in choosing a design for the proposed development on the meadow. This spurred the creation of their own campaign and latterly, from the Children's Wood, their own explicit vision for the urban meadow. Yet their class positionality becomes problematic when they make moves to establish their legitimacy as 'the' community, in its singular, neighbourhood sense. Legitimacy in this sense was fought for through deliberate policies of depoliticization, and tactics that positioned organizations as capable and organized, and which took recognizable form as charities. This is the sense in which groups stake a claim to the right to represent their constituency – in both the cases here, in geographical terms. But it can also be read as a kind of class politics, in which the dominance of both projects by middle-class White people becomes a continuation of a trend readily noted: the dominance in public life of the middle classes (Ray et al, 2003). The projects come to stand metonymically for an imagined neighbourhood community as some kind of unified and singular unit. In this context these differences are likely to disappear and the community project becomes the Community – that is, the ultimate partiality and fluidity of the community as practised (its myth of representation) is lost in its representative function. This reduces the sense in which either project might be considered deeply progressive or alternative, since it largely mirrors the status quo.

The dominant positions in the social hierarchy held by growers discomfits ideas of radical growing, as it presents in these particular case studies. This is also where the notion of community-led regeneration leads to – the key question of who gets to be the community (before, of course, any consideration of how sincere their participation gets to be). If one takes Rancière's (1999) position as primarily a critique of the notion that everything is (or can be) political, and therefore very little is truly political; this in-group position jostling becomes about as non-political as could be. On the level of class, this is not the production of alternatives, as Barry (2001) would have us assess politics. In response to those who position communal growing and urban agriculture as a kind of radical politics (Hodgkinson, 2005; Certomà and Tornaghi, 2015), this research questions how radical a largely middle-class escapist phenomenon can be considered. Rather than seeing this, however, as part of a narrative of co-option and neoliberal encroachment, this is more akin to the way that play figures as evading power (Thrift, 1997b; Jones, 2013). This is Rancière's (1999) challenge to those who would position all struggles as political – do they engage with the foundation of equality upon which democratic society rests? And if they do not, should we conceive of what they do as truly radical? In these terms, it is clear that growing projects cannot be conceived within the parameters of politics as rupture, yet they clearly engage in some kind of political manoeuvre in a smaller, mundane way. I have drawn on Holloway (2010) and Beveridge and Koch (2019) to argue that communal growing's evasion is a kind of politics in itself: a reinterpretation of everyday life, where the everyday is situated as a political terrain in and of itself.

As Olin Wright (2015) notes, escapism does not necessarily build a progressive future, so much as avoid the worst vicissitudes of capitalist society. In this, communal growing projects can be situated not as Nettle's (2014) prefigurative politics of example but as a protective, evasive space in the city: as escapist. Analytically, the politics of this are very much latent; pressured into strategic neutrality, with the spaces involved often held aloft from the lay associations of politics. The critical question then becomes not whether a community garden is or is not political, but what ideals they can enact (however partially), and what afterlives they have – how projects move, what trajectories, relations and outflows they produce.

This has implications when we consider community growing as a practice attuned to justice, as clearly the case studies here make the case for – as responses to specific perceived injustices, and as operationalizations of a vision of justice, whether of greater green space, welcoming community or fair access to food. Yet, when viewed from the perspective of social dominance, particularly in class terms, communal growing in these specific cases has tended to reproduce much of the same, rather than present a real alternative. This questions some of the suggestions that communal growing projects are places of inclusivity, though the moves of the Woodlands Community Development Trust in more recent years suggest a potential to shift and change in relation to inclusion as their main justice imaginary. Thus the limits and tensions within practices of justice emerge, particularly their imperfections and blind spots. In these cases specifically there are clear challenges at the intersection of community practices and attempts to actualize just urban life; though responding to such challenges should be seen as dynamic and evolving processes.

I have been concerned through this book to ask what transformative potential is possible within communal urban growing, what challenges are mounted to systemic inequalities and what alternatives posed. I argue that the contribution of growing is contextual and rhythmic. The volumes of food produced in communal growing projects tend to be symbolic, however, their potential capacity to provide spaces in which to encounter difference is greater than their actual disruption of food systems (Aptekar, 2015). Nettle (2014) argues this places them firmly in the politics of example, or demonstrating the possibility of another way of living the city. Contrarily, while I have argued there is an analytical politics to staking ground in the city, it is in these cases made more complicated by the intertwining of boundary-making and exclusionary practices with inclusionary dynamics. This diverges from interpretations of gardening as radical in that it does not assume alterity as a sufficient condition for political interpretation, nor does it argue that because communal growing works within bureaucratic systems as much as against them, that they are co-opted beyond their intentions. Instead, it suggests something far more incremental and everyday but not less critical: that these growing projects produce breathing space for conversation, contact and debate, in a circumscribed austerity setting that lends a specific shape to their emergence. Given the increasingly stark ideological divides that appear to dominate Western political debate, this stakes a normative way of living in the city in the everyday – it acts to bring people together, through the idea of community itself and performances of collectiveness.

While the COVID-19 pandemic may have a long tail, and its lasting impacts I will not hazard to predict, it clearly emphasized the importance of communal life. Esther's murder, alongside this global calamity, the challenges of deepening inequalities, and the ticking clock of climate change heighten the power and importance of collective life as a resource for social resilience and grounds for building towards transformative change. Although communal growing projects present only one everyday site of contest and negotiation, the possibilities of such spaces in providing social infrastructure become apparent in small ways via such urban interventions as the anti-racist library, the community café and the daily escapes of the meadow, suggesting the ways that such heterogeneous projects can hold space for a multitude of escapes.

Communal growing can be disruptive and in some ways alternative, but in the milieu of different possibilities within the city, it is not automatically political: it often lacks a distinct framing and strategic intention. As such, the opportunities and pressures in which communal growing projects emerge are important for understanding what possibilities can be located there. What this research has thus explored is community as an everyday contest and escape: a practice that fills peoples' lives with meaning and an idea towards which they orient their action as paradoxically an escape into responsibility. It is discontinuous and fluid, but functionally so. Nevertheless, within projects oriented towards this fluid and contested construct, some small hope can still be situated: in the everyday production of alternative ways of being in the city; and in the attempts at ever broadening its inclusive reach.

Notes

Chapter 1
[1] In Scotland, such surfaces were commonly made of blaes, a colliery by-product that gives a hard red or brown gritty surface. Respondents who were old enough to remember falling on such a surface described it as painful and were not sad to see its use decline and disappear over time.

Chapter 2
[1] Like Liverpool, and other global hubs during the British empire, this sometimes emerges as a 'second city' narrative – but it has been critiqued (see, for example, Kintrea and Madgin, 2019).
[2] This is based on a survey from 2015, with little reliable survey evidence since. It is likely to present an undercount, especially of smaller or more informal growing spaces.

Chapter 4
[1] See also http://www.poverty.org.uk/62/index.shtml.

Chapter 5
[1] The City of Glasgow Corporation ceased to exist in 1975, becoming first the City of Glasgow District Council and then Glasgow City Council in 1996 after the dissolution of Strathclyde Regional Council. But Alasdair as a former journalist and lifelong Glaswegian would refer to it by its former name, or even just as "the corpie".
[2] This has been the case for far longer in rural Scotland, as the oft-cited case of the local ownership of the island of Eigg demonstrates.
[3] The Children's Wood have given support to a campaign within Scotland called Upstart, which argues children should not start school until they are seven years old, akin to the Scandinavian model. The presence on the meadow of many home-educators means that often conversations on the meadow start from a set of presumptions that state education is flawed and should be changed.

Chapter 7
[1] In 2018 I facilitated this, inviting the manager of the WCDT to a food poverty and inequality international workshop to speak alongside myself and other academics on the topic of food insecurity in the UK.
[2] The Climate Challenge Fund is a Scottish Government funding stream offering 'grants and support for community-led organisations to tackle climate change by running projects that reduce local carbon emissions' (Keep Scotland Beautiful, nd). It became apparent in

this research that it is renowned among community garden workers for being restrictive in its funding and exacting in its monitoring.

Chapter 8
1. 'Fae' is Scots for 'from', thus refugees get a letter from a Glaswegian resident. More on Refuweegee at https://www.refuweegee.co.uk/.
2. The Transition Network, as it is now called, grew out of a series of very local experiments in sustainability and social change called Transition Towns, that emerged initially in Totnes in Devon, UK.
3. The 2014 referendum on Scottish independence was split 55 per cent to remain in the UK to 45 per cent voting for Scottish independence.

Chapter 9
1. This is the most common route to supplying community café style interventions (including some pantries and community fridges). FareShare in Scotland were awarded £1.6 million in 2020 (see https://fareshare.org.uk/news-media/press-releases/scottish-government-1-6m-to-help-tackle-food-insecurity/); and in successive years hundreds of thousands of pounds to support diverting food waste from the supply chain back into charitable use. These huge sums of money have been critiqued by some in the community food sector as money that could have been spent better elsewhere.
2. Esther was one of the people who early on in the research welcomed me into the garden and patiently explained how it all worked, and what it meant to her. Her death was widely reported in the press, and affected myself and many of the people in this research in intense ways that I cannot reflect fully on here. I have deanonymized her here (but not in earlier pages) in order to do justice to her legacy, which will be written into the space of Woodlands itself in the form of a memorial stone in a new rockery and wildlife area. I hope that rather than her violent death, Esther will be recalled in that sense of community, of welcoming others and caring for them in mundane ways, that she practised and that will outlive her in the garden.
3. A fuller write up of the Neighbourhood Food Service is found in Traill (2022); on the basis of an evaluation exercise I carried out with WCDT on their food work and its values.

References

Adams, D. and Hardman, M. (2014) 'Observing guerrillas in the wild: Reinterpreting practices of urban guerrilla gardening', *Urban Studies*, 51(6), pp 1103–19. Available at: https://doi.org/10.1177/0042098013497410.

Amin, A. (2005) 'Local community on trial', *Economy and Society*, 34(4), pp 612–33. Available at: https://doi.org/10.1080/03085140500277211.

Anderson, B. (2006) *Imagined Communities*. 2nd edn. London: Verso. Available at: https://doi.org/10.1080/1382557042000294701.

Anderson, S., Hamilton, K. and Tonner, A. (2018) '"They were built to last": Anticonsumption and the materiality of waste in obsolete buildings', *Journal of Public Policy and Marketing*, 37(2), pp 195–212. Available at: https://doi.org/10.1177/0743915618810438.

Andres, L. and Grésillon, B. (2013) 'Cultural brownfields in European cities: A new mainstream object for cultural and urban policies', *International Journal of Cultural Policy*, 19(1), pp 1–23. Available at: https://doi.org/10.1080/10286632.2011.625416.

Angelo, H. (2021) *How Green Became Good: Urbanized Nature and the Making of Cities and Citizens*. Chicago: Chicago University Press.

Anguelovski, I., Brand, A.L., Connolly, J.J.T., Corbera, E., Kotsila, P., Steil, J., et al (2020) 'Expanding the boundaries of justice in urban greening scholarship: Toward an emancipatory, antisubordination, intersectional, and relational approach', *Annals of the American Association of Geographers*, 110(6), pp 1743–69. Available at: https://doi.org/10.1080/24694452.2020.1740579.

Aptekar, S. (2015) 'Visions of public space: Reproducing and resisting social hierarchies in a community garden', *Sociological Forum*, 30(1), pp 209–27. Available at: https://doi.org/10.1111/socf.12152.

Arapoglou, V. and Gounis, K. (2015) *Poverty and Homelessness in Athens: Governance and the Rise of an Emergency Model of Social Crisis Management*. GreeSE Paper No. 90. London. Available at: http://www.lse.ac.uk/europeanInstitute/research/hellenicObservatory/CMS pdf/Publications/GreeSE/GreeSE_No90.pdf.

Armstrong, D. (2000) 'A survey of community gardens in upstate New York: Implications for health promotion and community development', *Health & Place*, 6(4), pp 319–27. Available at: https://doi.org/10.1016/S1353-8292(00)00013-7.

Atkinson, R. and Flint, J. (2004) 'Fortress UK? Gated communities, the spatial revolt of the elites and time–space trajectories of segregation', *Housing Studies*, 19(6), pp 875–92. Available at: https://doi.org/10.1080/0267303042000293982.

Auyero, J. (2011) 'Patients of the state: An ethnographic account of poor people's waiting', *Latin American Research Review*, 46(1), pp 5–29. Available at: www.jstor.org/stable/41261368.

Barnett, C. (2010) 'Publics and markets: What's wrong with neoliberalism?', in S.J. Smith, R. Pain, S.A. Marston and J.P. Jones (eds) *The SAGE Handbook of Social Geographies*. London and New York: SAGE, pp 269–96. Available at: https://doi.org/10.4135/9780857021113.

Barron, J. (2017) 'Community gardening: cultivating subjectivities, space, and justice', *Local Environment*, 22(9), pp 1142–58. Available at: https://doi.org/10.1080/13549839.2016.1169518.

Barry, A. (2001) *Political Machines: Governing a Technological Society*. London and New Brunswick: Athlone Press.

Bastian, M. (2014) 'The slow university and a collective politics of time', *Sustaining Time*. Available at: http://www.sustainingtime.org/home/the-slow-university-and-a-collective-politics-of-time.

Bates, L. (2015) 'Ten things you should know about the gender pay gap', *The Guardian*. Available at: https://www.theguardian.com/lifeandstyle/2015/nov/10/ten-things-you-should-know-about-the-gender-pay-gap.

Bauman, Z. (2000) *Liquid Modernity*. Cambridge: Polity.

Bell, C. and Newby, H. (1971) *Community Studies: An Introduction to the Sociology of the Local Community*. London: Allen & Unwin.

Belton, B. (2013) '"Weak power": Community and identity', *Ethnic and Racial Studies*, 36(2), pp 282–97. Available at: https://doi.org/10.1080/01419870.2012.676198.

Benson, M. and Jackson, E. (2013) 'Place-making and place maintenance: Performativity, place and belonging among the middle classes', *Sociology*, 47(4), pp 793–809. Available at: https://doi.org/10.1177/0038038512454350.

Benson, M. and O'Reilly, K. (2022) 'Reflexive practice in live sociology: Lessons from researching Brexit in the lives of British citizens living in the EU-27', *Qualitative Research*, 22(2), pp 177–93. Available at: https://doi.org/10.1177/1468794120977795.

Berlant, L. (2016) 'The commons: Infrastructures for troubling times', *Environment and Planning D: Society and Space*, 34(3), pp 393–419. Available at: https://doi.org/10.1177/0263775816645989.

Berlin, I. (1969) 'Two concepts of liberty', in *Four Essays on Liberty*. Oxford: Oxford University Press, pp 118–72.

Beveridge, R. and Koch, P. (2019) 'Urban everyday politics: Politicising practices and the transformation of the here and now', *Environment and Planning D: Society and Space*, 37(1), pp 142–57. Available at: https://doi.org/10.1177/0263775818805487.

Bialski, P. and Otto, B. (2015) 'Collective low-budget organizing and low carbon futures: An interview with John Urry', *Ephemera*, 15(1), pp 221–8.

Blake, M.K. (2019) 'More than just food: Food insecurity and resilient place making through community self-organising', *Sustainability*, 11(10), 2942.

Blokland, T. (2017) *Community as Urban Practice*. Cambridge: Polity.

Bonow, M. and Normark, M. (2018) 'Community gardening in Stockholm: Participation, driving forces and the role of the municipality', *Renewable Agriculture and Food Systems*, 33(6), pp 503–17. Available at: https://doi.org/10.1017/S1742170517000734.

Bresnihan, P. and Byrne, M. (2015) 'Escape into the city: Everyday practices of commoning and the production of urban space in Dublin', *Antipode*, 47(1), pp 36–54. Available at: https://doi.org/10.1111/anti.12105.

Brint, S. (2001) 'Gemeinschaft revisited', *Sociological Theory*, 19(1), pp 1–23. Available at: https://doi.org/10.1111/0735-2751.00125.

British Academy (2021) *The COVID Decade: Understanding the Long-term Societal Impacts of COVID-19*. London: British Academy. Available at: https://www.thebritishacademy.ac.uk/publications/shaping-the-covid-decade-addressing-the-long-term-societal-impacts-of-covid-19/.

Brubaker, R. (2013) 'Categories of analysis and categories of practice: A note on the study of Muslims in European countries of immigration', *Ethnic and Racial Studies*, 36(1), pp 1–8. Available at: https://doi.org/10.1080/01419870.2012.729674.

Buechler, S.M. (2004) 'The strange career of strain and breakdown theories of collective action', in D.A. Snow, S.A. Soule and H. Kriesi (eds) *Blackwell Companion to Social Movements*. Oxford: Blackwell, pp 47–66.

Byrne, D. (2005) 'Class, culture and identity', *Sociology*, 39(5), pp 807–16.

Caffentzis, G. and Federici, S. (2014) 'Commons against and beyond capitalism', *Community Development Journal*, 49(1), pp 92–105. Available at: https://doi.org/10.1093/cdj/bsu006.

Calhoun, C. (1998) 'Community without propinquity revisited: Communications technology and the transformation of the urban public sphere', *Sociological Inquiry*, 68(3), pp 373–97.

Care Collective (2020) *The Care Manifesto: The Politics of Interdependence*. London: Verso.

Carney, N. (2017) 'Multi-sited ethnography: Opportunities for the study of race', *Sociology Compass*, 11(9), pp 1–10. Available at: https://doi.org/10.1111/soc4.12505.

Certomà, C. and Tornaghi, C. (2015) 'Political gardening: Transforming cities and political agency', *Local Environment*, 20(10), pp 1123–31. Available at: https://doi.org/10.1080/13549839.2015.1053724.

Certomà, C., Sondermann, M. and Noori, S. (2019) 'Urban gardening and the quest for just uses of space in Europe', in C. Certomà, S. Noori and M. Sondermann (eds) *Urban Gardening and the Struggle for Social and Spatial Justice*. Manchester: Manchester University Press, pp 1–21. Available at: https://doi.org/10.7228/manchester/9781526126092.003.0001.

Chatterton, P. (2005) 'Making autonomous geographies: Argentina's popular uprising and the "Movimiento de Trabajadores Desocupados" (Unemployed Workers Movement)', *Geoforum*, 36(5), pp 545–61. Available at: https://doi.org/10.1016/j.geoforum.2004.10.004.

Chatterton, P. and Pickerill, J. (2010) 'Everyday activism and transitions towards post-capitalist worlds', *Transactions of the Institute of British Geographers*, 35(4), pp 475–90. Available at: https://doi.org/10.1111/j.1475-5661.2010.00396.x.

Chen, Y. (2013) '"Walking with": A rhythmanalysis of London's East End', *Culture Unbound*, 5, pp 531–49.

Claeys, G. (2022) *Utopianism for a Dying Planet: Life after Consumerism*. Oxford: Princeton University Press.

Cody, K. (2019) 'Community gardens and the making of organic subjects: A case study from the Peruvian Andes', *Agriculture and Human Values*, 36(1), pp 105–16. Available at: https://doi.org/10.1007/s10460-018-9895-z.

Coffey, A. (1999) *The Ethnographic Self*. London: SAGE.

Cohen, A. (1985) *The Symbolic Construction of Community*. London: Routledge. Available at: https://doi.org/10.2307/2803278.

Cooke, B. and Kothari, U. (2001) *Participation: The New Tyranny?* New York: Zed Books.

Cooper, D. (2013) *Everyday Utopias: On the Conceptual Life of Promising Spaces*. London: Duke University Press.

Crang, M. (2001) 'Rhythms of the city: Temporalised space', in T. May and N. Thrift (eds) *Timespace: Geographies of Temporality*. London: Routledge, pp 187–207.

Crawford, F., Beck, S. and Hanlon, P. (2007) *Will Glasgow Flourish? Glasgow Centre for Population Health Report*. Glasgow: Glasgow Centre for Population Health.

Cress, D.M. (1997) 'Non-profit incorporation among movements of the poor: Pathways and consequences for homeless social movement organizations', *The Sociological Quarterly*, 38(2), pp 343–60. Available at: https://doi.org/10.1111/j.1533-8525.1997.tb00481.x.

Crossan, J., Shaw, D., Cumbers, A. and McMaster, R. (2015) *Glasgow's Community Gardens: Sustainable Communities of Care*. Project Report. University of Glasgow, Glasgow.

Crossan, J., Cumbers, A., McMaster, R. and Shaw, D. (2016) 'Contesting neoliberal urbanism in Glasgow's community gardens: The practice of DIY citizenship', *Antipode*, 48(4), pp 937–55. Available at: https://doi.org/10.1111/anti.12220.

Cumbers, A., Shaw, D., Crossan, J. and McMaster, R. (2018) 'The work of community gardens: Reclaiming place for community in the city', *Work, Employment and Society*, 32(1), pp 133–49. Available at: https://doi.org/10.1177/0950017017695042.

Daily Record (2017) 'Local election results', *Daily Record*, 24 June. Available at: http://www.dailyrecord.co.uk/news/politics/local-election-results-live-counting-10359359.

de Angelis, M. (2017) *Omnia Sunt Communia: On the Commons and the Transformation to Postcapitalism*. London: Zed Books.

Delanty, G. (2003) *Community*. London: Routledge.

Desmond, M. (2016) *Evicted: Poverty and Profit in the American City*. London: Penguin. Available at: https://doi.org/10.1177/0887403416644013.

de Souza, M.L. (2006) 'Social movements as "critical urban planning" agents', *City*, 10(3), pp 327–42. Available at: https://doi.org/10.1080/13604810600982347.

Deutsch, F.M. (2007) 'Undoing gender', *Gender & Society*, 21(1), pp 106–27. Available at: https://doi.org/10.1177/0891243206293577.

Ding, X., Zhao, Z., Zheng, J., Yue, X., Jin, H. and Zhang, Y. (2022) 'Community gardens in China: Spatial distribution, patterns, perceived benefits and barriers', *Sustainable Cities and Society*, 84. Available at: https://doi.org/10.1016/j.scs.2022.103991.

Docherty, I. (2019) 'Stopped in its tracks? Transport's contribution to Glasgow's development', in K. Kintrea and R. Madgin (eds) *Transforming Glasgow: Beyond the Post-Industrial City*. Bristol: Policy Press.

Douglas, G.C.C. (2018) *The Help-Yourself City*. Oxford: Oxford University Press. Available at: https://doi.org/10.1093/oso/9780190691332.001.0001.

Drake, L. and Lawson, L.J. (2014) 'Validating verdancy or vacancy? The relationship of community gardens and vacant lands in the U.S.', *Cities*, 40, pp 133–42. Available at: https://doi.org/10.1016/j.cities.2013.07.008.

Draus, P., Haase, D., Napieralski, J., Roddy, J. and Qureshi, S. (2019) 'Wounds, ghosts and gardens: Historical trauma and green reparations in Berlin and Detroit', *Cities*, 93(June), pp 153–63. Available at: https://doi.org/10.1016/j.cities.2019.05.002.

Edensor, T. (2010) 'Walking in rhythms: Place, regulation, style and the flow of experience', *Visual Studies*, 25(1), pp 69–79. Available at: https://doi.org/10.1080/14725861003606902.

Egerer, M. and Fairbairn, M. (2018) 'Gated gardens: Effects of urbanization on community formation and commons management in community gardens', *Geoforum*, 96, pp 61–9. Available at: https://doi.org/10.1016/j.geoforum.2018.07.014.

Eizenberg, E. (2012) 'Actually existing commons: Three moments of space of community gardens in New York City', *Antipode*, 44(3), pp 764–82. Available at: https://doi.org/10.1111/j.1467-8330.2011.00892.x.

Eizenberg, E. (2016) *From the Ground Up: Community Gardens in New York City and the Politics of Spatial Transformation*. London: Routledge.

Elias, N. and Scotston, J.L. (1965) *The Established and the Outsiders: A Sociological Enquiry into Community Problems*. London: F. Cass.

Ellison, N. (2013) 'Citizenship, space and time: Engagement, identity and belonging in a connected world', *Thesis Eleven*, 118(1), pp 48–63. Available at: https://doi.org/10.1177/0725513613500271.

Erickson, I. and Mazmanian, M. (2016) 'Bending time to a new end: Investigating the idea of temporal entrepreneurship', in J. Wajcman and N. Dodd (eds) *The Sociology of Speed: Digital, Organizational, and Social Temporalities*. Oxford: Oxford University Press, pp 152–68.

Esposito, R. (2010) *Communitas: The Origin and Destiny of Community*. Edited and translated by T. Campbell. Stanford: Stanford University Press.

FCFCG (2016) 'Benefits of community growing, green spaces and outdoor education'. Federation of City Farms and Community Gardens. Available at: https://www.farmgarden.org.uk/sites/farmgarden.org.uk/files/benefits-community-growing-research-and-evidence.pdf.

Featherstone, D., Ince, A., Mackinnon, D., Strauss, K. and Cumbers, A. (2012) 'Progressive localism and the construction of political alternatives', *Transactions of the Institute of British Geographers*, 37(2), pp 177–82. Available at: https://doi.org/10.1111/j.1475-5661.2011.00493.x.

Ferris, J., Norman, C. and Sempik, J. (2001) 'People, land and sustainability: Community gardens and the social dimension of sustainable development', *Social Policy and Administration*, 35(5), pp 559–68.

Firth, C., Maye, D. and Pearson, D. (2011) 'Developing "community" in community gardens', *Local Environment: The International Journal of Justice and Sustainability*, 16(6), pp 555–68. Available at: https://doi.org/10.1080/13549839.2011.586025.

Franklin, A. (2010) *City Life*. London: SAGE.

Fraser, A. (2013) 'Street habitus: Gangs, territorialism and social change in Glasgow', *Journal of Youth Studies*, 16(8), pp 970–85. Available at: https://doi.org/10.1080/13676261.2013.793791.

Fraser, E. (2018) 'Unbecoming place: Urban imaginaries in transition in Detroit', *Cultural Geographies*, 25(3), pp 441–58. Available at: https://doi.org/10.1177/1474474017748508.

Fraser, N. (2008) *Scales of Justice: Reimagining Political Space in a Globalizing World*. Cambridge: Polity Press.

Garcia-Lamarca, M., Anguelovski, I., Cole, H., Connolly, J.J.T., Argüelles, L., Baró, F., et al (2021) 'Urban green boosterism and city affordability: For whom is the "branded" green city?', *Urban Studies*, 58(1), pp 90–112. Available at: https://doi.org/10.1177/0042098019885330.

GCFN (2021) *Glasgow, Tackling Food Poverty with a City Plan-Pathways to a Just Recovery*. Glasgow: Glasgow Community Food Network.

Gerstel, N. (2000) 'The third shift: Gender and care work outside the home', *Qualitative Sociology*, 23, pp 467–83.

Ghose, R. and Pettygrove, M. (2014) 'Urban community gardens as spaces of citizenship', 46(4), pp 1092–112. Available at: https://doi.org/10.1111/anti.12077.

Gibson-Graham, J.K. (1996) *The End of Capitalism (as We Knew It): A Feminist Critique of Political Economy*. Oxford: Blackwell.

Gibson-Graham, J.K. (2008) 'Diverse economies: Performative practices for "other worlds"', *Progress in Human Geography*, 32(5), pp 613–32. Available at: https://doi.org/10.1177/0309132508090821.

Ginn, F. (2016) *Domestic Wild: Memory, Nature and Gardening in Suburbia*. London: Routledge.

Ginn, F. and Ascensão, E. (2018) 'Autonomy, erasure, and persistence in the urban gardening commons', *Antipode*, 50(4), pp 929–52. Available at: https://doi.org/10.1111/anti.12398.

Glasgow City Council (nd) 'Stalled spaces application'. Available at: https://glasgow.gov.uk/index.aspx?articleid=17954.

Glasgow City Council (2019) 'Glasgow continues trend of regenerating vacant and derelict land sites', September. Available at: https://www.glasgow.gov.uk/article/24941/Glasgow-continues-trend-of-regenerating-vacant-and-derelict-land-sites.

Glasgow City Food Plan (2021) Available at: http://goodfoodforall.co.uk/home/glasgow-city-food-plan.

Glover, T.D. (2004) 'Social capital in the lived experiences of community gardeners', *Leisure Sciences*, 26, pp 143–62. Available at: https://doi.org/10.1080/01490400490432064.

Goffman, E. (1975) *Frame Analysis*. Harmondsworth: Penguin.

GOV.UK (nd) *National Minimum Wage and National Living Wage Rates*. Available at: https://www.gov.uk/national-minimum-wage-rates.

Graziano, V., Cangiano, S., Fragnito, M. and Romano, Z. (2020) 'Pirate care: How do we imagine the health care for the future we want?' *Medium*. Available at: https://medium.com/dsi4eu/pirate-care-how-do-we-imagine-the-health-care-for-the-future-we-want-fa7f71a7a21.

Green, M. and Lawson, V. (2011) 'Recentring care: Interrogating the commodification of care', *Social and Cultural Geography*, 12(6), pp 639–54. Available at: https://doi.org/10.1080/14649365.2011.601262.

Hall, S. (2011) 'The neo-liberal revolution', *Cultural Studies*, 25(6), pp 705–28.

Hall, S.M. (2011) 'Exploring the "ethical everyday": An ethnography of the ethics of family consumption', *Geoforum*, 42(6), pp 627–37. Available at: https://doi.org/10.1016/j.geoforum.2011.06.009.

Hall, S.M. (2013) 'Super-diverse street: A "trans-ethnography" across migrant localities', *Ethnic and Racial Studies*, 38(1), pp 1–14.

Hanmer, O. (2021) *Retirement and the Everyday Politics of Commoning in Urban Gardens*. PhD Thesis. Cardiff University.

Hardin, G. (1968) 'The tragedy of the commons', *Science*, 162(June), pp 1243–8. Available at: https://doi.org/10.1126/science.162.3859.1243.

Harris, A. (2012) 'Art and gentrification: Pursuing the urban pastoral in Hoxton, London', *Transactions of the Institute of British Geographers*, 37(2), pp 226–41. Available at: https://doi.org/10.1111/j.1475-5661.2011.00465.x.

Harvey, D. (2003) 'The right to the city', *International Journal of Urban and Regional Research*, 27(4), pp 939–41. Available at: https://doi.org/10.1111/1468-2427.00257.

Harvey, D. (2007) 'Neoliberalism as creative destruction', *The Annals of the American Academy of Political and Social Science*, 610, pp 21–44. Available at: https://doi.org/10.1177/0002716206296780.

Hensby, A. (2017) 'Open networks and secret Facebook groups: Exploring cycle effects on activists' social media use in the 2010/11 UK student protests', *Social Movement Studies*, 16(4), pp 466–78. Available at: https://doi.org/10.1080/14742837.2016.1201421.

Herd, C. (2021) *Urban Nature Glasgow: Map*. London: Urban Good CIC.

Herman, A. (2021) 'Governing Fairtrade: Ethics of care and justice in the Argentinean wine industry', *Social & Cultural Geography*, 22(3), pp 425–46. Available at: https://doi.org/10.1080/14649365.2019.1593493.

Hobart, H.J.K. and Kneese, T. (2020) 'Radical care: Survival strategies for uncertain times', *Social Text*, 38(1), pp 1–16. Available at: https://doi.org/10.1215/01642472-7971067.

Hodgkinson, T. (2005) 'Digging for anarchy', in N. Kingsbury and T. Richardson (eds) *Vista: The Culture and Politics of Gardens*. London: Francis Lincoln, pp 66–73.

Holloway, J. (2002) *Change the World without Taking Power: The Meaning of Revolution Today*. London: Pluto Press.

Holloway, J. (2010) *Crack Capitalism*. London: Pluto Press.

Honoré, C. (2004) *In Praise of Slow*. London: Orion.

Hoskins, G. and Tallon, A. (2004) 'Promoting the "urban idyll": Policies for city centre living', in C. Johnstone and M. Whitehead (eds) *New Horizons in British Urban Policy: Perspectives on New Labour's Urban Renaissance*. Aldershot: Ashgate, pp 25–40.

Ingold, T. (2014) 'That's enough about ethnography!', *HAU: Journal of Ethnographic Theory*, 4(1), p 383. Available at: https://doi.org/10.14318/hau4.1.021.

Iveson, K. (2013) 'Cities within the city: Do-it-yourself urbanism and the right to the city'. *International Journal of Urban and Regional Research*, 37(3), pp 941–56.

Jackson, E.K. (2017) 'Damned if you do ... banal gendered exclusions in academia, babies and "dinner with other candidates"'. *The Sociological Review blog*. Available at: https://www.thesociologicalreview.com/blog/damned-if-you-do-banal-gendered-exclusions-in-academia-babies-and-the-dinner-with-the-other-candidates.html.

Jafri, A., Mathe, N., Aglago, E.K., Konyole, S.O., Ouedraogo, M., Audain, K., et al (2021) 'Food availability, accessibility and dietary practices during the COVID-19 pandemic: A multi-country survey', *Public Health Nutrition*, 24(7), pp 1798–805. Available at: https://doi.org/10.1017/S1368980021000987.

Jerolmack, C. and Khan, S. (2014) 'Talk is cheap: Ethnography and the attitudinal fallacy', *Sociological Methods and Research*, 43(2), pp 178–209.

Jones, A. (2013) 'A tripartite conceptualisation of urban public space as a site for play: Evidence from South Bank, London', *Urban Geography*, 34(8), pp 1144–70. Available at: https://doi.org/10.1080/02723638.2013.784081.

Jorgensen, A. (2011) 'Introduction', in A. Jorgensen and R. Keenan (eds) *Urban Wildscapes*. London: Routledge, pp 1–14.

Kamvasinou, K. (2017) 'Temporary intervention and long-term legacy: Lessons from London case studies', *Journal of Urban Design*, 22(2), pp 187–207. Available at: https://doi.org/10.1080/13574809.2015.1071654.

Kanosvamhira, T.P. and Tevera, D. (2022) 'Urban community gardens in Cape Town, South Africa: Navigating land access and land tenure security', *GeoJournal* [Preprint]. Available at: https://doi.org/10.1007/s10708-022-10793-3.

Keep Scotland Beautiful (nd) 'What can the CCF fund?' Available at: http://www.keepscotlandbeautiful.org/sustainability-climate-change/climate-challenge-fund/applying-for-ccf-funding/ccf-grants/what-can-the-ccf-fund/.

Kintrea, K. and Madgin, R. (eds) (2019) *Transforming Glasgow*. Bristol: Policy Press. Available at: https://doi.org/10.2307/j.ctvt6rk5x.

Klinenberg, E. (2019) *Palaces for the People: How Social Infrastructure can Help Fight Inequality, Polarization, and the Decline of Civic Life*. London: Penguin.

Kurtz, H. (2001) 'Differentiating multiple meanings of garden and community', *Urban Geography*, 22(7), pp 656–70. Available at: https://doi.org/10.2747/0272-3638.22.7.656.

Langegger, S. (2013) 'Emergent public space: Sustaining Chicano culture in North Denver', *Cities*, 35, pp 26–32.

Lawler, S. (2012) 'White like them: Whiteness and anachronistic space in representations of the English white working class', *Ethnicities*, 12(4), pp 409–26. Available at: https://doi.org/10.1177/1468796812448019.

Lawson, L. and Kearns, A. (2014) 'Rethinking the purpose of community empowerment in neighbourhood regeneration: The need for policy clarity', *Local Economy*, 29(1–2), pp 65–81. Available at: https://doi.org/10.1177/0269094213519307 .

Lefebvre, H. (1991) *The Production of Space*. Edited by D. Nicholson-Smith. Oxford: Blackwell. Available at: https://doi.org/10.1027/1618-3169/a000129.

Lefebvre, H. (1996) *Writings on Cities*. Edited and translated by E. Kofman and E. Lebas. Cambridge, MA: Blackwell.

Lefebvre, H. (2004) *Rhythmanalysis: Space, Time and Everyday Life*. London: Bloomsbury.

Leith, M.S. (2012) 'The view from above: Scottish national identity as an elite concept', *National Identities*, 14(1), pp 39–51. Available at: https://doi.org/10.1080/14608944.2012.657081.

Linebaugh, P. (2010) 'Enclosures from the bottom up', *Radical History Review*, 108, pp 11–27. Available at: https://doi.org/10.1215/01636545-2010-007.

Littler, J. (2011) 'What's wrong with ethical consumption?', in T. Lewis and E. Potter (eds) *Ethical Consumption: A Critical Introduction*. London: Routledge, pp 27–39.

Loopstra, R. (2020) *Vulnerability to Food Insecurity since the COVID-19 Lockdown: Preliminary Report*. Available at: https://foodfoundation.org.uk/publication/vulnerability-food-insecurity-covid-19-lockdown.

Loughran, K. (2014) 'Parks for profit: The high line, growth machines, and the uneven development of urban public spaces', *City and Community*, 13(1), pp 49–68. Available at: https://doi.org/10.1111/cico.12050.

Loukaitou-Sideris, A. (1996) 'Cracks in the city: Addressing the constraints and potentials of urban design', *Journal of Urban Design*, 1(1), pp 91–103. Available at: https://doi.org/10.1080/13574809608724372.

Lyon, D. (2016) 'Doing audio-visual montage to explore time and space: The everyday rhythms of Billingsgate Fish Market', *Sociological Research Online*, 21(3), pp 1–12. Available at: https://doi.org/10.5153/sro.3994.

Maantay, J. (2013) 'The collapse of place: Derelict land, deprivation, and health inequality in Glasgow, Scotland', *Cities and the Environment*, 6(1), pp 1–52.

Mabon, L. and Shih, W.Y. (2018) 'What might "just green enough" urban development mean in the context of climate change adaptation? The case of urban greenspace planning in Taipei Metropolis, Taiwan', *World Development*, 107, pp 224–38. Available at: https://doi.org/10.1016/j.worlddev.2018.02.035.

Macleod, G. (2012) 'From urban entrepreneurialism to a "revanchist city"? On the spatial injustices of Glasgow's renaissance', in N. Brenner and N. Theodore (eds) *Spaces of Neoliberalism: Urban Restructuring in North America and Western Europe*. Oxford: Blackwell, pp 254–76. Available at: https://doi.org/10.1002/9781444397499.ch11.

Madden, D.J. (2017) 'Pushed off the map: Toponymy and the politics of place in New York City', *Urban Studies*, 55(8), pp 1–16. Available at: https://doi.org/10.1177/0042098017700588.

Martinez, M. (2009) 'Attack of the butterfly spirits: The impact of movement framing by community garden preservation activists', 8(4), pp 323–39. Available at: https://doi.org/10.1080/14742830903234213.

Massey, D. (1994) *Space, Place, and Gender*. Minneapolis: University of Minnesota Press. Available at: http://www.jstor.org/stable/10.5749/j.cttttw2z.

Masud-All-Kamal, M. and Nursey-Bray, M. (2021) 'Socially just community-based climate change adaptation? Insights from Bangladesh', *Local Environment*, 26(9), pp 1092–108. Available at: https://doi.org/10.1080/13549839.2021.1962829.

Matejowsky, T. (2013) 'Backyard and community gardening in the urban Philippines', *Locale: The Australasian-Pacific Journal of Regional Food Studies*, 3, pp 29–50.

McCarthy, J.D., Britt, D.W. and Wolfson, M. (1991) 'The institutional channeling of social movements by the state in the United States', *Research in Social Movements, Conflicts and Change*, 14, pp 45–76.

McClintock, N. (2014) 'Radical, reformist, and garden-variety neoliberal: Coming to terms with urban agriculture's contradictions', *Local Environment*, 19(2), pp 147–71. Available at: https://doi.org/10.1080/13549839.2012.752797.

McCrone, D. (2001) *Understanding Scotland: The Sociology of a Nation*. 2nd edn. London: Routledge.

McKay, G. (2011) *Radical Gardening: Politics, Idealism and Rebellion in the Garden*. London: Francis Lincoln.

Miraftab, F. (2009) 'Insurgent planning: Situating radical planning in the global south', *Planning Theory*, 8(1), pp 32–50. Available at: https://doi.org/10.1177/1473095208099297.

Moffatt, S., Brown, J., Sowden, S., Patterson, R.A., Holding, E., Dennison, A., et al (2014) 'Public health implications of UK welfare reform: Qualitative research in a North East England community: Suzanne Moffatt', *European Journal of Public Health*, 24(suppl_2). Available at: https://doi.org/10.1093/eurpub/cku161.083.

Mooney, G. (2004) 'Cultural policy as urban transformation? Critical reflections on Glasgow, European city of culture 1990', *Local Economy*, 19(4), pp 327–40. Available at: https://doi.org/10.1080/0269094042000286837.

Morris, A.D. and Staggenborg, S. (2004) 'Leadership in social movements', in D.A. Snow, S.A. Soule and H. Kriesi (eds) *Blackwell Companion to Social Movements*. Oxford: Blackwell, pp 171–96.

Mould, O., Badger, A., Cole, J. and Brown, P. (2022) 'Mutual aid: Can community fridges bring anarchist politics to the mainstream?', *The Conversation*. Available at: https://theconversation.com/mutual-aid-can-community-fridges-bring-anarchist-politics-to-the-mainstream-174491.

Mulligan, M. (2015) 'On ambivalence and hope in the restless search for community: How to work with the idea of community in the global age', *Sociology*, 49(2), pp 340–55. Available at: https://doi.org/10.1177/0038038514534008.

Nancy, J.-L. (1991) *The Inoperative Community*. Minneapolis: University of Minnesota Press.

National Records of Scotland (2014) 2011 Census data. Available at: www.scotlandscensus.gov.uk/.

Neal, S., Bennett, K., Cochrane, A. and Mohan, G. (2018) 'Community and conviviality? Informal social life in multicultural places', *Sociology*, pp 1–26. Available at: https://doi.org/10.1177/0038038518763518.

Németh, J. and Langhorst, J. (2014) 'Rethinking urban transformation: Temporary uses for vacant land', *Cities*, 40, pp 143–50. Available at: https://doi.org/10.1016/j.cities.2013.04.007.

Neo, H. and Chua, C.Y. (2017) 'Beyond inclusion and exclusion: Community gardens as spaces of responsibility', *Annals of the American Association of Geographers*, 107(3), pp 666–81. Available at: https://doi.org/10.1080/24694452.2016.1261687.

Nettle, C. (2014) *Community Gardens as Social Action*. Farnham: Ashgate.

Olin Wright, E. (2015) 'How to be an anti-capitalist today', *Jacobin*, February. Available at: https://www.jacobinmag.com/2015/12/erik-olin-wright-real-utopias-anticapitalism-democracy/

Oliver, M. and Barnes, C. (2010) 'Disability studies, disabled people and the struggle for inclusion', *British Journal of Sociology of Education*, 31(5), pp 547–60. Available at: https://doi.org/10.1080/01425692.2010.500088.

Oncini, F. (2021) 'Food support provision in COVID-19 times: A mixed method study based in Greater Manchester', *Agriculture and Human Values*, 38(4), pp 1201–13. Available at: https://doi.org/10.1007/s10 460-021-10212-2.

Osterman, P. (2006) 'Overcoming oligarchy: Culture and agency in social movement organizations', *Administrative Science Quarterly*, 51(4), pp 622–49. Available at: https://doi.org/10.2189/asqu.51.4.622.

Ostrom, E. (1990) *Governing the Commons: The Evolution of Institutions for Collective Action*. Cambridge: Cambridge University Press.

Osuteye, E., Koroma, B., Macarthy, J.M., Kamara, S.F. and Conteh, A. (2021) 'Fighting COVID-19 in Freetown, Sierra Leone: The critical role of community organisations in a growing pandemic', *Open Health*, 1(1), pp 51–63. Available at: https://doi.org/10.1515/openhe-2020-0005.

Paddeu, F. (2017) 'Demystifying urban agriculture in Detroit', *Metropolitics*, pp 1–8.

Paddison, R. (2002) 'From unified local government to decentred local governance: The "institutional turn" in Glasgow', *GeoJournal*, pp 11–21. Available at: https://doi.org/10.1023/B:GEJO.0000006566.14616.87.

Pánek, J., Glass, M.R. and Marek, L. (2020) 'Evaluating a gentrifying neighborhood's changing sense of place using participatory mapping', *Cities*, 102. Available at: https://doi.org/10.1016/j.cities.2020.102723.

Parkins, W. (2004) 'Out of time', *Time & Society*, 13(2–3), pp 363–82. Available at: https://doi.org/10.1177/0961463X04045662.

Paton, K. (2014) *Gentrification: A Working-class Perspective*. Aldershot: Ashgate.

Paton, K., Mooney, G. and Mckee, K. (2012) 'Class, citizenship and regeneration: Glasgow and the Commonwealth Games 2014', *Antipode*, 44(4), pp 1470–89. Available at: https://doi.org/10.1111/j.1467-8330.2011.00966.x.

Paton, K., Mccall, V. and Mooney, G. (2016) 'Place revisited: Class, stigma and urban restructuring in the case of Glasgow's Commonwealth Games', *Sociological Review*, 65(4), pp 578–94. Available at: https://doi.org/10.1111/1467-954X.12423.

Payne, G. and Grew, C. (2005) 'Unpacking "class ambivalence"', *Sociology*, 39(5), pp 893–910. Available at: https://doi.org/10.1177/003803850 5058371.

Peck, J. and Tickell, A. (2002) 'Neoliberalizing space', *Antipode*, 34(3), pp 380–404. Available at: https://doi.org/10.1111/1467-8330.00247.

Peck, J. and Whiteside, H. (2016) 'Financializing Detroit', *Economic Geography*, 92(3), pp 235–68. Available at: https://doi.org/10.1080/00130 095.2015.1116369.

Peck, J., Theodore, N. and Brenner, N. (2009) 'Neoliberal urbanism: Models, moments, mutations', *SAIS Review of International Affairs*, 29(1), pp 49–66. Available at: https://doi.org/10.1353/sais.0.0028.

Pitt, H. (2014) 'Therapeutic experiences of community gardens: Putting flow in its place', *Health and Place*, 27, pp 84–91.

Polletta, F. (1998) 'Contending stories: Narrative in social movements', *Qualitative Sociology*, 21(4), pp 419–46.

Power, M., Doherty, B., Pybus, K.J. and Pickett, K.E. (2020) 'How COVID-19 has exposed inequalities in the UK food system: The case of UK food and poverty', *Emerald Open Research*, 2, p 11. Available at: https://doi.org/10.35241/emeraldopenres.13539.2.

Prior, N. (2009) *The Slug and the Juggernaut? Museums, Cities, Rhythms.* Edinburgh University Working Paper, No. 38. Edinburgh.

Pudup, M.B. (2008) 'It takes a garden: Cultivating citizen-subjects in organized garden projects', *Geoforum*, 39, pp 1228–40. Available at: https://doi.org/10.1016/j.geoforum.2007.06.012.

Purcell, M. (2006) 'Urban democracy and the local trap', *Urban Studies*, 43(11), pp 1921–41. Available at: https://doi.org/10.1080/00420980600897826.

Rancière, J. (1999) *Disagreement*. Minneapolis: University of Minnesota Press.

Raneng, J., Howes, M. and Pickering, C.M. (2023) 'Current and future directions in research on community gardens', *Urban Forestry and Urban Greening*, 79, 127814. Available at: https://doi.org/10.1016/j.ufug.2022.127814.

Ray, K., Savage, M., Tampubolon, G., Warde, A., Longhurst, B and Tomlinson, M. (2003) 'The exclusiveness of the political field: Networks and political mobilization', *Social Movement Studies*, 2(1), pp 37–41.

Rigolon, A. and Németh, J. (2020) 'Green gentrification or "just green enough": Do park location, size and function affect whether a place gentrifies or not?', *Urban Studies*, 57(2), pp 402–20. Available at: https://doi.org/10.1177/0042098019849380.

Robertson Trust (nd) *How to Apply*. Available at: http://www.therobertsontrust.org.uk/how-to-apply/levels-of-funding.

Rogaly, B. (2016) '"Don't show the play at the football ground, nobody will come": The micro-sociality of co-produced research in an English provincial city', *Sociological Review*, 64(4), pp 657–80. Available at: https://doi.org/10.1111/1467-954X.12371.

Rosa, H. (2003) 'Social acceleration: Ethical and political consequences of a desynchronized high-speed society', *Constellations*, 10(1), pp 1–33.

Rosa, H. (2005) 'The speed of global flows and the pace of democratic politics', *New Political Science*, 27(4), pp 445–59. Available at: https://doi.org/10.1080/07393140500370907.

Rosol, M. (2010) 'Public participation in post-Fordist urban green space governance: The case of community gardens in Berlin', *International Journal of Urban and Regional Research*, 34(3), pp 548–63. Available at: https://doi.org/10.1111/j.1468-2427.2010.00968.x.

Rosol, M. (2012) 'Community volunteering as neoliberal strategy? Green space production in Berlin', *Antipode*, 44(1), pp 239–57. Available at: https://doi.org/10.1111/j.1467-8330.2011.00861.x.

Rough Guides (2014) *Friendliest Cities in the World*. Available at: https://www.roughguides.com/gallery/the-worlds-friendliest-cities-as-voted-by-you/#/15.

Safransky, S. (2014) 'Greening the urban frontier: Race, property, and resettlement in Detroit', *Geoforum*, 56, pp 237–48. Available at: https://doi.org/10.1016/j.geoforum.2014.06.003.

Saguin, K. (2020) 'Cultivating beneficiary citizenship in urban community gardens in Metro Manila', *Urban Studies*, 57(16), pp 3315–30. Available at: https://doi.org/10.1177/0042098019897035.

Samanani, F. (2022) 'Convivality and its others: For a plural politics of living with difference', *Journal of Ethnic and Migration Studies*, 49(9), pp 2109–28. Available at: https://doi.org/10.1080/1369183X.2022.2050190.

Savage, M., Bagnall, G. and Longhurst, B. (2001) 'Ordinary, ambivalent and defensive: Class identities in the northwest of England', *Sociology*, 35(4), pp 875–92.

Sayer, A. (2002) 'What are you worth? Why class is an embarrassing subject', *Sociological Research Online*, 7(3).

Sayer, A. (2005) 'Class, moral worth and recognition', *Sociology*, 39(5), pp 947–63. Available at: https://doi.org/10.1177/0038038505058376.

Schmelzkopf, K. (1995) 'Urban community gardens as contested space', *American Geographical Society*, 85(3), pp 364–81. Available at: https://doi.org/10.1038/126199a0.

Schmelzkopf, K. (2002) 'Incommensurability, land use, and the right to space: Community gardens in New York City', *Urban Geography*, 23(4), pp 323–43. Available at: https://doi.org/10.2747/0272-3638.23.4.323.

Scott, J.C. (1998) *Seeing Like a State: How Certain Schemes to Improve the Human Condition have Failed*. New Haven and London: Yale University Press.

Scottish Index of Multiple Deprivation (2016) Available at: http://statistics.gov.scot/.

Sempik, J., Aldridge, J. and Becker, S. (2005) *Growing Together*. Bristol: Policy Press.

Sharma, S. (2014) *In the Meantime: Temporality and Cultural Politics*. Durham, NC: Duke University Press. Available at: https://doi.org/10.2307/j.ctv11cw801.

Sharma, S. (2016) 'Speed traps and the temporal: Of taxis, truck stops, and TaskRabbits', in J. Wajcman and N. Dodd (eds) *The Sociology of Speed: Digital, Organizational, and Social Temporalities*. Oxford: Oxford University Press, pp 131–51. Available at: https://doi.org/10.1093/acprof.

Skeggs, B. (2014) 'Values beyond value? Is anything beyond the logic of capital?', *British Journal of Sociology*, 65(1), pp 1–20. Available at: https://doi.org/10.1111/1468-4446.12072.

Smith, M. and Harvey, J. (2021) 'Social eating initiatives and the practices of commensality', *Appetite*, 161. Available at: https://doi.org/10.1016/j.appet.2021.105107.

Solnit, R. (2014) *Men Explain Things To Me*. Chicago: Haymarket Books.

Soule, D.P.J., Leith, M.S. and Steven, M. (2012) 'Scottish devolution and national identity', *National Identities*, 14(1), pp 1–10. Available at: https://doi.org/10.1080/14608944.2012.657085.

Southerton, D. (2009) 'Re-ordering temporal rhythms: Co-ordinating daily practices in Britain 1937 and 2000', in E. Shove, F. Trentmann and R. Wilk (eds) *Time, Consumption and Everyday Life: Practice, Materiality and Culture*. Oxford: Berg, pp 49–63.

Spataro, D. (2015) 'Against a de-politicized DIY urbanism: Food Not Bombs and the struggle over public space', *Journal of Urbanism: International Research on Placemaking and Urban Sustainability*, 9(2), pp 185–201. Available at: https://doi.org/10.1080/17549175.2015.1056208.

Spinney, J. (2010) 'Performing resistance? Re-reading practices of urban cycling on London's South Bank', *Environment and Planning A*, 42(12), pp 2914–37. Available at: https://doi.org/10.1068/a43149.

Springer, S. (2020) 'Caring geographies: The COVID-19 interregnum and a return to mutual aid', *Dialogues in Human Geography*, 10(2), pp 112–15. Available at: https://doi.org/10.1177/2043820620931277.

Standing, G. (2017) *Basic Income: And How We Can Make It Happen*. London: Pelican.

Stavrides, S. (2016) *Common Space: The City as Commons*. London: Zed Books.

St Clair, R., Hardman, M., Armitage, R.P. and Sherriff, G. (2018) 'The trouble with temporary: Impacts and pitfalls of a meanwhile community garden in Wythenshawe, South Manchester', *Renewable Agriculture and Food Systems*, 33(6), pp 548–57. Available at: https://doi.org/10.1017/S1742170517000291.

St Clair, R., Hardman, M., Armitage, R.P. and Sherriff, G. (2020) 'Urban agriculture in shared spaces: The difficulties with collaboration in an age of austerity', *Urban Studies*, 57(2), pp 350–65. Available at: https://doi.org/10.1177/0042098019832486.

Strong, S. (2020) 'Food banks, actually existing austerity and the localisation of responsibility', *Geoforum*, 110, pp 211–19. Available at: https://doi.org/10.1016/j.geoforum.2018.09.025.

Studdert, D. (2016) 'Sociality and a proposed analytic for investigating communal being-ness', *Sociological Review*, 64(4), pp 622–38. Available at: https://doi.org/10.1111/1467-954X.12430.

Studdert, D. and Walkerdine, V. (2016a) 'Being in community: Re-visioning Sociology', *Sociological Review*, 64(4), pp 613–21. Available at: https://doi.org/10.1111/1467-954X.12429.

Studdert, D. and Walkerdine, V. (2016b) *Rethinking Community Research: Interrelationality, Communal Being and Commonality*. Basingstoke: Palgrave Macmillan. Available at: https://doi.org/10.1057/978-1-137-51453-0.

Sullivan, O. and Gershunny, J. (2018) 'Speed-up Society? Evidence from the UK 2000 and 2015 time use diary surveys', *Sociology*, 52(1), pp 20–38.

Sultana, F. (2007) 'Reflexivity, positionality and participatory ethics: Negotiating fieldwork dilemmas in international research', *ACME*, 6(3), pp 374–85. Available at: https://doi.org/10.1016/j.ijedudev.2008.02.004.

Swann, R. and Hughes, G. (2016) 'Exploring micro-sociality through the lens of "established-outsider" figurational dynamics in a South Wales community', *The Sociological Review*, 64(4), pp 681–98.

Tan, L.H.H. and Neo, H. (2009) '"Community in Bloom": Local participation of community gardens in urban Singapore', *Local Environment: The International Journal of Justice and Sustainability*, 14(6), pp 529–39. Available at: https://doi.org/10.1080/13549830902904060.

Thrift, N. (1997a) 'The rise of soft capitalism', *Cultural Values*, 1(3), pp 29–57. Available at: https://doi.org/10.1080/14797589709367133.

Thrift, N. (1997b) 'The still point: Resistance, expressive embodiment and dance', in S. Pile and M. Keith (eds) *Geographies of Resistance*. London: Routledge, pp 124–51.

Tonkiss, F. (2013) 'Austerity urbanism and the makeshift city', *City*, 17(3), pp 312–24. Available at: https://doi.org/10.1080/13604813.2013.795332.

Traill, H. (2021) 'The idea of community and its practice: Tensions, disruptions and hope in Glasgow's urban growing projects', *Sociological Review*, 69(2), pp 484–99. Available at: https://doi.org/10.1177/00380 26120982272.

Traill, H. (2022) *'Addressing the Community Need': Exploring and Evaluating Woodlands Community Café and Neighbourhood Food Service*. Glasgow: WCDT.

Tronto, J. (1987) 'Beyond gender difference to a theory of care', *Signs*, 12(4), pp 644–63.

Tronto, J. (1993) *Moral Boundaries: A Political Argument for an Ethic of Care*. New York and London: Routledge.

Tronto, J. (2017) 'There is an alternative: Homines curans and the limits of neoliberalism', *International Journal of Care and Caring*, 1(1), pp 27–43. Available at: https://doi.org/10.1332/239788217X14866281687583.

Trussell Trust (2022) *End of Year Statistics 2021–22 Data Briefing*. London: Trussell Trust.

Tyler, I. (2013) *Revolting Subjects: Social Abjection and Resistance in Neoliberal Britain*. London: Zed Books.

Valle, G.R. (2021) 'Learning to be human again: Being and becoming in the home garden commons', *Environment and Planning E: Nature and Space*, 4(4), pp 1255–69. Available at: https://doi.org/10.1177/2514848620961943.

Voicu, I. and Been, V. (2008) 'The effect of community gardens on neighboring property values', *Real Estate Economics*, 36(2), pp 241–83.

von Benzon, N. (2017) 'Confessions of an inadequate researcher: Space and supervision in research with learning disabled children', *Social & Cultural Geography*, 18(7), pp 1039–58. Available at: https://doi.org/10.1080/14649365.2016.1257148.

Wajcman, J. and Dodd, N. (2016) 'The powerful are fast, the powerless are slow', in J. Wajcman and N. Dodd (eds) *The Sociology of Speed: Digital, Organizational, and Social Temporalities*. Oxford: Oxford University Press, pp 1–10.

Walker, S. (2016) 'Urban agriculture and the sustainability fix in Vancouver and Detroit', *Urban Geography*, 37(2), pp 163–82. Available at: https://doi.org/10.1080/02723638.2015.1056606.

Walkerdine, V. (2016) 'Affective history, working-class communities and self-determination', *Sociological Review*, 64(4), pp 699–714. Available at: https://doi.org/10.1111/1467-954X.12435.

Walkerdine, V. and Studdert, D. (2012) 'Concepts and meanings of community in the social sciences'. *AHRC Discussion Paper*. Available at: http://www.ahrc.ac.uk/documents/project-reports-and-reviews/connected-communities/concepts-and-meanings-of-community-in-the-social-sciences/.

Walkerdine, V. and Studdert, D. (2015) 'Community as micro – sociality and the new localism agenda'. AHRC Connecting Communities discussion paper.

Wallace, A. (2010) 'New neighbourhoods, new citizens? Challenging "community" as a framework for social and moral regeneration under new labour in the UK', *International Journal of Urban and Regional Research*, 34(4), pp 805–19. Available at: https://doi.org/10.1111/j.1468-2427.2009.00918.x.

Walsh, D., McCartney, G., Collins, C., Taulbut, M. and Batty, D. (2016) *History, Politics and Vulnerability: Explaining Excess Mortality in Scotland and Glasgow*. Glasgow: Glasgow Centre for Population Health.

Watt, P. (2009) 'Living in an Middle-class disaffiliation and selective belonging in an English suburb', *Environment and Planning A*, 41(12), pp 2874–92. Available at: https://doi.org/10.1068/a41120.

Weakley, S. (2021) 'Glasgow socio-economic indicators in the Covid-19 crisis: Drivers of poverty', in Glasgow Community Food Network (ed) *Glasgow, Tackling Food Poverty with a City Plan: Pathways to a Just Recovery*. Glasgow: Glasgow Community Food Network.

Weber, R. (2002) 'Extracting value from the city: Neoliberalism and urban redevelopment', *Antipode*, 34(3), pp 519–40. Available at: https://doi.org/10.1002/9781444397499.ch8.

Wheeler, S.M. and Rosan, C.D. (2021) *Reimagining Sustainable Cities: Strategies for Designing Greener, Healthier, More Equitable Communities*. Oakland: University of California Press.

Whyte, B. and Ajetunmobi, T. (2012) *Still 'the Sick Man of Europe'? Scottish Mortality in a European Context 1950–2010: An Analysis of Comparative Mortality Trends*. Glasgow: Glasgow Centre for Population Health Report.

Whyte, B., Young, M. and Timpson, K. (2021) *Health in a Changing City: Glasgow. A Study of Changes in Health, Demographic, Socioeconomic and Environmental Factors in Glasgow over the Last 20 Years*. Glasgow: Glasgow Centre for Population Health Report.

Williams, A., Goodwin, M. and Cloke, P. (2014) 'Neoliberalism, Big Society, and progressive localism', *Environment and Planning A*, 46, pp 2798–815. Available at: https://doi.org/10.1068/a130119p.

Williams, M.J. (2016) 'Justice and care in the city: Uncovering everyday practices through research volunteering', *Area*, 48(4), pp 513–20. Available at: https://doi.org/10.1111/area.12278.

Wilson, A.D. (2013) 'Beyond alternative: Exploring the potential for autonomous food spaces', *Antipode*, 45(3), pp 719–37. Available at: https://doi.org/10.1111/j.1467-8330.2012.01020.x.

Wolch, J.R., Byrne, J. and Newell, J.P. (2014) 'Urban green space, public health, and environmental justice: The challenge of making cities "just green enough"', *Landscape and Urban Planning*, 125, pp 234–44. Available at: https://doi.org/10.1016/j.landurbplan.2014.01.017.

Worldwatch Institute (2016) *Can a City be Sustainable?* Washington, DC: Island Press.

Young, I.M. (1990) *Justice and the Politics of Difference*. Princeton: Princeton University Press.

Index

A

acceleration hypothesis 41
activism
  anti-racist 51–2, 127
  'can do' spirit of 75, 108–9
  class and issue disparities in 21
  networks 23, 25, 26–7
  subjective politicization and 130–2
  threat levels motivating 116
aesthetics 87–9
alterity 48, 89–91, 124
Anderson, B. 4, 49, 91, 92, 102
anti-racist
  activism 51–2, 127
  library 136, 140–1
anti-social behaviour 59, 141
arrhythmia 45
austerity 19–20, 29–30, 157
  operating within state of 36–8
Australia 9, 28
autonomous space 32, 35, 38, 107
autonomy 38, 87, 88, 89, 107
  politics of alterity and 89–91
awareness-raising 130

B

Baltic Street Adventure Playground 148
"bams" 59, 60
bat boxes 80, 81, 122
benefits system 34, 35, 36–7, 38
Berlin, I. 95, 106, 107
Black Lives Matter 51–2, 138, 140
'blight' 22, 78
Blokland, T. 5, 6, 92, 94, 105, 139
BMX runs 81
boundary work 49–50, 56–7, 91, 149
  fragmentary boundaries 102–4
  in-group, out-group 100–2
  safe spaces 13
  see also inclusion
box schemes 51
Brown, Esther 136, 144

C

café *see* Woodlands Community Café
'can do' attitude 75, 87, 108–9
capitalism 10
  in cracks of 86–7, 90
  creative destruction 22, 78
  food systems 8, 128, 129
  resistance to 8, 36, 90
  spaces away from pressures of 38–41, 42, 47, 90, 106
  time pressures 41–2
care, practices of 78, 93–4, 142–3
  friendships and 97–100
  imagining community and 95–7
challenges, evolving 140–4
charitable status 121
Children's Wood committee 26, 27, 80, 123, 131
  attitude to council planning committee 134–5
  campaign lobbying tactics 131
  efforts at greater inclusion 60–2
  gap between some meadow users and culture of 62–3
  motivations for getting involved with 131–2
  transformational work with teenagers 141–2, 143
  universalist position on outdoors 63–5
  see also North Kelvin Meadow and Children's Wood
city
  -as-freedom 105
  reimagining 75–6, 76–7
  rhythm 41–3
  right to 4, 25–6, 28, 74–5, 88
City Properties 80
class 155–6
  community growing and 130
  meadow and 58–9, 155
    assumed universality of outdoors 63–5
    middle class and the other 59–63, 141–2
  and racial divide between Woodlands and local area 54–7
  talk 58

INDEX

climate action 113, 151
Climate Challenge Fund 112, 115, 159–60n2
collective escape 3–5, 141, 150
  positive freedom of 107
  into responsibility and care 93–109
  rhythms of 31–48
  those who get to escape 49–72
collective rhythm 47–8
'common justice' 132–5, 155
Common Knowledge UK 53
common ownership 79–86
  meadow 79–82, 85
  Woodlands 82–6
commons 74, 86–9, 95
  from commons to community 91–2
communal growing projects 3, 6–8
  around world 28–30
  awareness-raising 130
  contributing to social change 154–8
  flexibility of practice 129
  freedom of 81, 84–5, 105–6
  in Glasgow 23–4, 152
  increased support for 152–3
  justice 10–12
  'meanwhile use' 22–3
  neoliberalism and 9–10, 33, 111, 155
  North Kelvin Meadow and Children's Wood 27, 81–2
  over time 139–40, 151–3
  politics and 8–10, 16, 124, 125–6, 127–30, 150–1, 155
  politics of alterity and autonomy 89–91
  researching 14–18
  right to the city 74–5
  as sites of commoning 86–9
  taxonomies 6–7
  utopian element 12
  see also Woodlands Community Garden
communities of care 96
community
  as above politics 122–3, 133
  from commons to 91–2
  'within a community' 100–2
  cultivating 5–8
  derived from collective obligation 106, 107
  as an idea 6, 8, 94–5, 97, 130, 139, 154–5
  imagined 92, 95–7, 102, 156
  political focus on 6
  practising care 93–4, 95–7
Community Clean-Ups 113
Community Empowerment Act (Scotland) 2015 6, 30, 152
consumption, spaces away from 38–41
Cooper, D. 5, 86, 94
co-option 90, 111, 118, 119
  vs. radicalism 120, 156, 157
COVID-19 pandemic 4, 6, 139, 144–5, 151–2
  emergency food in 146–8

  impact in Glasgow 19–20
  meadow in 139, 142–3, 146, 147
  Woodlands in 139, 145, 146, 147, 149
criminal activity 59, 60
crises, emerging 144–6

D

derelict sites 18–19, 20–2, 78, 79
  narratives of dereliction 22
Detroit, Michigan 29
development
  community-led 25, 77
  as fixing problem spaces 77, 78
  housing 18–19, 21
  and narratives of dereliction 22
  sustainable 153
  WCDT and 76–7
development, North Kelvin Wood campaign to prevent site 26–7, 57–8, 90
  'can do' attitude 108–9, 134
  'common justice' rather than 'a political act' 132–5
  direct political action 115, 123, 131
  a mothers' campaign 65–8
  non-alignment policy 115, 121–4, 132, 134–5
  oppositional organizing 114–17, 118
  political parties' support for 122
  protest at meadow 116–17, 134
  public representation 66–7
  reimagining city 75–6
  signing of a 25 year lease 135, 143
  staking claim to history 73–5
  urgency vs. longevity in 46–7
development trust *see* Woodlands Community Development Trust (WCDT)
Development Trust Association Scotland 119, 123
disability, inclusion and 52–3
diversity 54–7
'DIY urbanism' 89
dog walkers 27, 31, 82, 103

E

eating together 99, 120, 141
educational programmes 50, 51, 53, 62, 82
employment, paid 35–6, 37
  escape from margins of 37–8
environmental movement 132, 140, 153
Esposito, R. 92, 94–5, 106
eurhythmia 43
Everard, Sarah 52, 136, 138, 140, 144
everyday utopias 5, 86, 94

F

families
  and motivation to become activists 131–2
  perception of privileged 58
  use of meadow 60, 62, 66, 70, 103, 132
  at Woodlands 70–1

female labour 65–8
financial situations, sensitivity to 35–6
food
  emergency food in pandemic 146–8
  insecurity 29, 120, 141, 145, 147
  networks in Glasgow 152
  organic 130, 136
  relationship to time 44–5
  systems, capitalist 8, 128, 129
  waste food 141
  see also Woodlands Community Café
food banks 145, 147–8
'foreign' gardeners 54
Fraser, N. 11, 12, 50, 72, 137
freedom
  city-as-freedom 105
  community gardens and sense of 81, 84–5, 105–6
  negative (freedom from) 106
  positive (freedom to) 95, 106–7
friendships 97–100
funders
  aligning with aims of 110–11, 118
  appeasing 112, 114, 115, 118, 136
  independence from 118, 119–20
funding
  meadow 115, 143
  WCDT 37, 110–14, 117, 118, 119, 120, 121, 143

G

G20 Youth Club 143, 146
  food deliveries 147, 148
  making a space for 141–2, 143
'garden babies' 70
gendered labour
  meadow 65–8
  Woodlands 68–71
gentrification 11, 22, 29, 77, 78, 79
Glasgow 5, 18–23
  abandoned space and derelict sites 18–19, 20–2, 78, 79
  anti-racist activism 127
  austerity 29–30
  community gardens 23–4, 152
  comparing with other countries 28–30
  as 'Dear Green Place' 18
  East End 18, 21
  friendliest city 126
  impact of COVID-19 pandemic in 19–20
  partisan history 126–7
  post-industrial context 5, 18, 29–30
  structural inequalities 19–20
  sustainability 11
  West End 14, 15, 20–1
Glasgow Botanical Gardens 93
Glasgow City Council
  City Properties 80
  decision to sell meadow 46, 47, 58

development of food plan 152
financial pressures 29–30
indictment of campaigners 81
lobbying 131, 132
negative views of 134
planning committee meadow site visit 134
public hearing on development planning application 66–7, 75
signs 25-year lease on meadow 135, 143
Stalled Spaces programme 21, 22, 79
Woodland's relationship with 114, 117–18, 135
Glasgow City Food Plan 152
Glasgow Community Food Network 23, 148, 152
Glasgow Food Growing Strategy 152
Glasgow Living Wage Employer scheme 37
Glasgow Old People's Welfare Association 50, 51
global South 28, 29
Goffman, E. 7, 95
'good enough' attitude 87–8
'grassroots' connections 50–1
Green Party 93, 121, 122
guerrilla gardening 8, 80, 121

H

Harvey, D. 9, 22, 32, 75, 88
Herd, C. 18
history, staking claim to 73–5
Holloway, J. 36, 38, 86, 89, 90, 91, 156
home-educators use of meadow 39
housing development 18–19, 21
  see also North Kelvin Meadow and Children's Wood, campaign to save

I

inclusion 4, 11, 50, 71, 129–30, 140, 150, 157
  disability and 52–3
  limits of 71–2
  at meadow 79–80
    efforts of Children's Wood committee 60–2
    'everybody's space' 48, 57–9
    middle class and the other 59–63, 141–2
  at Woodlands 38, 50–4
    limits of 54–7, 71
  see also boundary work
independence, maintaining 118–21
institutional channelling 111

J

justice 50, 140, 150–1
  'common' 132–5, 155
  common garden justice 10–12
  land use value and issues of 78–9
  and reimagining city 75–6
  responsibility and 105–7
  see also social justice

INDEX

K

knowing, patterns of 105

L

labour
  gendered 65–8, 68–71
  valued 32–5, 47
land use
  land value, land use value and 77–9
  legislation 30
Lefebvre, H. 4, 13–14, 25, 32, 43, 45, 47, 75, 150
legibility 76, 115, 119
legitimacy 76, 77, 119, 155
library, anti-racist 136, 140–1
littering 93–4
living wage 37
lobbying 115, 123, 131

M

Maryhill 21, 59–60
  efforts to include more people from 60–1
Maryhill Park 143, 146
masculinity, space for development of 67–8, 71
'meanwhile use' of space 22–3, 79
mental health, gardening as a positive impact on 42–3, 146
methodology 14–17
mosque, conflict with local 55
mothers as campaigners 65–8
murder
  of Esther Brown 144
  of Sarah Everard 52, 136, 138, 140, 144

N

Nancy, J.-L. 7, 94, 107
nature
  'Nurture in Nature' sessions 43
  reconnecting with 2, 18, 41, 42–3, 45–6, 146
negative freedom (freedom from) 106
Neighbourhood Food Service (NFS) 147, 148
neoliberalism 9, 78
  community gardening and 9–10, 33, 111, 155
neutrality, strategic 130, 156
  meadow campaign 115, 121–4, 132, 134–5
  WCDT 112, 113–14, 117–18
New York
  community gardens 28, 57, 76, 86, 116
  impact of High Line park 78
non-commodified spaces 38–41
non-profit status 121
North Kelvin Meadow and Children's Wood 1–2
  as above politics 122–3, 133

campaign to save 26–7, 57–8, 90
  'can do' attitude 108–9, 134
  'common justice' rather than 'a political act' 132–5
  direct political action 115, 123, 131
  a mothers' campaign 65–8
  non-alignment policy 115, 121–4, 132, 134–5
  oppositional organizing 114–17, 118
  political parties' support for 122
  protest at meadow 116–17, 134
  public representation 66–7
  reimagining city 75–6
  signing of a 25 year lease 135, 143
  staking claim to history 73–5
  and threat levels 115–17
  urgency vs. longevity in 46–7
commitment to social justice 129–30
community gardening 27, 81–2
contrasting Woodlands with 23–4, 104
in COVID-19 pandemic 139, 142–3, 146, 147
decommodified space 38–41
'a depressurizing chamber' 31
DIY aesthetic 87
'everybody's space' 48, 57–9
fragmentary boundaries 102–4
funding 115, 143
gendered labour 65–8
middle class and the other 59–63, 141–2
ownership 79–82, 85
politics of alterity and autonomy 90
practices of care 93–4, 95–7
responding to ecological overuse 143, 145–6
rhythm of 31, 41, 42, 48, 105–6
site 26–8
tensions between meadow and Children's Wood 82, 102–4, 116
transformational work 138, 141–3, 149, 151
value structure 64
see also Children's Wood committee
'Nurture in Nature' sessions 43

O

the other, middle class and 59–63, 141–2
outdoor culture, assumed universality of 63–5
ownership, common 79–86
  meadow 79–82, 85
  Woodlands 82–6

P

paid work 35–6, 37
  escape from margins of 37–8
parents 60–1, 62, 71, 102–3
  becoming activists 131–2
  on benefits of meadow 39–40

183

and 'garden babies' 70
mothers' campaign to save meadow 65–8
participation 119, 155
  gaps 51, 58
  and unwillingness to participate 62–3
partnerships 50–1
permaculture 45
political imagination
  interpretations, ambiguity and 125–7
  and moral ambivalence to politics 133–5
  variations in interpretations in community gardening 127–30
political non-alignment 130, 156
  meadow campaign 115, 121–4, 132, 134–5
  WCDT 112, 113–14, 117–18
politicization, subjective 130–2
politics
  of alterity and autonomy 89–91
  ambivalence towards 133–5
  communal growing projects and 8–10, 16, 124, 125–6, 127–30, 150–1, 155
  community as above 122–3, 133
  and oppositional organizing at meadow 114–17
  over time 135–8
  Scottish regional 122
  urban everyday 89
positionality, researcher 15, 16
positive freedom (freedom to) 95, 106–7
pregnant women 69–71

R

racial divide between Woodlands and local area 54–7
radical gardening 8, 10, 80, 124, 156
radicalism vs. co-option 120, 156, 157
raised beds
  in meadow 81–2
  at Woodlands 2, 36, 45, 82–4, 100–2
Rancière, J. 124, 156
Refuweegie 127
representation
  issues of 50–4, 155–6
  see also inclusion
researching community growing projects 14–17
responsibility
  and idea of community 94–5
  justice and 105–7
  practices of care and 93–4, 95–7
rhythm 2, 13–14
  alternative urban 31, 32, 38, 41–3
  collective 47–8
  differences between meadow and Woodlands 105–6
  as an heuristic 31–2
  planetary 44–5
right to the city 4, 25–6, 28, 74–5, 88
'right to urban life' 75
Robertson Trust 112

S

Scottish National Party (SNP) 122, 131
seasonality 13, 43–6
Singapore 28, 107
Slow movement 40, 41
slowness 13, 40, 41, 42, 43
social abjection 59
social change 130, 137, 140, 154–8
  see also transformational work
social justice 107, 150, 157
  commitment to 126, 127, 129–30
social movements
  difficulties of working with funders 136
  institutional channelling 111
  non-profit status 121
  social ties facilitating activism 132
  threat levels and 116
space 13
  abandoned 18–19, 20–2, 78, 79
  autonomous 32, 35, 38, 107
  decommodified 38–41
  illegible 22
  'meanwhile use' of 22–3, 79
Stalled Spaces programme 21, 22, 79
supermarkets 45
surplus, sharing 98–9
sustainability 4, 11, 153–4

T

teenagers *see* youths
threat, mobilization and levels of 116–18
time 13–14
  capitalist pressures of 41–2
  'circumscribed' 42
  communal growing projects over 139–40, 151–3
  interconnection of place and 32
  politics over 135–8
  relationship to food 44–5
  slowing down and speeding up of 40–1
  'thick' 13
  urgency vs. longevity in meadow 46–7
transformational work
  at meadow 138, 141–3, 149, 151
  at Woodlands 113, 136–8, 140–1, 151
Trussell Trust 145, 148

U

urban everyday politics 89
urban green space 11, 19, 21, 33
'urban idyll' 88–9
utopias, everyday 5, 86, 94

V

value
  alternative spaces of 32–5, 37, 38, 43, 47

INDEX

land use, land use value and land structures at meadow 77–9, 64
veganism 113, 137, 141
volunteering 33–5, 44, 52
  boundary between employment and 36
  gender and 68–9
  in-groups and out-groups 100–2
  valuing volunteers 88
vulnerability 52–3

W

welfare reforms 9, 36–7
West Princes Street 57, 77, 113, 121, 128
Whiteness, problem of 54, 57
wilderness and wildness 19
Women of Woodlands 136–7
Woodlands Community Café 51, 128, 147
  eating together 99, 120, 141
  funding 112–13, 148
  refusal to use waste food 141
  vegan food 137, 141
  volunteers 69
Woodlands Community Development Trust (WCDT) 24, 25, 37
  anti-racist library 136, 140–1
  board 51, 57
  funding 37, 110–14, 117, 118, 119, 120, 121, 143
  'grassroots' structure 51
  keeping private the difficulties with the council 117–18
  non-profit status 121
  as a recognized community 119, 120
  responses to field pressures 118–21
  staking a claim to city 76–7
  strategic neutrality 112, 113–14, 117–18
  transformational work 113, 136–8, 140–1, 151
  Workspace project 55, 114, 117
Woodlands Community Garden 2
  contrasting with North Kelvin meadow 23–4, 104
  in COVID-19 pandemic 139, 145, 146, 147, 149
  DIY aesthetic 87–8
  'foreign' gardeners 54
  freedom of the garden 84–5
  friendships 97–100
  gendered labour 68–71
  in-group, out-group 100–2
  inclusive practices 38, 50–4
    limits of 54–7, 71
  murder of Esther Brown 144
  outreach activities 50, 51, 53
  ownership 82–6
  paid employment 35–6, 37
  politics of alterity and autonomy 90
  racial and class divide between local area and 54–7
  raised beds 2, 36, 45, 82–4, 100–2
  rhythm of 2, 41, 42–3, 47–8, 106
  sharing surplus 98–9
  site 2, 24–6
  tensions with gardener of Algerian origin 56
  valued labour 32–5, 47
  volunteering 33–5, 88, 100–2
  working within austere state 36–8
work-programmes 34
Workspace project 55, 114, 117
world, community gardening around 28–30
Wyndford 40, 59, 138, 146, 147
  efforts to include more people from 60–1

Y

youths 47, 61, 85
  associations with criminality 59, 60
  invited into 'useful' activity 90
  making a space for 141–2, 143
  see also G20 Youth Club

www.ingramcontent.com/pod-product-compliance
Lightning Source LLC
Chambersburg PA
CBHW051547020426
42333CB00016B/2141